Studies in German Literature, Linguistics, and Culture:
Literary Criticism in Perspective

About *Literary Criticism in Perspective*

Books in the series *Literary Criticism in Perspective* trace literary scholarship and criticism on major and neglected writers alike, or on a single major work, a group of writers, a literary school or movement. In so doing the authors — authorities on the topic in question who are also well-versed in the principles and history of literary criticism — address a readership consisting of scholars, students of literature at the graduate and undergraduate level, and the general reader. One of the primary purposes of the series is to illuminate the nature of literary criticism itself, to gauge the influence of social and historic currents on aesthetic judgments once thought objective and normative.

The German Novella:
Two Centuries of Criticism

Siegfried Weing

The German Novella:
Two Centuries of Criticism

CAMDEN HOUSE

ISBN 1-879751-64-X

Library of Congress Cataloging-in-Publication Data

Weing, Siegfried, 1942-
     The German novella : two centuries of criticism / Siegfried Weing.-- 1st ed.
     p.   cm. -- (Studies in German literature, linguistics, and culture. Literary
criticism in perspective)
     Includes bibliographical references and indexes.
     ISBN 1-879751-64-X (alk. paper)
     1. Short stories, German--History and criticism--Theory, etc. 2. German
fiction--History and criticism--Theory, etc. I. Title. II. Series.
     PT747.S6W45 1994
     833'.0109--dc20   93-39186
                                                                                CIP

Acknowledgments

I owe debts of gratitude to several people and organizations who aided me in the completion of this project. The staff at Preston Library, especially Elizabeth Hostetter and Wylma Davis, were more than diligent in helping me acquire materials. Robert Goebel proofread the manuscript and Mike Monsour encouraged me in many ways. I wish to thank the VMI Research Committee and those officials in the VMI Foundation and Administration who supported this project in the form of grants and released time. Janet Cummings provided invaluable computer advice and services. Finally, I wish to thank my family, Lori, Andy, and Jeremy, for their patience and forbearance during the course of this project.

Contents

Preface xi

1: Origins of the Novella 1
Precursors of the Novella 2
The Romance Novella 3
Early German Novellistic Narratives 9

2: The Age of Goethe (1795-1832) 18
Goethe 19
The Brothers Schlegel 26
From the Schlegels to Goethe's Death 31

3: The Age of Realism (1833-1914) 37
Biedermeier and Young Germany 37
Poetic Realism 43
Precursors of the Modern Age 52

4: Between the Great Wars (1915-1945) 57

5: Planting the Seeds of Doubt (1946-1959) 76

6: Doubt Established (1960-1970) 96

7: Modern Criticism (1971-1980) 117

8: Contemporary Criticism (1981-1991) 137

Conclusion 159

Works Consulted 161

Index 179

Preface

BOCCACCIO, GENERALLY ACKNOWLEDGED as the originator of the novella, refers to the hundred narratives of his *Decameron* as "stories [novellas], or fables, or parables, or histories [novelle o favole o parabole o istorie], or whatever you wish to call them" (1352, 3). Boccaccio's medium (prose) and format (a cyclical collection of framed stories) became popular and led to scores of imitations in the Romance countries and England. Most commentators agree that the novella did not become part of the German genre repertoire until the end of the eighteenth century. Upon transplantation from Romance to German soil, it retained the original medium and, at times, also the frame, but quickly abandoned the cyclical format. Since the genre came to dominate the literary landscape of nineteenth-century Germany, it became the object of a great deal of artistic and critical speculation that involved the question of what constituted a novella. Attempts to answer this question, which began in 1772 with Christoph Martin Wieland, continue unabated into the present.

In the nineteenth century artists dominated the efforts to define the genre and presented theories that were representative of either historical, thematic, or formal viewpoints. These attempts led to such postulates that the novella is the narration of an unprecedented event that took place (Goethe), that it contains a turning point (Ludwig Tieck), and, to name a last example, that it features a concrete symbol (Paul Heyse). These notions acquired, for artists and critics alike, the force of normative prescription. Yet, a few commentators were quite pessimistic about defining the form. Wilhelm Meyer, one such skeptic, likened the genre to a chameleon that constantly changed its colors and stubbornly mocked all attempts to clap it into the irons of theory. The first half of the twentieth century, interrupted twice by the catastrophe of world war, witnessed a shift in the nature of the commentary as well as a change in the identity of the commentators. Artists fall silent and academics begin to dominate the discussion by focusing upon theories advanced during the previous century. After the Second World War the skeptical stance, first advanced by a handful of nineteenth-century critics, begins to become a significant theme in the rhetoric of the novella. Walter Pabst, for instance, asserts that there is no such genre as the novella. Modern liter-

ary discourse about the topic can be classified into three groups: rigorists, who insist that the novella has a distinct set of formal features; latitudinarians, who either dismiss all features or advance the idea that the novella is a narrative of medium length; and moderates, who fall between these two groups and postulate, in undogmatic fashion, that there is such a genre as the novella and that it tends to have several recognizable features.

Three *Forschungsberichte* (critical summaries of research) have appeared: Walter Pabst's "Die Theorie der Novelle in Deutschland (1920-1940)" (1949), Heinz Otto Burger's "Theorie und Wissenschaft von der deutschen Novelle" (1951), and Karl Konrad Polheim's *Novellentheorie und Novellenforschung: Ein Forschungsbericht (1945-1964)* (1965). All three works provide sound analyses of the literature, but are limited by scope and other causes. Pabst's approach is dominated by the traditions of Romance novella scholarship and seems to be colored, from the beginning, by the belief that there is no such genre as the novella. Burger's analysis, aimed at pedagogues, is limited in its usefulness because he undertakes too much: he attempts to provide the history of the genre as well as a summary of the theory and criticism — all within the confines of twenty-five pages. Polheim's study, the best and most scholarly of the three reports, at times seems to be driven by the subtext that the novella and the *Erzählung* (narrative, tale, story) are identical genres.

No monographic attempt to illuminate the theory and criticism of the German novella from its inception to the present has been undertaken in either English or German. This study, commensurate with the goals of the series *Literary Criticism in Perspective*, presents a chronological, selective orientation to the literature on the topic (unpublished dissertations are excluded for the sake of spatial economy). Since surveys of novella literature originating on the Continent at times minimize and even leave out the scholarly efforts of other countries, I have attempted to fill this critical gap by incorporating into this survey British and North American studies. Such criticism, I believe, has made a substantial contribution to the development of novella theory.

I have anglicized two German words in the text. I use the noun *novellist* to refer to a writer of such narratives and the adjective *novellistic* to refer to a story that has the qualities of a novella.

1: Origins of the Novella

THE ENGLISH WORD *novella* (German *Novelle*, French *nouvelle*, Spanish *novela*) traces its origins to the Italian *novella*, which in turn is derived from the Latin *novella*, a diminutive of the adjective *novus*. Early Roman writers, Cicero and Virgil, used the term to describe something young in plant or animal husbandry. Later writers, Ovid and Pliny, employed the term to describe anything new or current. In the sixth century the word acquired a legal meaning and also began to refer to the laws that were added as sections 528-35 to the Justinian Code. In addition to the above meanings, the dictionary defines *novus* as "fresh," "novel," "strange," "unusual," or "unheard-of." By the twelfth century the Italian noun *novella*, in its literary application, referred to a short prose account of an unusual, new event (Wiese 1963, 1). In the mid-fourteenth century, by the time Boccaccio published *The Decameron* (considered by many critics the first novella collection), the term encompassed three basic meanings: "young or new," "news," and "a story that could be true or fictional, new or simply unusual, written or recited." Boccaccio, in his proem to the *Decameron*, refers to his stories as *cento novelle* (Clements and Gibaldi 1977, 4-6).

The adoption of *Novelle* as a literary term came to Germany late. In the early stages *novella* was translated as a new *Historie*, *Fabel*, or *Geschichte*, as seen in the title of the first complete translation of *The Decameron* by Heinrich Schlüsselfelder: *decameron, daz ist cento novelle in welsch Und hundert histori oder neüe fabel in teutsche* (c. 1472). Boccaccio's work became so popular in Germany that over the course of the next century and a half more than a dozen editions appeared. In every version *cento novelle* was translated into an orthographic variant of *hundert newer historien*. This interpretation continued until the middle of the eighteenth century. In 1751 Lessing translated the title of Cervantes's *Novelas ejemplares* as *Neue Beispiele*. The German word *Novelle* was not used until well into the second half of the eighteenth century. The term did not gain wide-spread currency in German literary discourse until after 1820 (for more complete information, see Mitchell 1915b, 3-8; Hirsch 1928, 13-14 and 20-22; and Bennett 1934, 20).

Precursors of the Novella

As a literary genre the novella has antecedents in the many anecdotes, myths, tales, legends, fables, *Schwänke*, and similar narratives that were transmitted orally and that circulated freely throughout Europe from the beginning of the Middle Ages onward. Since such secular stories were regarded as trivial entertainment, they were of minor consequence and deemed unworthy of the trouble and expense of being preserved on parchment. Despite this loss, the tradition of oral narration survived and a number of such stories eventually found their way onto paper as novellas.

Scholars generally agree that another predecessor of the novella is the *exemplum*, a rhetorical device dating from Aristotle's time that originally involved an anecdotal interpolation serving as an example. Later, c. 100 B.C., the meaning of the word expanded to encompass also an exemplary character, a person who was considered the embodiment of some admirable principle or moral quality. In Christian times, beginning at the end of the sixth century, the clergy began to incorporate such anecdotes into their sermons in order to pique and hold the interest of their parishioners and to simplify difficult theological points. Since *exempla* were interpreted to be similar to Christ's parables, the church hierarchy sanctioned their use and the clergy began to collect them in written form to serve mainly as reference materials for the preparation of illustrative moral and ethical points in sermons. The first such collection, the *Disciplina clericalis* by Petrus Alfonsi, was written c. 1110 and was soon followed by other collections. There were two types of *exempla*, the allegorical and the literal, both serving the dual purposes of useful, moral instruction and amusement — *utilitas* and *delectatio* — with the former being of far greater importance. *Exempla* became popular among both the clergy and the laity and eventually found their way into secular, traditional forms of imaginative literature. Dante, for example, incorporated exemplary characters from the collections of Baudri of Bourgueil (1046-1130) and John of Salisbury (c. 1115-1180) into twelve cantos of his *Purgatorio*. Baudri collected *exempla* from both pagan and biblical sources and regarded them as excellent vehicles for pedagogy.

Forbears of the novella from classical times include some historical materials from Herodotus, Petronius's *Satyricon*, and Apuleius's *Metamorphoseon libri XI*. Medieval antecedents involve many *Volksbücher, Die*

Geschichte von den sieben Weisen, and *Gesta Romanorum*. Significant oriental predecessors encompass such works as the *Panchatantra*, *Alf laila wa
laila*, and *Tuti-Nameh*, with the first of these works, in *exemplum* fashion,
exhibiting strong moralistic overtones. Several oriental works incorporated the frame or cyclical narrative structure that later came to be
associated with the novella and that began in western literature with
Boccaccio's *Decameron*.

A last set of precursors of the novella include the biographies, *Lais*,
and *Fabliaux* of the medieval French troubadours. Critics note that in
these works there is a gradual and significant shift in the hitherto expected functions of literature that not only espoused, but required that
moral instruction be primary and entertainment secondary. This shift,
while not immediately reversing these functions, began to emphasize
recreation and entertainment at the expense of moral edification. Boccaccio, in "The Author's Conclusion" to the *Decameron*, expresses the
same view when he suggests that this process was noticeably at work in
the *exempla* that were interwoven into contemporary sermons. In many
cases, he observes, the sermons contain "nonsense, jokes, and foolishness"
(688). This new emphasis eventually leads to a reversal of functions and
becomes a distinguishing feature of the novella, a development that can
be seen not only in *The Decameron*, but in many later novella collections
as well (for a more complete orientation on the background of the novella, see Pabst 1953, 7-27; Himmel 1963, 9-12; Ehrismann, I, 1932, 98;
Clements and Gibaldi 1977, 14 and 37-40; Curtius 1948, 59-60 and
362-64; Foulkes and Lohner 1969, 2; Aust 1990, 55; and Hirsch 1928,
93-94).

The Romance Novella

Upon introducing the new genre, Boccaccio opened the flood gates
of novella production. In the three centuries following the publication of
The Decameron, Romance Europe and England became inundated with
more than a hundred novella collections. Despite their popularity in the
rest of western Europe, novellas failed to cross the Alps or the Rhine for
decades and, in the opinion of many scholars, German authors did not
produce novellas until the late eighteenth century. Once Goethe transplanted the novella from Romance to German soil, it flourished and
came to dominate the literary landscape of nineteenth century Germany.

The works known to have most influenced German writers, especially Goethe, include *The Decameron* (c. 1353), *Les Cent nouvelles nouvelles* (1460), Marguerite de Navarre's *Heptameron* (1558), and Cervantes's *Novelas ejemplares* (1613). The ensuing discussion leans heavily upon two important books that deal with the history and theory of the Romance novella: Pabst's *Novellentheorie und Novellendichtung* (1953) and Clements and Gibaldi's *Anatomy of the Novella* (1977). These works, it might be noted, also reflect two branches of critical opinion that have dominated German novella theory since the Second World War: Pabst insists that while there may be many individual narratives labelled novellas, there is no such genre as the novella; Clements and Gibaldi draw the opposite conclusion and insist that the novella can be characterized and even defined.

Pabst analyzes *The Decameron* for a possible novella theory by devoting his attention to the "Preface," the "Introduction," the framework, Boccaccio's intrusion on the fourth day, and "The Author's Conclusion." In these places Boccaccio pays lip service to the traditional functions of medieval literature by claiming that his work both edifies and entertains. Yet Boccaccio rebelled against this moralistic tradition — "er ist ein Rebell gegen das 'Gesetz'" (30) — and meant only to entertain. His subterfuge was discovered and he came under attack. This attack involved several reasons, with the primary one centering on the belief that the work was alien to the noble spirit of art. Censors also condemned Boccaccio because many of his stories were erotic. The problem was not so much his salaciousness, but his failure to draw morally exemplary conclusions. Another problem involved stories that were silly and farcical. The prevailing aesthetic canon declared such tales unworthy of an artist who should have been drawing inspiration from the muses on Mount Parnassus. In addition, Boccaccio presented old stories and motifs in a new way and in a new spirit: he was censured not for his failure to invent new stories, but for casting them in the inartistic medium of prose. And, as a last reason, Boccaccio was considered a lecher who engaged in the frivolous and unseemly enterprise of entertaining women — attempting, thereby, to inveigle himself into their graces.

Boccaccio defended himself by appealing to literary tradition and to nature. In his intrusion on the fourth day, he remains aggressive in his unrepentance because he is following the precedent set by Dante, who also honored women. Since "heaven made" his body "to love" women, he

determines to ignore his critics, but before doing so, he maliciously implies that they are sexual perverts (244-50). In "The Author's Conclusion" Boccaccio again responds to criticism. He first defends himself
against the charge of libertinism: "nothing is so indecent that it cannot
be said to another person if the proper words are used to convey it." In
addition, since his stories "were not told in a church," but in "a place
suited for pleasure," he should not be held responsible if his work is mis-
used. Boccaccio also defends his stories against charges of lengthiness,
lack of beauty, and frivolity of content. He concludes by rededicating his
work to women and by imploring them to think of him if they find
"some little pleasure" in reading his tales (684-89).

Erich Auerbach believes that Boccaccio's genius manifested itself in
the discovery that well-crafted prose, too, can function as an artistic
medium in which "actual occurrences in contemporary life can become
polite entertainment." Furthermore, Boccaccio's break with the medieval
literary tradition signals a new literary function: "narrative no longer
serves as a moral exemplum ... it serves as a pleasant diversion" (1946,
188-89). Pabst, after agreeing with Auerbach, observes that since Boccaccio was rebelling against the established norms of literature, he had
no interest at all in developing new ones. Pabst concludes his study of
The Decameron with a forewarning: whoever seeks either a theory, a
genre, a norm, or a proto-form of the novella in Boccaccio's work will
find only sharp disappointment (39-41).

Upon turning his attention to *Les Cent nouvelles nouvelles*, Pabst focuses on the "Dedication," which at first blush seems to contain a five-
point novella theory. The first element of this theory is that novellas
must narrate new stories. Boccaccio, therefore, was unjustified in calling
his tales novellas because he used old stories. Yet since twenty-one of the
novellas in *Cent nouvelles nouvelles* are borrowed from Poggio Bracciolini's *Liber Facetiarum*, the anonymous author confounds himself. Thus,
the first point of the theory is merely a ruse through which the author
attempted to ascribe to his work a characteristic it lacked. Pabst analyzes
and refutes the other four points of the theory and concludes that the
author of this novella collection can lay claim to originality primarily because he refuses to make any claims for traditional didactic or exemplary
functions (168-74).

After examining several other Romance novella collections, Pabst
cites as a recurrent feature the authors' game of hiding entertainment

behind a mask of pedagogy. Marguerite de Navarre, in *The Heptameron* (1558), reverses this pattern of dissimulation because she hides her pedagogic intentions behind the mask of entertainment (187). This reversal is not immediately apparent, for her "Prologue" seems to be a close imitation of Boccaccio's "Preface to the Ladies." In both works a natural catastrophe (in the former, the plague and in the latter, floods) isolates a small group of noble men and women and forces them to while away time by telling stories. Initially there seems to be no other goal than that of entertainment and the enactment of a precious conceit. This conceit revolves around a frame character's suggestion that the group create a "Decameron" and preempt Marguerite de Navarre's reputed effort to create an imitation of Boccaccio's work. Yet their stories should differ from the original in that "every history therein contained shall be the truth." The primary concern thus seems to be focused upon devising a pleasant pastime so that "the day be passed joyously" (6-9).

Marguerite's true agenda begins to reveal itself when another frame character insists that the best pastime consists of reading scripture. After discussion, the group decides to devote mornings to religious activities and afternoons to telling tales. Yet these stories are neither accounts of events that took place nor are they tales told for the sake of entertainment. They are, instead, pretexts for neo-Platonic and Christian moralizing. The moral of each story, often abundantly clear from the tale itself, is further underscored by the discussions of the frame characters. In this way Marguerite deceived her readers into believing that a moral dialog featuring an *exemplum* was entertainment (Pabst, 192).

In the "Prologue" to the *Novelas ejemplares* (1613), Cervantes claims a dual purpose for his novellas: since they conform to "Christian conduct" and "afford a useful example," he has given them "the title of Exemplary;" yet like billiards, they also provide "decent and pleasant pastimes" (5). Cervantes, much like Boccaccio, pays only grudging lip service to the demands of a literary dogma that in Spain was strongly promulgated by the Church. Cervantes rebelled against the dogmatic function of literature since his novellas mock and satirize the tradition of the *exemplum* and ultimately refute the claims made in the "Prologue." Pabst observes that it is almost always a mistake to lend credence to the theoretical utterances of the Renaissance authors (122).

Pabst ends his study of the Romance novellas by calling attention to the antinomic relationships that arise when the demands of literary

dogma, as obligatorily set forth in proems and frameworks, clash with the artistic freedom demanded and exercised by the authors in their novellas. Since there is a decided lack of congruence between novella theory and practice, and since there is a wide divergence of opinion among individual authors, Pabst believes that a universally accepted definition or theory of the Romance novella is both elusive and illusive. He concludes with a brief statement that has reverberated loudly in the annals of modern novella scholarship: there are novellas, but there is no such genre as the novella — "es gibt weder die 'romanische Urform' der Novelle noch 'die Novelle' überhaupt. Es gibt nur Novellen" (245).

In counterpoint to Pabst's inductive analysis, Clements and Gibaldi's deductive approach in *Anatomy of the Novella* (1977) differs not only in method, but also yields commensurately different results. They analyze the Romance collections (as well as a few English ones) and identify a number of structural and thematic characteristics which, taken in their totality, comprise a theory of the Renaissance novella. This theory, formulated in two chapters entitled "The Renaissance Theory of the Novella" (1-35) and "The Structure of the Novella Collection" (36-61), informs the following discussion.

Oral vs. written medium. For the earliest authors, a novella was a story that could be either true or fictional, new or old, written or recited. The framework fused these two modes of narrative transmission since the stories are simultaneously fixed on paper as well as recounted orally by a fictional storyteller.

Function of the novella. The Church demanded that literature be either the handmaiden of Philosophy or the vassal of Theology. In either case, art should reflect the requisite *utilitas* and *delectatio* demanded by the *exemplum* and by the almost identical dictates of Horace's *Ars Poetica* — *prodesse* and *delectare*. A small number of writers hew close to this mark, but most only nod perfunctorily in that direction because their true purpose is recreation and delight.

Invention and variety. The medieval mind was suspicious of innovation. Early novellists attained variety by assembling a large number of stories that contained a wide range of subjects. Invention did not necessarily mean the author created stories — it often meant that he reworked well-known stories and cast them in the new artistic medium of prose. Late in the development of the Romance novella, Cervantes strikes out in a new direction by stating that his novellas are "neither imitated nor

stolen. My mind conceived them, my pen brought them forth ..." (1613, 6).

Verisimilitude. Horatian aesthetics set *probabilitas, veritas,* and *verisimilitudo* as goals for all literary activity. Many novellists embraced these ideas by insisting, albeit spuriously, that the narrators in the frame were historical personages and that the stories they tell are accounts of events that occurred. With such claims, the authors attempted to shield themselves from criticism by attributing the stories to their frame characters. In keeping with this realism, there also seems to be a tendency to avoid elements and stories that smack of the miraculous, the utterly fantastic, or the fairy tale.

Unity and harmony. Seldom published individually, novellas are normally housed in a framework and arranged in groups of ten around preselected topics. Individual novellas possessed the unity of the stated theme, had a clear beginning, middle, and end, and needed to be well-told. Boccaccio, with the story of Oretta (1352, 382-84) and Marguerite, with the story of the unnamed lady (1558, 340-41), emphasize well-wrought narratives by providing examples of poorly crafted ones. Boccaccio's narrator botches his story by repeating episodes, mixing up names, and returning to the beginning several times. Marguerite's narrator bungles the punchline, thereby making herself into a laughingstock.

Language and style. Since novella authors intend their works to be read or narrated to a mixed company of the upper classes, they tend to avoid crude language and favor euphemisms. Boccaccio calls the sex act making "the nightingale sing" (339), whereas Marguerite, in an overtly scatological story, refers to the ordure of a privy as "the lees of Bacchus and the corn of Ceres, passed through the bellies of the Gray friars" (79).

Brevitas. The early Renaissance novellas are short and can be recounted in ten to twenty minutes. Later novellas tend to be longer since the printing press causes the oral tradition to disappear. Cervantes's individual novellas, for example, take an average of two hours to narrate. Nevertheless, injunctions are often made either by the author himself or by a character in the frame that the novellas be brief and that all extraneous materials or episodes be excluded.

The Cornice Tradition. Many novella collections have a frame which may be an inheritance from oriental sources (*Arabian Nights*) and from episodic divisions of the medieval romances. Frames also provide a structure in which to house many stories and thereby justify the costs of

reproduction. If the stories were found offensive, blasphemous, too long, or obscene, the frame allowed the author to dodge responsibility by claiming he was only a scribe. Boccaccio notes that "some stories here might well have been omitted ... but I could do nothing but write down the tales as they were told ..." (687).

Unity by time, theme, title. The frame contributed to unity by allowing authors to tell a pre-established number of stories within a given number of days. Dante's hundred cantos in the *Divine Comedy* may have inspired Boccaccio's human comedy. Willi Hirdt notes that *The Decameron* is a unified whole and is composed in agreement with the principle of *numerus perfectissimus* (1981, 29). The author of *Cent nouvelles nouvelles* also tells a hundred tales and Marguerite, likewise, aimed for the same number but died after only seventy-two novellas were completed — hence the posthumous title *Heptameron*. Both Boccaccio and Marguerite structure their works so that ten novellas are told each day. The unity of theme is observed because the narrators recount tales in agreement with a pre-selected topic. Clements and Gibaldi end their analysis of the theory of the novella by speculating that the Renaissance authors pursued unity, harmony, and balance in their works to attain "artistic legitimacy" and to transform the "popular new literary type into an art form consistent with the aims of Renaissance classicism" (1977, 59).

Early German Novellistic Narratives

While there is general scholarly agreement that Boccaccio originated the novella during the Italian Renaissance, there is no equivalent consensus about when the novella initially appeared in Germany. The dominant opinion postulates that the novella did not become part of the German genre repertoire until Goethe published his *Unterhaltungen deutscher Ausgewanderten* in 1795. Walter Silz asserts that Goethe wrote "the first true Novellen in Germany" (1954, 1) and Johannes Klein echoes this sentiment (1954, 3). Roger Paulin, while acknowledging a strong Romance influence, opines that "the modern German Novelle grew out of an existing body of eighteenth-century narrative." These narratives, written by obscure writers such as Wezel, Spiess, Meißner, Eckartshausen, and Langbein, lacked literary quality or merit. Such inferior works, Paulin argues, "made it possible for works of greater quality" by more

prominent authors such as Wieland, Tieck, and Goethe "to find an entry" (1985, 17-18).

Another view is advanced by critics who believe that German novellas originated in the Middle Ages and thus predate even Boccaccio. Walter Silz, for example, hedges his assertion by citing Hartmann von Aue's *Der arme Heinrich* (c. 1200) as "a sort of Novelle" and suggests that this genre "represents something like a 'natural' form in literature" (1954, 10). Wolfgang Stammler believes that the novella was created in the late thirteenth century when Konrad von Würzburg's "Engelhard" was translated into a short prose novella. Another sign of interest in the novella was exhibited when a Latin version of the frame narrative *Die Geschichte von den sieben Weisen* was translated into German in the fourteenth century. This oriental work acquired such popularity that by the end of the sixteenth century it had become, in Stammler's view, a German chapbook (1954, 1058).

Hellmuth Himmel presents yet another opinion by noting that originally there was no separation between myths, fables, fairy tales, legends, and novellas. Himmel then identifies *diu getriu kone* (1257-1275) by Herrand von Wildonie as a verse novella ("eine echte Novelle in Versen") and lists additional examples of early German novellistic narratives such as the anonymous *Moriz von Craon* (1180-1190), Wernher der Gärtner's *Meier Helmbrecht* (1250-1280), and der Stricker's *Die Schwänke des Pfaffen Amis* (c. 1230). Yet these works, while individually representing a novellistic event ("novellistische Begebenheit"), collectively do not constitute an early form of the German novella since the authors of these works fail to establish a tradition (1963, 10-12). Johannes Klein expresses the same view by referring to the verse novellas not only of this early literary period, but of other, later ones as well, as exceptional cases (1954, 27-28).

Joachim Heinzle, while eschewing the term novella, provides an overview of the short epics of the Middle Ages and the Age of Humanism. In agreement with the opinions of Ehrismann, Pabst, and Himmel, Heinzle too states that an enormous number of narratives were disseminated throughout Europe by *Spielmänner*, merchants, journeymen, clergymen, poets, and other wanderers and travelers. These narratives, some in verse and others in prose, were regularly converted from one medium to the other. Early examples of verse narratives include *Das Annolied* in

the *Kaiserchronik*, *Meier Helmbrecht*, Hartmann von Aue's *Der arme Heinrich*, and Konrad von Würzburg's *Herzmäre* (1981, 17-24).

While only a few prose narratives appeared during the twelfth and thirteenth centuries, the end of the fourteenth century witnessed an awakening of interest in the Romance novellas and their precursors. This interest intensified in the second half of the fifteenth century and manifested itself in translations by the early humanists. Representative examples include:

1461 - Heinrich Steinhöwel translated Petrarch's *Griseldis*. This story, also the last novella in Boccaccio's *Decameron*, was first translated into German prose by Erhart Gross in 1432 (Stammler 1954, 1059).

1462 - Niklas von Wyle translated Aeneas Silvius's *Eurialus und Lucretia* and Boccaccio's novella *Guiscard und Sigismunde* (Hirsch 1928, 107-116).

1472 - Albrecht von Eyb published his *Ehebüchlein* in which he incorporated translations of *Griseldis*, *Guiscard und Sigismunde*, and *Marina* (this motif was also treated in the last novella of *Les Cent nouvelles nouvelles* and later became the source of Goethe's "Prokurator" novella in the *Unterhaltungen*).

1472 - Heinrich Schlüsselfelder (Arigo), translated the whole *Decameron*.

1475 - Heinrich Steinhöwel published *Buch und Leben des Fabeldichters Esopi*. This work includes not only translations of Aesop's fables, but also of stories from Petrus Alfonsi's *Disciplina clericalis* and adaptations of Poggio's facetiae (Heinzle 1981, 27).

1478 - Niklas von Wyle published *Translatzion oder Tütschungen*, a work consisting of eighteen narratives translated from Aeneas Silvius, Petrarch, Poggio, and Boccaccio.

These examples, also discussed by Hans Rupprich (1970, 570-79), suggest that interest in the novella during the fifteenth century did not focus so much upon the creation of original novellas as it did upon translating and adapting the Romance examples (Aust 1990, 56). This interest was so great that Haslinger regards it as tantamount to a German appropriation ("Eindeutschung") of antique, Italian motifs (1981, 39).

The Protestant Reformation, which shredded many German social fabrics, also led to a considerable diminution of interest in the arts. During the first half of the sixteenth century only two works of novellistic consequence, both strongly influenced by Poggio, appeared: Heinrich von Bebel's *Facetiae* (1509-1514) and Johannis Pauli's *Schimpf und Ernst* (1522). In 1555 the Peace of Augsburg led to a respite from religious hostilities and ushered in a new literary epoch. This era, inaugurated by Jörg Wickram's *Rollwagen-Büchlein* (1555), is characterized by Willi Hirdt and Richard Newald as the age of the *Schwank*. Wickram's *Rollwagen* not only shows strong influences from the works by Pauli, Poggio, and Boccaccio, but also contains stories by these authors. Wickram's work became immensely popular and inspired such imitations, among others, as Frey's *Gartengesellschaft* (1556), Montanus's *Wegkürzer* (1557), Lindner's *Katzipori* (1558) and *Rastbüchlein* (1558), and Schumann's *Nachtbüchlein* (1559).

Willi Hirdt characterizes these works and the Zeitgeist that produced them in terms of a strong societal need for rest and diversion from the rigors of prolonged religious strife. This entertainment was channeled by a moral tone much reminiscent of the medieval demands for literary *utilitas*. *The Decameron*, excoriated by Boccaccio's contemporaries, now also came under German attack. Labeled Boccaccio's book of harlots ("hurenbuch Bocatii"), it came to be included among a group of nasty books ("unnützen, unzüchtigen und garstigen Büchern") and eventually earned a listing in the Index. The moralistic climate of the times prompted many authors to attempt at all costs to avoid the label of obscenity. Thus the avowed purpose of the *Schwank* literature, as noted in many proemial statements, was to banish melancholia and to enliven and to reconstitute, in Jacob Frey's words from *Gartengesellschaft*, flagging spirits — "die schwaeren verdroßnen gemueter" (Hirdt 1981, 30-35).

Hirdt reports that in 1583, with the sixteenth-century *Schwank* literature drawing to a close, Sigmund Feyerabend published a book entitled *Kurtzweilige und Laecherliche Geschicht Und Historien Die wol in Schimpff und Ernst moegen gelesen werden. Darinnen allerley Welthaendel, warhaffte Exempel, Gleichnussen, merckliche Historien.... Hierzu seindt kommen die hundert neuwe Historien, sonst Cento Nouelle* [i.e., The Decameron] *genannt ... Sampt einem kurzen Außzug der fuernembsten Historien des Rollwagens, Gartengesellschaft und Wegkuertzers.* From symbolic as well as literal viewpoints, this unwieldy yet remarkably descrip-

tive title (here shortened) recapitulates in compendium form much of the history of novellistic narration from its inception. Three reasons — the contents of this work, the conviction that much of the *Schwank* literature was greatly influenced by and derivative of *The Decameron*, and the belief that Goethe, too, was greatly influenced by Boccaccio — prompt Hirdt to crown not Goethe, but Boccaccio as the creator of the German novella (28).

The next phase in the development of the German novella, the short prose narratives written during the Baroque era, becomes problematic because of divergent critical opinions. In remarks describing the novella of the seventeenth century, Benno von Wiese ignores all German literary production and comments only on the influence of Cervantes's *Novelas ejemplares* upon the later German novellas (1963, 38-40). Himmel too emphasizes Cervantes's novellas and, upon discussing possible German examples, confines his remarks to brief descriptions of the prose works of Rist, Harsdörffer, and Anton Ulrich, the Duke of Braunschweig. None of these works, however, qualifies as a genuine novella (1963, 18). Richard Newald and Harry Steinhauer also examine the novellistic production of the period and single out only Grimmelshausen's *Courasche*, *Springinsfeld*, and *Vogelnest* for comment. Newald believes these works are a continuation of the *Schwank* literature of the sixteenth century (1965, 376), whereas Steinhauer considers them to be "three long novellas" (1977, xv).

This diversity of opinion arises, at least partially, from a paucity of research. In comparison with the other genres of seventeenth-century literature, the novella remains, in Adolf Haslinger's words, a stepchild of scholarship. The scant research that is extant reveals that the writers of this era, much like their colleagues from earlier epochs, apparently also labored under the injunction of literary *utilitas*, since the short prose narrative often illustrated a moral thesis. Haslinger classifies novellistic narratives from this period into three chronologically arranged phases: appropriation and continuation of the sixteenth-century German *Exemplum* and *Schwank* literature, transplantation and adaptation of the Romance novellas (now also including Cervantes's *Novelas ejemplares*), and incorporation of divers novellistic narratives into novels (1981, 39-40).

In the earliest phase, writers such as Sandrubs, Liechtensee, Memel, and Lundorf compiled new editions, translations, or adaptations of *Schwänke* from collections published in previous centuries. Also in need

of inclusion at this point is Niclas Ulenhart's translation and adaptation, under the misleading title *Historie von Isaak Winckelfelder und Jobst von der Schneid* (1617), of the Spanish picaresque novel *Lazarillo de Tormes* and Cervantes's novella "Rinconte y Cortadillo" from the recently published *Novelas ejemplares* (1613). In another form of this first literary phase clergymen like Templin, Cochem, Strobl, and Abraham a Sancta Clara published their sermons, many of which contained a *Predigtmärlein*, the baroque equivalent of the *exemplum*. The collected works of Abraham a Sancta Clara, for example, include over four hundred *Schwänke*, *exempla*, and *Predigtmärlein*. The contents of many of these narratives transcend the normal bounds of sermons. In a development reminiscent of Boccaccio's characterization of the sermons of his day, Newald remarks that these narratives belong to the realm of trivial literary entertainment (1965, 419).

The second phase of the short prose narrative, adaptation of Renaissance novellistic works, is perhaps best represented by Georg Philipp Harsdörffer's *Frauenzimmer-Gesprächsspiele* (1641-1649), a framed compilation of narratives from classical, French, Italian, and Spanish sources. In two other works, *Der Schauplatz jämmerlicher Mordgeschichte* (1650) and *Der Große Schauplatz Lust- und Lehrreicher Geschichte* (1650), Harsdörffer published nearly one thousand narratives that Hugo Aust categorizes as "Novellen" (1990, 57).

The final phase of the baroque short narrative, adaptation and incorporation of novellistic stories into longer works, can be found in the novels of Grimmelshausen, Ulrich, and Lohenstein. Haslinger cites as examples of this phenomenon the "Beau-Alman" and the "Jupiter" sections of Grimmelshausen's *Simplizissimus*. Grimmelshausen borrowed the "Beau-Alman" material from Harsdörffer, who borrowed it from a French source. This unnamed French source in turn borrowed the material from an Italian source, Matteo Bandello's *Novelle*. The history of the Jupiter chapters is equally convoluted because the original source again can be traced first to Harsdörffer, then to a French novel by Sorel, and finally to Cervantes's *Don Quixote* and "Man of Glass" from *Novelas ejemplares*. Such literary appropriations were common during the age and, rather than being viewed as plagiarism, were evaluated positively as demonstrations of scholarliness (Haslinger 1981, 50-51).

The last stage in the development of the pre-Goethean novellistic narrative, the short prose story of the eighteenth century, suffers from

the same neglect as did the story of the Age of Baroque. This lack of critical attention is exemplified by Richard Newald's volume in the standard history of German literature, *Geschichte der deutschen Literatur*. Newald's treatise on the short prose narratives of the period amounts to a six-page, annotated bibliography (1957, 477-82). In the most recent edition of this volume, Jørgensen, Bohnen, and Ohrgaard accord these narratives even shorter shrift than did Newald (1990, 208). Paulin, as previously noted, dismisses these narratives because of their poor quality. In a more positive vein, Jürgen Jacobs points out that the era produced a wealth of short narratives. Since many of these works have not fallen under scholarly scrutiny, Jacobs, in agreement with Newald, Himmel, and other critics, classifies these stories into three categories that appeared in the following sequence: moral narratives, philosophical narratives, and fairy tales (1981, 56-57).

The initial phase, inspired by Addison and Steele's *The Tatler* (1709) and *The Spectator* (1711), led to the founding of similar German periodicals. The purpose of these periodicals, to develop the facility for aesthetic and moral evaluation (Himmel 1963, 20) and to increase the general knowledge of readers, once again seems to resonate with the medieval tradition of *utilitas*. These periodicals published moral tales initially known as *moralische Beispielerzählungen*. Such narratives, through the influence of Marmontel's *contes moraux* (collected 1761), evolved into the genre of *moralische Erzählung*. These tales appeared in dozens of book-length collections and were written by Pfeil, Spiess, Wezel, Meißner, Merck, Eckartshausen, and others. The most noteworthy and perhaps best example of this genre in terms of quality is Sophie von LaRoche's *Moralische Erzählungen im Geschmack Marmontels* (1782-1784).

The German philosophical tales, considerably less popular than their moral relatives during this period, trace their origins to Voltaire's *Contes philosophiques*, especially to *Zadig* (1748) and *Candide* (1759). The purpose of such narratives, as defined by Jacobs, was to propagate and to illustrate a general philosophical thesis by casting it in the form of a fictional story. Examples of such narratives include stories by Pfeil, Wezel, and Meißner, as well as Wieland's *Koxkox und Kikequetzel* (1770), a number of Anton Wall's *Bagatellen* (1783), and many of Ramdohr's *Moralische Erzählungen* (1799).

The origin of the third type of eighteenth-century prose narrative, the fairy tale, once again is of French provenance. Fairy tales became

popular in the court of Louis XIV and Charles Perrault either created or jotted down many and eventually published them in 1679 as his Mother Goose tales. Such narratives remained popular until the Revolution and, having crossed the Rhine in their original versions, began to be published in translation in 1760 (Jacobs 1981, 57-65). German involvement with the collection and production of fairy tales quickly ensued and became evident in multi-volume collections such as Musäus's *Volksmärchen der Deutschen* (1762-1786), Wieland's *Dschinnistan* (1786-89), and Bertuch's *Blaue Bibliothek aller Nationen* (1790-1800).

One other type of narrative in the development of the German novella, hitherto unmentioned, involves the *Kriminalgeschichten* of the last quarter of the eighteenth century. The criminal story, regarded by a number of scholars as a sub-genre of the *moralische Erzählung*, is exemplified by Lenz's *Zerbin* (1776) and by several stories in Meißner's *Skizzen* (1777) and Spiess's *Selbstmörderbiographien* (1785). Richard Newald considers Lenz's narrative as one of the first examples of the modern German novella (1957, 272). The purpose of such stories, many of them apparently accounts of events that took place, was to understand a character better, to prevent hasty, pharisaical judgments (Jacobs 61), and to foster a more humane and objective sense of justice (Himmel 23).

The most famous *Kriminalgeschichte*, Schiller's *Verbrecher aus verlorener Ehre* (1786), is an adaptation of a true story that Schiller heard from his teacher Abel about the execution of Friedrich Schwan in 1760. Schiller's narrative, which according to Jacobs is modelled on Meißner's tales, is thematically typical of the genre. The main character, here called Christian Wolf, in the beginning characterized as neither better nor worse than the normal man, is driven to commit a crime. After being imprisoned and released, he finds himself stripped of his honor and identity. For lack of an alternative, Wolf becomes a professional criminal and, upon suffering from remorse, seeks out his well-earned punishment.

Schiller's narrative has not suffered from the same critical inattention as have many of the other works alluded to earlier. Yet the spectrum of opinion formulated by only a few representative scholars cited below is startling in its disparity. E. K. Bennett, Bernhard von Arx, Arnold Hirsch, and Josef Kunz fail even to mention this work as a novella in their monographs devoted to the history and theory of the genre. Richard Newald, Jürgen Jakobs, and Roger Paulin call the work a *Kriminalgeschichte*, whereas Hugo Aust in sundry fashion labels it a true story, a

moral tale, and a historical report (1990, 60). Johannes Klein characterizes *Verbrecher* as a proto-novella — "[eine] Keim-Novelle, die für eine Erzählung zu sehr, für eine Novelle zu wenig gesammelt ist" (1954, 61). Himmel allies himself with Klein's position, for after identifying a number of novellistic elements in the work, he, too, avoids the rubric novella (1963, 24). In similar fashion, Benno von Wiese flirts with the term when he describes the work as a preliminary draft of a novella — "eine Erzählung, die gleichsam wie der Vorentwurf zu einer Novelle anmutet" (1956, 46). Despite his reservations, Wiese nevertheless includes an interpretation of this story in the first volume of *Die deutsche Novelle von Goethe bis Kafka*. Emil Staiger completes the opinion spectrum when he declares Schiller's narrative to be the prototype of the modern German novella — "[*Verbrecher*] gilt mit Recht als erste große Novelle des neueren deutschen Schrifttums. Sie ist zu einer Art Modell geworden" (1966, 513).

2: The Age of Goethe (1795-1832)

AS NOTED EARLIER, the term *Novelle* was adopted in Germany late. In 1759, eight years after incorrectly translating the title of Cervantes's *Novelas ejemplares* as *Neue Beispiele*, Lessing employed a cognate by referring to a French novella writer as a "Nouvellenschreiberin." Shortly thereafter, Wieland introduced the German term in the foreword of *Don Sylvio von Rosalva* (1764) by listing it as one of three types of narratives: "die Arabischen und Persianischen Erzählungen, und die *Novellen* und Feenmärchen." Three years later Lessing also used the German word when he criticized the English dramatist Banks for transforming a French "Novelle" into a drama by merely converting it into dramatic dialogue. The context in which Lessing employed the term provides "the first hint" of the "close relationship existing between the drama and the *novelle*" (see Mitchell 1915b, 2-4). Of collateral interest here is that in 1779 Lessing himself adapted a novella, the story of Melchizedek from *The Decameron*, for his drama *Nathan der Weise*.

Wieland, in the second edition of *Don Sylvio* (1772), attempted to define the genre by its short compass: "Novellen [sind] eine Art von Erzählungen" that can be differentiated from the novel "durch die Simplizität des Plans und den kleinen Umfang der Fabel." Or, in terms of an analogue, novellas are related to novels in the same way as "die kleinen Schauspiele" are related "[zu] der großen Tragödie und Komödie" (1). This definition strikes two notes that later critics develop more fully: the first delimits the novella in terms of scope, whereas the second is in tune with the comparison to drama. In 1780, in a letter to Sophie von LaRoche, Wieland again described the novella by size, calling it a small, interesting narrative that contains one main situation (see Hoffmeister 1990, 44). Although Wieland's letter remained unpublished until 1820, his views about size were echoed a decade later by Johann Eschenburg, who referred to novellas as "kleinere prosaische Erzählungen" (1783, 2). In the following decade, C. F. von Blanckenburg called them small novels (1792, 3). Christian Friedrich Schwan expanded on the definition by describing novellas as small, invented stories and wondrous events that serve only as entertainment — "kleine erdichtete Erzählungen und wunderbare Begebenheiten, die blos zur Unterhaltung dienen sollen" (1791, 2). Three years later the terms *Begebenheit* and *Unterhaltung* ac-

quired considerable significance for Goethe, although it is unclear whether he adopted the terms from Schwan or, what may well be more likely, developed the ideas from his study of the Romance novellas.

Goethe

Roughly three decades after the term *Novelle* was coined, the genre made a debut in its German form with Goethe. This development came about in 1794 after Goethe agreed to contribute to Schiller's new journal, *Die Horen*. On 26 October, Goethe submitted a poem and asked whether Schiller needed additional works from him. In response, Schiller reminded Goethe of an earlier project: "so erinnere ich Sie an Ihre Idee, die Geschichte des ehrlichen Prokurators aus dem Boccaz zu bearbeiten" (*Goethe-Schiller Briefwechsel* 1794-1795, 25). Schiller's mistaken reminder — the real source of the "Prokurator" is the ninety-ninth novella of *Les Cent nouvelles nouvelles* — led Goethe to begin working not on the above story, but on a story cycle entitled *Unterhaltungen deutscher Ausgewanderten*. In a letter to Körner, Schiller described this work in terms of a Boccaccian novella cycle — "eine zusammenhängende Suite von Erzählungen im Geschmack des Boccaz" (*Schillers Briefe* 1794, 54).

An examination of Goethe's first venture into the realm of the novella confirms Schiller's assessment. Boccaccio, in the "Introduction," describes how the plague and its attendant social and medical disasters prompt a group of young Florentine men and women to flee to a country estate where they decide to "live happily." In pursuit of this goal, they choose a leader "whose only thought shall be to keep us happily entertained." A part of this entertainment, they all agree, will involve the telling of stories (18). In similar fashion, the framework of *Unterhaltungen* describes how the convulsions of the French Revolution force a German baroness's family and entourage to flee from their home on the west bank of the Rhine to an estate on the east bank. There they are joined by another noble German family, but because of a heated political disagreement the visitors leave. The baroness becomes distraught and upbraids her nephew Karl for expressing his opinions so immoderately. Determined to restore and to maintain social harmony, the baroness enjoins her household to avoid all controversial topics and to seek amusement in harmless pursuits. The family chaplain then informs the

baroness that he has a collection of stories with which he could entertain the group (Goethe 1795, 142).

A lengthy discussion ensues which, in the opinion of many critics, comprises a significant part of Goethe's novella theory. Luise, the baroness's daughter, accuses the chaplain of having compiled either a scandalous chronicle ("skandalöse Chronik") or a collection of bawdy tales ("lüsterne Späße") — precisely the type of stories found so often in the Italian and French novella collections. The chaplain, a Catholic priest, demurs by saying he finds such tales repugnant. He does acknowledge to Luise that nothing quickens the interest of an audience more than novelty ("die Neuheit"). Yet, the chaplain also dislikes such stories because they lead, all too often, only to malice ("Tücke und Schadenfreude"). His tales are not based on grand historical events ("der grossen Geschichte" or on "Weltbegebenheiten"), but on events as they occur in everyday life ("im gemeinen Leben"). These stories, therefore, possess a charm that exceeds that of novelty ("einen schöneren Reiz, als den Reiz der Neuheit"), for they involve an ingenious twist ("eine geistreiche Wendung"), reveal hidden aspects of human nature ("die menschliche Natur und ihre inneren Verborgenheiten"), or portray strange instances of tomfoolery ("sonderbare Albernheiten"). They also deal with situations where chance impinges upon human foibles — "wo der Zufall mit der menschlichen Schwäche und Unzulänglichkeit spielt" (141-45).

These remarks lead the baroness to assume that the chaplain's stories deal with events that occurred within her own social circle. She finds it difficult to believe that any of the events she witnessed or in which she participated merit inclusion in a story collection. Luise shares her mother's opinion regarding the veracity of these stories and looks forward to identifying friends and neighbors in them. The chaplain reveals that a number of his stories come from old books and, if he happens to confound his audience with one of them, he will enjoy pulling out an old folio to prove that the story had either occurred or been invented several hundred years earlier. On the other hand, his listeners may be tempted to believe that one of his stories is an old fairy tale when it actually took place in their proximity. The chaplain concludes by claiming, in compliance with the baroness's original request, that his collection should be regarded only as light, tasteful entertainment (144-46). At this point the first installment of *Unterhaltungen* ends.

Upon receiving the installment Schiller comments on its pronounced realism by noting Goethe had created the impression that a real event had taken place — "daß etwas wirklich Vorgefallenes im Spiele sei" (*Briefwechsel* 28). Goethe replies by informing Schiller that the next installment would include the story and that he intended to proceed like the narrator in *Arabian Nights* (29). Yet the second installment did not consist of "Der Prokurator," as Goethe had promised, but of four stories. The first, "Antonelli," involves an episode from the life of Marmontel's mistress, the French actress Hippolyte Clairon. The next story, "Das Klopfen," repeats an anecdote originally told by a Herr von Pannwitz in Weimar. The last two stories, "Die Krämerin" and "Der Schleier," are events taken from the memoirs of the French Marshal de Bassompierre. All four stories in some way are historical accounts of unresolved mysteries about which the refugees speculate. Thus Goethe, like Marguerite de Navarre, also employs a conceit in that he has fictional frame characters who seem "real" speculate about "real" events that seem fictional.

The transition between stories shows Goethe employing two different, yet related narrative techniques that appear to have been inspired by Scheherazade. After the first and third tales have been told, the refugees begin to ponder the mysterious events. Goethe, however, cuts off all speculation by having a frame character recount yet another tale. Since no acceptable solution for either mystery is ever advanced, these stories lack a satisfactory ending. Yet the *Ausgewanderten* hardly seem to notice, for their interest has been aroused by the mystery of the new stories. In the other technique, found after the second and fourth narratives, Goethe curtails all speculation by inventing a mysterious event that takes place among the frame characters. In the first instance, when these characters are attempting to solve the puzzle of the knocking in "Das Klopfen," their speculations are interrupted by the resounding crack of a splitting desk top. The *Ausgewanderten* lose all interest in "Das Klopfen" and now devote their attention to this mysterious occurrence. The other incident takes place after "Der Schleier" is told. Luise at first attempts to dismiss this story as a fairy tale, but her brother Friedrich will not allow such an interpretation, for he insists that the tradition of the talismans described in the story exists in their own family. Luise's interest is piqued and she demands more information. Friedrich announces that it is a secret passed on from father to eldest son and, with an air of smugness, leaves by saying that he already has revealed too much (166). Friedrich's

departure signals the end of the second installment and Luise, not to mention the reader, is left in the air about both the story and the family tradition of a talisman.

The next morning the frame characters reassemble and the chaplain again volunteers to tell a story. The baroness, who had been absent the previous evening, welcomes his offer but warns him about the type of stories she dislikes:

> Jene Erzählungen machen mir keine Freude, bei welchen nach Weise der 'Tausendundeinen Nacht' eine Begebenheit in die andere einge-schachtelt, ein Interesse durch das andere verdrängt wird, wo sich der Erzähler genötigt sieht, die Neugierde ... durch Unterbrechung zu rei-zen und die Aufmerksamkeit, anstatt sie durch eine vernünftige Folge zu befriedigen, nur durch seltsame und keineswegs lobenswürdige Kunstgriffe aufzuspannen. Ich tadle das Bestreben, aus Geschichten, die sich der Einheit des Gedichts nähern sollen, rhapsodische Rätsel zu machen und den Geschmack immer tiefer zu verderben. (166)

This passage reveals Goethe realized that with his first four stories he had departed from the principles of sound story telling. The baroness's lines, which in tone and tenor are reminiscent of the poor story telling in Boccaccio's account of Oretta, constitute a pithy, yet remarkably apt piece of literary self-criticism: through the voice of the baroness, Goethe con-demns, in the space of a few lines, the stories and the narrative technique that he himself had chosen for the second installment.

This criticism suggests that in the two months between installments Goethe gained new insights into the artistic nature of short prose fiction. As a result, he does not limit the baroness to negative criticism, but also has her describe, with criteria that could have been taken from Aristotle's *Poetics*, the ideal characteristics of not only this epic genre, but also of other literary efforts. Goethe realized that since the stories had unsatis-factory endings, they failed to meet the Aristotelian notion of a complete action and lacked unity. The baroness therefore emphasizes, in her later remarks, that such narratives should possess the unity of a poem. Be-cause of its compass, the story should portray only a few people and events, be well thought out, true, natural, and out of the ordinary. The plot ought to advance at an appropriate pace and the characters should be interesting rather than exceptional. The baroness concludes by ad-monishing the chaplain that his story should be entertaining, satisfying, and upon completion, lead to further, quiet contemplation. The chaplain

at first complains about her strict demands (166-67), but then complies by narrating the previously-mentioned "Der Prokurator." The ending of this novella coincides with the ending of the third installment.

The chaplain apparently has met the baroness's criteria, for in the next installment she praises the novella as entertaining and instructive, awards it the honorary title of a *moralische Erzählung*, and calls for a parallel story. Luise then requests that the next story be a family portrait ("Familiengemälde") and, in a development that echoes the proem of *Les Cent nouvelles nouvelles*, she also asks that the story take place at home rather than in some exotic place. The chaplain accedes to both requests, but forewarns that all such narratives are the same and lack novelty. Yet, he will venture to tell one and hopes to make it new and interesting by emphasizing what took place in the mind — "was in den Gemütern vorging." Before recounting the story of Ferdinand, the chaplain says he will narrate only one illuminative event that affected his whole life — "nur eine Begebenheit, die seinen ganzen Charakter ins Licht setzt und in seinem Leben eine entschiedene Epoche machte" (185-88). The chaplain tells the tale and the installment ends with what seems to be the conclusion of the story.

In the beginning of the fifth installment Luise praises "Ferdinand" because the story, although originating in everyday life ("aus dem gemeinen Leben"), is not common ("alltäglich"). She then requests that the chaplain, having narrated the development, now tell the ending. The chaplain at first demurs, announcing that the story has ended, but then he goes on to finish. These two conclusions to the story indicate that Goethe, despite his earlier resolution as stated by the baroness, again encountered difficulties in creating a satisfactory ending. After the chaplain complies with Luise's request, the frame characters are in the mood for a fairy tale. Since such a story comprises a distinct genre, Karl requests that it exclude that which actually occurred ("was wirklich geschehen ist"). The chaplain allows Karl to make this one, but no other demands, because such a tale, he insists, is a venture of the imagination ("ein Produkt der Einbildungskraft") and, as a distinct genre, is borne aloft by its own, unique aesthetic principles (204-209). The chaplain promises to tell a fairy tale that evening and the fifth installment ends. The sixth and final installment consists exclusively of "Das Märchen." Since subscriptions to *Die Horen* were lagging, the journal ceased publication and *Unterhaltungen* stops at this point and remains a fragment.

Many critics credit this work with introducing the novella into the mainstream of German letters. Yet there is no mention of the word *Novelle* in either the *Unterhaltungen* or in the correspondence. Goethe and Schiller both refer exclusively to *Geschichte* or *Erzählung*. Four months after stopping work on *Unterhaltungen*, Goethe reveals he is familiar with the German word, for he writes Schiller that he considers Cervantes's "Novellen" a treasure (*Briefwechsel* 89). For more than a decade Goethe remains silent on the subject. In 1807, however, he begins working on a number of short prose narratives that he eventually incorporated into *Wilhelm Meisters Wanderjahre*. Goethe again avoids the term, for he writes in his *Tag- und Jahresheften*: "Die kleinen Erzählungen beschäftigten mich in heitern Stunden, und auch die 'Wahlverwandtschaften' sollten in der Art kurz behandelt werden" (1809, 670). An entry in the *Annalen* shows that while writing these "Erzählungen," Goethe studied the Romance novella collections. Yet, even here the term is missing: "Veranlaßt, in das Feld der Märchen und kleinen Geschichtchen mich zu wagen, las ich gar manches schon Vorhandene dieser Art: Tausendundeine Nacht, Anekdoten der Königin von Navarra, dann den Decameron des Boccaz" (1809, 604).

Two years after writing this entry Goethe once more reverses himself. In *Die Wahlverwandtschaften* the visiting nobleman asks his companion to provide entertainment by telling stories and anecdotes from his large collection. The companion complies and concludes "mit einer zwar sonderbaren, aber sanfteren Begebenheit" (Goethe 1809, 434), the story "Die wunderlichen Nachbarskinder." This narrative bears the subtitle "Novelle." After this novella has been recounted, Charlotte becomes distraught because this event took place — "diese Begebenheit hatte sich … wirklich zugetragen" (442).

In 1827, upon completing a story that he originally had conceived in the form of an epic poem in 1797, Goethe found himself at a loss for a title. After considering and rejecting a number of unsuitable ones, Goethe finally settled upon a title and, in the process, delivered his now famous definition:

> 'Wissen Sie was,' sagte Goethe, 'wir wollen es die *Novelle* nennen; denn was ist eine Novelle anders als eine sich ereignete unerhörte Begebenheit. Dies ist der eigentliche Begriff, und so vieles, was in Deutschland unter dem Titel Novelle geht, ist gar keine Novelle, sondern bloß Erzählung oder was Sie sonst wollen. In jenem ursprüng-

lichen Sinne einer unerhörten Begebenheit kommt auch die Novelle in den Walhlverwandtschaften vor.' (Eckermann 1836, 170-71)

Goethe's involvement with the novella spanned more than three decades. Early in this process he failed to refer to his own works — and at times to the Romance collections — as novellas. Yet, an examination of *Unterhaltungen* in the light of the practices and criteria described earlier for the Renaissance novella reveals so many parallels it seems clear that Goethe was intent upon mastering the art of this genre. In long-standing novellistic tradition Goethe, too, claims that his stories are meant to entertain. But, just as Pabst noted about Marguerite de Navarre, Goethe also has a moralistic intent that harks back to *utilitas* and *delectatio*. This intent is initially hinted at when the chaplain remarks that he cannot abide bawdy tales. The same sentiment is expressed by the baroness when she pronounces "Der Prokurator" as not only entertaining ("unterhaltend"), but also instructive ("unterrichtend"). Goethe himself, moreover, confirmed these intentions when he praised Cervantes's novellas as a treasure ("Schatz") in terms of "Unterhaltung und Belehrung" and noted that he felt fostered ("gefördert") in his own literary efforts (*Briefwechsel* 89). Parallels between the criteria drawn by Clements and Gibaldi for the Renaissance novella and *Unterhaltungen* include not only the framework, but also such categories as invention (Goethe too borrowed freely), unity (the baroness's call for "die Einheit des Gedichts"), verisimilitude (the presumption that the stories took place), and, as a last example, language and style (the emphasis that the stories be fit entertainment for polite society: "gute Gesellschaft").

A comparison of Goethe's novellistic practices with those of the more recent past reveals additional similarities. Much like the novellists of the Renaissance and the humanists of the late fifteenth century, Goethe, too, translated, adapted, and revised stories from other sources. This tradition of borrowing, it might be mentioned, goes back to ancient Greece, for Aristotle noted on several occasions that the poet was at liberty to take either a "ready-made [story] or invent it himself" (c. 340 B.C., 313). Goethe's sources include *Cent nouvelles nouvelles*, Bassompierre, Clairon, and Pannwitz. Grimmelshausen and other baroque writers incorporated novellas into their novels and, in similar fashion, Goethe embedded "Die wunderlichen Nachbarskinder" into *Die Wahlverwandtschaften* and a half dozen novellas, written in 1807, into *Wanderjahre* (1829). One of these novellas, "Die pilgernde Törin," is a translation from the French

"Cahiers de lecture" published by Reichardt in 1789. Goethe, incidentally, first published five of the *Wanderjahre* novellas as independent "Taschennovellen" in Cotta's *Damenkalender* between 1809 and 1818. In *Unterhaltungen* Goethe simultaneously replicates not only the novellistic traditions of the past, but also those of his own era, for he has the baroness call both "Der Prokurator" and "Ferdinand" *moralische Erzählungen*. The latter story represents a "Familiengemälde" and, in at least one respect, a *Kriminalgeschichte*. "Das Märchen," of course, reflects the fairy tales that became popular during the late eighteenth century.

Goethe's definition of the novella as an unprecedented event that occurred ("eine sich ereignete unerhörte Begebenheit"), much like his novellistic practice, also recaptures the past. Although Goethe delivered this epigrammatical definition in 1827, he had already used a cognate in 1809 to characterize a story that he himself labelled a novella when he described "Die wunderlichen Nachbarskinder" as a strange event that had taken place — "[eine] sonderbare ... Begebenheit" (434), "[die] sich ... wirklich zugetragen [hatte]" (442). Individual elements of Goethe's epigram, as noted in the earlier discussion, also can be found in either incipient or cognate form in passages cited from *Unterhaltungen*. Thus, it is meet that Goethe apply this definition not only to his own works, but also to the Romance novellas from which he derived inspiration, models, and, ultimately, the definition itself. After all, as Goethe tells Eckermann, "der eigentliche Begriff" of a novella, "in jenem *ursprünglichen* [emphasis added] Sinne," is "eine unerhörte Begebenheit."

The Brothers Schlegel

The above discussion abandoned chronology in order to present Goethe's ideas in unified fashion. A return to chronological sequence leads to Friedrich and August Wilhelm Schlegel, both of whom began to theorize about the characteristics of the genre shortly after Goethe published *Unterhaltungen*. Unlike Goethe, they used the term *Novelle* with consistency.

Friedrich, in his various disconnected *Fragmente* and *Ideen zu Gedichten*, develops a number of postulates that are in accord with theories of the novella discussed earlier. Like Wieland, Friedrich too believes that a novella is a streamlined novel ("Roman ohne Psychologie") and that many novels, conversely, are only chains of novellas ("eigentlich nur

Ketten oder Kränzen von Novellen"). The novella, the poetry of high
society, is a well-told "Begebenheit" that is true ("wahr") and that deals
with a singular and arresting oddity ("Seltsamkeit"). Commensurate
with its name, a novella eternally retains its novelty because it is striking
— "überraschend," "unzerstörbar," "frappant." Since both Boccaccio and
Goethe adapted older material, Friedrich also noted, in remarks suggestive of those made by the chaplain about "Ferdinand," that the subject
matter of the novella need not be new as long as the spirit is. Novellas
also exhibit an all-encompassing unity even stricter than the one formulated by Goethe's baroness: "In einer Novelle ist die Einheit zugleich
philosophisch, ethisch und poetisch." In several allusions to Shakespeare,
Friedrich remarks on the close kinship of the novella to the drama. After
noting that a number of Shakespeare's plays are adaptations of novellas,
he even claims that the formal elements of Shakespeare's plays cannot be
understood without a knowledge of novellas — "ohne Novellen zu ken-
nen, kann man Shakspeare's Stücke nicht verstehen der Form nach"
(1797-1801, 3-9).

In 1801 Friedrich wrote an essay on the works of Boccaccio. After
first granting Boccaccio paternity rights to the novella, Friedrich attempts to analyze the characteristics of the genre in a more organized
fashion than he did in the *Fragmente*. The most striking feature of the
novella, he observes, arises from the author's narrative approach, which is
simultaneously objective and subjective. He elaborates on this paradox by
noting that the basis of the novella is an historical event ("ursprünglich
Geschichte"). Hence, the genre normally inclines the author toward objectivity by emphasizing exactitude of detail (history provides "das Lo-
kale und Costum gerne mit Genauigkeit"). This overt, surface objectivity allows the author to superimpose his covert subjectivity ("indirekte
und verborgene Subjektivität"). Thus, even if the novella is a reworking
of a known story, the tension that emanates from this bifurcated narrative stance lends the novella both uniqueness ("jede Novelle [hat] ihre
eigene Signatur") and artistic charm — "Zauber" (9-14). Friedrich also
attempts to consolidate his theory by weaving the various strands with
which he characterizes the novella into one cloth:

> Es ist die Novelle eine Anekdote, eine noch unbekannte Geschichte,
> so erzählt, wie man sie in Gesellschaft erzählen würde, eine Geschich-
> te, die ... interessieren können muß ... [und die, die] Ironie ... mit auf
> die Welt bringt. Da sie interessieren soll, so muß sie in ihrer Form ir-

gend etwas enthalten, was vielen merkwürdig oder lieb sein zu können verspricht. (1801, 12)

Friedrich's characterizations of the novella in many instances come close to duplicating Goethe's remarks in *Unterhaltungen* and, thus, anticipate Goethe's definition of 1827. Such similarities are attributable to the circumstance that the theories of both Goethe and Friedrich were partially shaped by their study of Boccaccio.

Contemporaneously with Friedrich, August Wilhelm also began theorizing about the novella and, much like his brother, developed many of his ideas from his study of the works of Boccaccio, Cervantes, and Goethe. In a review of *Die Horen* in 1796, August Wilhelm comments on *Unterhaltungen* and describes the similarities between the works of Goethe and Boccaccio, but refers to both novella collections as a series of narratives — "Reihe von Erzählungen" (85) — rather than novellas. Two years later, however, he begins his analysis of the genre under the rubric "Die Novelle" by noting that the wellspring of the novella, *The Decameron*, has often been castrated. He points out in *Vorlesungen über schöne Literatur und Kunst* that this operation was performed because the work has been viewed as a scandalous chronicle ("scandalöse Chronik") since most of the stories are considered offensive. August Wilhelm, it should be noted, employs the same phrase Luise initially used to characterize the chaplain's story collection. August Wilhelm then presents an Aristotelian defense against this indictment by pointing out that the stories simply mime reality, "die Welt ist durchaus anstößig." He observes that Cervantes, apparently aware of the pitfalls of such offensiveness, attempted to avoid them by setting high moral standards for his works. Although August Wilhelm lauds this effort, he believes that Cervantes paid too heavy an aesthetic price — he severely limited the thematic scope of the genre and ensnared himself by falling into artificiality, "ins manierirte."

Very much in line with Goethe and his brother Friedrich, August Wilhelm then describes novellas as accounts of incidents that occurred ("wirklich geschehenen Dingen") and that constitute remarkable events ("merkwürdige Begebenheiten"). Since the events actually took place, Schlegel emphasizes that the driving force behind the genre is action: "in der Novelle muß etwas geschehen." In a statement reminiscent of Goethe's chaplain (whose stories involved private matters rather than world-shaking events), August Wilhelm notes that the novella is a story

outside of history ("eine Geschichte außer der Geschichte") because the incident described, although interesting, would normally not merit inclusion in "der eigentlichen Historie." Much like Wieland, he describes the novella as a short novel ("bloß ein Roman im Kleinen"). But since August Whilhelm holds an exceedingly low opinion of novels, he is quick to claim that the novella is superior to the novel because the novel contains neither truth nor action ("erstens enthalten [Romane] keine Wahrheit, sondern Fratzen, und zweytens geschieht auch nichts darin"). This view in some ways parallels Aristotle's claim in the *Art of Poetry* that the tragedy was superior to the epic (340 B.C., 325). Since the function of the novella is one of entertainment ("Erholung" and "Unterhaltung"), August Wilhelm places great value upon the educated and socially accomplished narrator who has the ability to attract and hold the attention of polite society. In terms again reminiscent of both Aristotle and Goethe's chaplain, August Wilhelm describes the contents of novellas as ranging between the serious and farcical ("von ernsten Begebenheiten mit tragischer Katastrophe bis zur bloßen Posse"), with the one type yielding "die tragischen und ernsten" and the other "die komischen Novellen." Irrespective of case, the events should in all instances remain in the real world ("in der wirklichen Welt").

Friedrich noticed an inherent tension in the novella that emanates from a bilateral narrative approach. August Wilhelm noticed a similar tension arising from a dualistic thematic content. Aristotle indicated that although the artist was at liberty to portray "things ... and men as they are," he should avoid the ordinary and present only such objects for mimesis that "stir our wonder" and are "incredible" (320-23). August Wilhelm, in what seems to be a mirroring of these ideas, dictates that the novella should portray reality in its everyday, pedestrian manifestations ("den Weltlauf ... wie er ist"). Concomitantly, it must depict people in their normal, natural condition, with all their foibles ("Schwächen, Leidenschaften und selbstischen Trieben"). Simultaneously, however, the event described also must be extraordinary ("außerordentlich ... einzig ... unwahrscheinlich"). He continues by observing that the demands of these two conflicting criteria, the commonplace versus the extraordinary, not only constitute the dynamic tension of the novella, but also pose a dilemma for the author. August Wilhelm, much like Aristotle, does not shy away from providing practical advice toward resolving this dilemma. Since the most unusual is often the most real ("das Unwahrscheinlichste

... [ist] oft gerade das Wahrste"), he advocates that novella writers give short shrift to the commonplace and emphasize the extraordinary — they should be daring by treating "das alltägliche ... so kurz als möglich" and by concentrating upon the "Außerordentlichen und Einzigen." Writers should not attempt to prop up an improbable event in unseemly fashion ("auf ungehörige Art aufstutzen zu wollen"), but should, instead, simply set it down ("positiv hinstellen") and boldly demand belief ("Glauben dafür fo[r]dern"). These injunctions come remarkably close to Aristotle's observation that "the incredible" is at home in "the epic" and that "a plausible impossibility is always preferable to an implausible possibility" (320-21). Simultaneously, this advice seems to be an oblique reiteration of the baroness's criticism of the first four stories in *Unterhaltungen*.

Friedrich's remarks about the novella and Shakespeare's drama apparently influenced his brother, for August Wilhelm, too, maintains that one cannot understand those plays that Shakespeare adapted from novellas without first studying the original. The relationship between these two genres is such, he speculates, that every novella may be convertible to a drama ("möglich mag es vielleicht seyn, alle Novellen zu dramatisieren"). This theory involving the kinship of genres again seems to be based, at least in part, on Aristotle's *Poetics*. August Wilhelm's strong emphasis on realism ("wirklich geschehenen Dinge") and action ("[es] muß etwas geschehen") reflects not only the Aristotelian mimetic intent of representing "human beings in action" (292), but also the contention that characters are subsidiary to action. Such representation led to comedy and tragedy in the drama and, as just noted, to correspondingly serious and humorous novellas. Aristotle emphasized the functions of reversal and discovery in radically changing the direction of the plot for both tragedies and epics. Goethe's chaplain in similar fashion noted that a number of his stories involved an ingenious twist ("eine geistreiche Wendung"). August Wilhelm, on a parallel track, observes that the novella requires decisive turning points ("die Novelle bedarf entscheidender Wendepunkte") and that the genre shares this need not with the novel, where reversals tend to come about only gradually, but with the drama — "dieß Bedürfnis hat auch das Drama" (1798-1804, 15-21).

From the Schlegels to Goethe's Death

The brothers Schlegel fell silent on the theory of the novella shortly after the turn of the century. A number of other authors and critics developed an interest and began to speculate about the characteristics of the genre, albeit at times with fragmented and only marginally significant commentary. Thus, for the next two decades, these comments, all too often, either lack originality, restate earlier opinions, or are simply deprecatory. In an illustration of the latter, Schelling dismisses the genre by disdaining to involve himself with a minor sub-genre — "Untergattung" (1802-1803, 27). In a passage duplicating Luise's request in *Unterhaltungen*, Wieland notes in *Die Novelle ohne Titel* (1804) that the incidents described by a novella should not take place in "Dschinnistan" or some other exotic place, but in the real world ("in unserer wirklichen Welt") where the events ("Begebenheiten") are not commonplace ("nicht alltäglich") and could occur ("zutragen könnten") at any time (2). In a similar vein Christian Clodius describes the novella as a "kleine Erzählung von Begebenheiten der geselligen Welt" (1804, 28). Friedrich Ast defines it as "eine einzelne Begebenheit und Geschichte" (1805, 29). In an unusual twist Johann Eberhard, upon describing epic poems ("die epischen Gedichte"), lists as undifferentiated examples "Erzählungen … Novellen … und … Mährchen" (1805, 30). Friedrich Bouterwerk aligns himself with ideas expressed in *Unterhaltungen* by observing that novellas narrate "interessante Begebenheiten aus der Sphäre des gemeinen Lebens in eine Art von Anekdotenstyl." Since such works are in either prose or verse and vary greatly in length, Bouterwerk concludes that no theory is possible ("so ist gar keine Theorie des Romans möglich"). Although Bouterwerk seems to be talking about the novel, his conclusion, by extension, applies to the novella, since a novel is merely a large novella — "eine Novelle im Großen" (1806, 30-33). Three years later Aloys Schreiber observes that a novella is simply a prose "Erzählung" of only one "Situation" (1809, 33).

As described earlier, Goethe published a story that he himself labelled a novella, "Die wunderlichen Nachbarskinder," in *Die Wahlverwandtschaften* (1809). Although the novel immediately attracted a great deal of attention, neither the interpolated "Nachbarskinder" nor the genre it represented occasioned much commentary. On the contrary, almost a full decade elapsed before another critic paid any attention to the

genre. In 1817 Georg Reinbeck, like other critics before him, calls the novella a short novel ("ein Roman im Kleinen") that portrays one event — "[eine] einzelne ... Thatsache" (33). In 1819 Friedrich Schleiermacher describes the novella as an "Anekdote" of an historically real event ("geschichtlich wahre Begebenheit") and notes that since it presents only a single event, it is considerable shorter than the novel (22-25). In almost identical fashion Franz Nüsslein describes the novel as depicting a whole world, whereas the novella, which depicts one event ("die prosaische Erzählung einer einzelnen Begebenheit, einer Situation"), resembles one episode of a novel (1819, 39).

In many of the above instances (as well as numerous ones yet to come), the Aristotelian differentiation between the epic and the tragedy seems to have played a significant, albeit unacknowledged role in novella theory. In a sub-chapter entitled "Epic and Tragedy Compared," Aristotle argues for the superiority of tragedy because it "contains everything to be found in the epic." Since the drama "attains its end in shorter compass," the "concentrated effect" of the tragedy is more "pleasurable" than the "diffused" one of the epic. Since an "epic is made up of a number of separate actions" and contains enough material for a "number of tragedies," it has "less unity" than a tragedy. In defense of epics, however, Aristotle notes that the *Iliad* and the *Odyssey* "have many ... parts, each with a magnitude of its own." Each of these parts "is as perfect, and approaches as nearly to the representation of a single action, as possible" (325). Earlier in his treatise, Aristotle had noted that the epic "comprises a number of stories" (314). Many of the critics cited above, through association and extrapolation, seem to have transferred either the differences that Aristotle cites between the epic and the tragedy or the difference between the whole epic and one of its parts to the differences between the novel and the novella.

An examination of the theory of the novella before 1820 corroborates the claim made by Mitchell and Hirsch that, with the exceptions of Goethe and the Schlegel brothers, the term novella did not gain wide circulation in Germany until after 1820. The few comments made by the other critics are either traceable to Aristotle, Goethe's *Unterhaltungen* (his famous definition of 1827 remains unpublished until 1836), or the brothers Schlegel. This tradition persists for much of the remainder of the century, since many critics either reiterate or explicate previous opinions. Yet, other critics strike out on original pathways. Willibald

Alexis, a representative of this group, remarks that a new direction ("ein ganz neuer Kreis") has appeared within the genre of the novella and cites as its best example Ludwig Tieck's *Die Gemälde* (1821). Alexis, apparently unaware of the earlier commentary by Goethe and the Schlegels, believes that no novella theory had yet been formulated and postulates that significant features of the genre include brevity and completeness ("Kürze, Vollendung und Rundung"). Since the novella deals with few events and people, it is, and he uses Aristotle's word, "concentrirt" (1821, 39-41). Two years later, Alexis also acknowledges Cervantes and Goethe as masters of the novella, but continues to insist that Tieck broke new ground with his *Gemälde* (1823, 41). Only four years after Alexis announced the advent of a new novellistic direction, there are indications that the novella had become as popular, and apparently as debased, as the *moralische Erzählungen* of the previous century. Thus, in his review of Tieck's latest novellas in 1825, Alexis first notes that the contemporary literary scene presents a novellistic maze ("[ein] Irrgarten" of stories "welche den Namen Novelle auf dem Titel führen"). Tieck's novellas are by far superior to these works — the qualitative distance is "himmel-weit" — because they comprise (in unwitting, but direct opposition to the theories of the Schlegel brothers) neither an interesting event ("eine interessant verwickelte Begebenheit") nor a story with surprising turns ("eine Erzählung mit überraschenden Wendungen"). On the contrary, in Tieck's novellas, much like in those of Cervantes, a significant theme ("ein bedeutendes Thema") rather than action ("die Handlung") is paramount. Alexis, after noting that the form of the genre is yet to be established, emphasizes that Tieck's novellas have at least one classical characteristic, they possess unity ("einen organischen Zusammenhang"). Upon concluding his review, Alexis seems to confound part of his theory by noting that all of Tieck's novellas contain a surprising turn — "eine überraschende Wendung" (1825, 42-45).

In 1823 Carl Rumohr called attention to the origins of the novella by noting that *novella* originally referred to a novelty or to a news report, and that the Italians, in their novellas, intertwined real with invented events. Rumohr therefore divides novellas into two categories, the poetic and the historical, and believes that the latter serve as sources ("Hülfsquellen") for historical research. The principal determinant of the novella, however, does not depend upon the veracity of the story, but rather upon its verisimilitude, "Wahrheit der Schilderung" (46). Four

years later Karl Rosenkranz observes that novels and novellas are being confused with one another and differentiates between the two genres: novels describe characters who are undergoing a process of formation or education ("Bildung"), whereas novellas contain characters who are already fixed — "von vorn herein bestimmte Individualitäten" (1827, 55).

Only a few months before formulating his famous definition, Goethe echoes Willibald Alexis and other critics of the time by grousing about the state of the contemporary German novella. He writes Wilhelm von Humboldt in 1826 that peculiar things ("gar vieles wunderliche Zeug") are sailing under the flag novella (1795, 723). A few months later, upon delivering the definition itself, he expresses the same view by telling Eckermann "so vieles ... ist gar keine Novelle, sondern bloß Erzählung oder was Sie sonst wollen."

Wilhelm Hauff also complains about the many scribblers ("Almanachsliteraten") flooding the German literary market with their peculiar wares that bear the label novella. Hauff is willing to wager that few, if any, of these two hundred novellists ever bother to think either about the nature ("über die innere Natur") or the rules ("über die Gesetze") of the genre. Only a year later Hauff himself published several novellas. In a satirical foreword, which takes the form of a letter addressed to a Dr. Spöttlich ("Dr. Mockly"), Hauff confesses that as a writer lacking in talent, he, too, felt the urge to ferret out a novella. He therefore joined his colleagues and sought inspiration for novellas by listening to stories told in cafés and taverns. Since this effort met with no success, he sought out elderly women in all parts of Germany and carefully set down their words. Hauff concludes his letter by solemnly assuring Dr. Spöttlich that his method faithfully reflects contemporary novella writing — "wie man beim Novellenschreiben zu Werke geht" (1828, 58-60).

In 1828 Theodor Mundt supported Hauff's views about the popularity of the genre when he remarked that the novella was the centerpoint of contemporary literary activity ("Mittelpunkt der poetischen Bestrebungen"). He too notes, in a reflection of prevailing critical opinion, that many novellas consist of botched efforts ("formlose Machwerke") that were written because the genre was the latest fashion ("um die Mode mit zu machen"). Like Alexis, Mundt also regards Tieck as the creator of the genre, but emphasizes that this author's works transcend by far the "Machwerke." Mundt theorizes that novellas describe a microcosm, as opposed to the novel, which describes a macrocosm. In form,

the novel is linear, whereas the novella is circular and encompasses a midpoint (a "Centrum" or "Mittelpunkt") from which all action radiates and that in natural fashion determines the ending (64-65).

In 1829 Tieck, who until as late as the early twentieth century was credited by critics as the originator of the modern German novella (see Biese 1909, II, 397), also enters the arena of theory by observing that his contemporaries mistakenly label all prose narratives novellas. Tieck traces the word *Novelle* to Italy where it was used to characterize incidents or stories that were new or unknown ("neu noch nicht bekannt"). He cautions that *Novelle* should not be construed as identical with narrative forms such as "Begebenheit, Geschichte, Erzählung, Vorfall, oder gar Anekdote." A novella is distinguishable from these narratives in that it takes an incident and illuminates it with the brightest of lights ("[stellt] einen ... Vorfall in's hellste Licht"). This incident, which is of such a nature that it could take place in the real world, is wondrous or singular ("wunderbar, vielleicht einzig"). Tieck believes that once the singularity of the event in the novella becomes self-evident, it is accompanied by a natural, yet dramatic change of direction in the story line that leads to an unforeseen, but logical ending. Tieck, like Mundt, first calls this change the midpoint ("Mittelpunkt") and, five lines later, the turning point ("Wendepunkt"). Tieck accords the novella great latitude of form and content but insists, in seeming direct opposition to Willibald Alexis, that a genuine ("ächte") novella will always have the turning point — "jenen sonderbaren auffallenden Wendepunkt" — as its distinguishing feature (74-76).

Tieck's much-celebrated "Wendepunkt" will come to represent, along with Goethe's definition and the yet-to-be discussed falcon theory of Paul Heyse, one of the three most significant elements in modern discussions of the novella. The idea of the "Wendepunkt" is not unique to Tieck, since it can be traced back first to Aristotle and his theories about the epic and the drama and, when applied to the novella, to Tieck's contemporaries — Goethe, August Wilhelm Schlegel, and Mundt. Tieck's presentation of the "Wendepunkt/Mittelpunkt," moreover, is confusing since it remains unclear whether he intended one such point as did Mundt, or several as did Aristotle and A. W. Schlegel. When he theorizes about the genre, Tieck uses the singular form and notes that he is providing an example ("ein Beispiel") from Goethe's "Ferdinand" in the *Unterhaltungen*. Yet, he lists two such points. He singles out Ferdinand's

chance discovery of the broken lock (the chaplain had called it "ein son-
derbarer Zufall") as such a turning point, since it provides Ferdinand
with an opportunity to steal money when he most urgently desires it.
Tieck also cites a later, equally significant turning point when he comments on Ferdinand's repentance and determination to mend his ways
and to restore the money (1829, 75). Tieck's description of the novella as
a "Vorfall" placed "ins hellste Licht" comes remarkably close to duplicating the chaplain's characterization of the Ferdinand novella as "eine Begebenheit" that sets Ferdinand's character "ins Licht."

    In the same year Tieck develops his "Wendepunkt," Wilhelm Meyer
vents his frustration by observing that the attempt to define the novella
is an exceedingly unrewarding task ("ein mißliches Ding"). The genre
not only resembles a chameleon, but mocks all attempts to clap it into
the irons of theory. After complaining about the execrable quality of
many current novellas, Meyer interprets the popularity of the genre as a
sign of youthful exuberance that, upon maturity, would produce works of
better quality. He next describes the novella as portraying a remarkable
inversion ("eine auffallende Verirrung oder Verkehrtheit") that involves a
puzzling moral phenomenon ("eine rätselhafte Erscheinung in der
moralischen Welt"). Aristotle had noted that the drama portrays one
episode of the epic. Meyer argues, analogously, that the novella lifts a
single moment or an interesting scene out of a larger drama. Aristotle
had observed that "every tragedy falls into two parts — the complication
or 'tying up' and the resolution or 'unraveling'" and that "many poets are
good at tying the knot but poor at untying it" (313-14). Meyer completes the Aristotelian paradigm for the novella when he observes that
the novella ties a knot which it attempts to unravel — "ja das Eigentliche und Wesentliche der Novelle möchte wohl sein, daß sie ... einen
Knoten schürzt, den sie auf geschickte Art zu lösen sucht" (1829-1830,
79-82).

3: The Age of Realism (1833-1914)

IN THEIR DISCUSSION of the novella Clements and Gibaldi observe that the Renaissance critics had failed to develop a theory for the genre because they had been at a loss when it came to evaluating prose as an artistic medium. They attribute this failure to the circumstance that both the ancient Greek and Roman aestheticians had ignored prose (1977, 6-7). Early German theorists, as discussed in the previous chapter, found themselves in similar straits. Several critics began to adapt and to transfer Aristotelian aesthetic principles to the novella. These adaptations, Aristotle's original theories, and the ideas developed by Goethe, the Schlegel brothers, Tieck, and other writers combined over the course of years to form a central core of criticism and theory to which later critics could react.

Biedermeier and Young Germany

In the year following Goethe's death, Theodor Mundt returns to the theory of the novella. He traces the origins of the genre to the anecdote which, he notes, was told for the sake of its "Pointe." To Mundt, the novella is so distinct a form that it could not possibly be confused with the novel. The novel has a clear beginning and, as a cycle ("Cyclus") of relationships and moments ("Verhältnissen und Momenten"), deals with a sequence of events ("Reihe von Begebenheiten"). The novella, in contrast, has an unfocused beginning and depicts only a single relationship and moment in life — "[ein] Verhältnis und Lebensmoment." The novel has a diffuse ending, whereas the novella, which is concentrated around the "Mittelpunkt," rushes toward a well-defined, concluding "Pointe," which is an obvious development or outgrowth of the "Mittelpunkt." Much as he did five years earlier, Mundt continues to believe that in form the novel is linear and the novella circular. Mundt sees his theory reflected in Tieck's *Der Aufruhr in den Cevennen*. In this novella, which portrays only one human life, Tieck does not concentrate upon the development of his main character, but upon one significant "Moment" that becomes the "Mittelpunkt" of the narrative. Not only is every character in the novella in one way or another affected by this "Moment," but all action either emanates from or revolves around this "Mittelpunkt."

Mundt concludes his analysis by remarking that Tieck's novella embod-
ies the circularity ("die zirkelartige Construction") he considers the hallmark of the genre (1833, 64-69). Mundt, it might be noted, is one of
only a few critics of the period who attempts to gauge his theory against
an example of the genre.

A year later Mundt criticizes the Biedermeier attitude of his fellow
Germans. Instead of becoming politically informed and engaged, his
countrymen retreat into the secure confines of their homes to read novellas. This genre has acquired such immense popularity in Germany during the last few decades that Mundt feels justified in calling it a German
house pet — "[ein] deutsches Hausthier." Since Germans rarely go out
— and when they do, it is only to see a farce by Kotzebue — Mundt intends to capture their political attention surreptitiously through the novella. He regards the novella as a splendid field for political allegory and,
as a political activist and advocate of "das junge Deutschland," intends to
cultivate this potentially productive field — "Ich säe und ärnte auf ihrem
Acker" (1834, 69-71).

While Mundt is developing interesting and original genre theories,
Karl Immermann is rehearsing ideas from the past: a novella is short and
narrates a strange incident that seems to have occurred. The mainspring
of the novella, he concludes is the plot — "Die Hauptsache bei einer
Novelle ist die Fabel" (1833, 85-86).

Heinrich Laube, yet another "young German," notes that the concept
of the novella has become diffuse — "breit und vag." After abandoning
the simplicity of Boccaccio, and after enduring decades of degradation
inflicted first by the Rationalists and then by the Romantics, the genre
has become mired in a deep swamp. One artist, Ludwig Tieck, has risen
above the creation of novellistic swamp creatures, for with his works he
has reestablished the novella as a superior narrative form. Laube also
distinguishes between the novella and the novel. The former deals with
the process of becoming, the latter with the finished product of this
process ("die Novelle beschäftigt sich mehr mit dem Werden, der Roman mit dem Gewordenen"). He then assumes the role of matchmaker
by advocating nuptials between the two genres because such a union
would produce the perfect form, the "Roman-Novelle" (1833, 86-89).
Since confusion about these two genres persists, Laube two years later
again emphasizes the differences. The novella depicts the external world,
whereas the novel strives for an exhaustive portrayal of both external and

internal life. The novella presents a segment of life ("einen Ausschnitt des großen Lebenskreises") in a more condensed form ("schärfer, spitzer, kürzer, wiederum einseitiger, überraschender") than that of the all-encompassing novel (1835, 89-90).

Eduard von Bülow, in the foreword to a collection of a hundred older novellas, expresses the hope that through the examples he has chosen, he will be able to clarify the modern notions involving the novella. In recent times ideas about this genre have gone awry since every narrative is mistakenly labelled a novella. Bülow, while advancing no theory of the novella, seems to be the first critic to recognize and to praise Heinrich von Kleist as one of Germany's earliest master novella writers (1834, 92).

More than a decade after his original attempt to come to grips with the genre, Carl Friedrich von Rumohr writes a satire in which a number of characters engage in a critical discussion of the novella. The "Dichter" notes that the contemporary novellist, all too often, is nothing but a gossip ("Klätscher"). Another character, "die Putzmacherin," observes that the word has lost all meaning, for upon attempting to define the genre, one comes to the conclusion that novellas are novellas. Yet another character makes an identical discovery about another genre: "die eigentliche Erzählung ... ist eben nur Erzählung." After an exchange of similarly unedifying discourse, Rumohr concludes his satire by having a fourth character, "der Kenner," describe the novella as an impenetrable mystery — "[ein] Strudel und Wasserwirbel ... ein bewegter Abgrund voll unaufgeklärter, undurchdringlicher Räthsel" (1835, 47-54).

The novella next attracts the attention of Karl Gutzkow and Franz Grillparzer. Despite their stature in the world of German letters, neither author contributes much in the way of original ideas to the theory of the novella. Gutzkow, like many critics of the time, observes that this noble genre, which incorporates more dramatic than epic elements, is being denigrated by having its name affixed to every poor piece of short prose fiction (1835, 93). Grillparzer, the author of two famous works generally regarded as novellas, *Das Kloster bei Sendomir* (written 1827) and *Der arme Spielmann* (written 1832), observes somewhat rhapsodically that the novella represents the descent of poetry to prose, the novel represents the striving of prose to ascend to poetry — "die Novelle ist das Herabneigen der Poesie zur Prosa, der Roman das Hinaufstreben der Prosa zur Poesie" (1837, 96).

Friedrich Hebbel, initially responding more to Tieck's works than attempting to define the genre, believes this author creates such a noticeably strong tension in his novella characters that it becomes evident they must change ("die Menschen können nicht so bleiben, wie sie sind"). Tieck's novellas, therefore, seem to depict characters who are in the process of becoming while his novels deal with fully developed characters (1838, 96). Three years later Hebbel remarks that the epic, although long dead, had left a number of heirs, one of which is the novella. Hebbel, apparently after reading Eckermann's recently published *Gespräche mit Goethe* (1836), becomes one of the first writers to concur with and to apply Goethe's definition (1841, 98-99). Hebbel continues to embrace this definition for some time, since fourteen years later he writes to Arnold Schloenbach that the unprecedented event is the mainspring of the novella — "die neue, unerhörte Begebenheit ... ist und bleibt in der Novelle die Hauptsache" (1855, 101).

Hermann Marggraff characterizes the novella as an expanded anecdote ("erweiterte Anekdote") that narrates a single "Begebenheit" and is, therefore, a reduced novel. Although he makes no original observations, Marggraff joins many of his contemporaries by delivering a diatribe against the current state of the novella. This genre, which the old Italians and Spaniards had mastered to a high degree, has degenerated: the former "Kunstform" has become a "Mißform" and, in the hands of modern German writers, has been transformed from an "Art der Kunst" into an "Abart" (1839, 103-106).

In an historically oriented essay, "Die Novelle. Didaskalie," Ernst Freiherr von Feuchtersleben accuses his compatriots of being overly intellectual because they demand a metaphysical theory for every trivial sphere of human activity, including, presumably, the novella. Thus, he first criticizes one element of Goethe's definition, the term "unerhört," on an etymological basis because a novella is nothing but something new ("Neuigkeit"). The definition is exaggerated because Goethe formulated it only to characterize his *Novelle* of 1828 which, along with the earlier "Nachbarskinder," Feuchtersleben considers as both peculiar and devoid of soul ("seltsam [und] seelenlos"). He considers it fortunate that Goethe's *Unterhaltungen* and *Wanderjahre* contain novellas that are as charming ("anziehend niedlich") as are those of Boccaccio. Feuchtersleben acknowledges Goethe and Tieck as masters of the German no-

vella and laments that Heinrich von Kleist, very much their artistic equal, has remained so long unrecognized.

Upon considering other aspects of theory, Feuchtersleben observes that the novella too long has been defined as a short novel. Such a definition is mistaken because it implies that the novella merely is a foreshortened, insufficiently developed novel. The two genres can best be differentiated by their portrayal of character. The novel develops character through a series of events, the novella reveals character through a single catastrophe. The nature of catastrophe differs by genre: in the drama, it is violent; in the novel, it is either continual or repeated; and in the novella, it falls between these extremes. Employing Aristotelian terms, Feuchtersleben notes that the catastrophe in the novella gradually unravels one simple knot. As a result, the novella is intolerant of multiple episodes and concentrates only upon the main event, usually a single, protracted moment of one deed — "[ein] einziges retardirendes Moment bei Einer That." Feuchtersleben is loath to characterize the novella further because all norms ("Gesetze") in the realm of art, including the ones he has just formulated for the novella, must be regarded as "negativ." Such matters, he advocates, are best left to the creative spirit of the artist (1841, 106-12).

Twenty-four years after first describing the novella as a small novel, Georg Reinbeck feels compelled to attempt a clarification of the theory of the novella since literary novices and experts alike are confusing this genre with the novel. He differentiates among the various types of prose narratives and initially describes the novella as a poetic tale that transmits an event that could have taken place. Not every such poetic narrative is a novella. If the narrative is broad in scope and depicts a series of events that logically belong together to form an organic unity, it is an epic ("Epopöe"); if these events portray cultural life ("Culturleben") it is a novel; and if they deal with nature ("Naturleben"), it is an idyll. If the narrative portrays only one situation or event and originates in nature, it is still an (presumably short) idyll; if in the world of fantasy, a fairy tale; if in religion, a legend; if in folk tradition, a saga; and if in cultural life, a novella.

Since both novel and novella deal with cultural life, they can be distinguished by scope. The novel normally encompasses a significant portion of a human life, a whole life, or even more than one life. The novel, stated briefly, is a poetic biography. The novella, on the other hand, deals

with only one unusual situation in a human life. The novella shares this concentration upon one event with the drama. Owing to its episodic structure, the reading of a novel can be interrupted without destroying the total impact of the work or the reader's interest. Since the novella is strictly narrative in form ("rein erzählend") and heir to a long oral tradition, the reader lacks interest in peripheral issues or the narrator's opinions and is anxious to read the work in one sitting. Reinbeck also observes that since a novella is a streamlined narrative, motivation is only casually suggested — "beiläufig angedeutet." Despite this casual approach, every detail needs, nevertheless, to have the appearance of adequate motivation (1841, 34-38).

Oscar Wolff describes the original Italian novella as a well-narrated novelty that, despite its brevity, consists of a complete "Begebenheit." The Spaniards and French expanded the novella into an *Erzählung* and the Germans stretched it even further. The novella in Germany has therefore become a hermaphroditic genre — "ein Zwitter von Erzählung, Novelle und Roman, oft dies Alles zusammen" (1841, 112-13).

In his multi-volume *Geschichte der Deutschen Dichtung* Georg Gervinus cites Tieck as the originator of both the German fairy tale and the German novella. In Tieck's early career his writings resembled the medieval tales of fantasy that the Romantics seemed so much to admire. His more recent works (novellas), commencing in the 1820s, deal with an individual coping with problems in a modern setting. Tieck's primary models were the novellas of Cervantes and Goethe. Through the efforts of Goethe and Tieck, the novella became the most popular genre of the period. This popularity, along with the involvement of many other authors, has led to a generic amorphousness. Gervinus, in scholarly fashion, cites the conclusions of earlier theoreticians in an attempt to capture the essence of the genre. He notes the novella "verhält sich zum Roman wie die poetische Erzählung zum Epos" (Aristotle and Wieland). It is a "vereinzelte Begebenheit" (Goethe) or "eine Situation" (Reinbeck) that, unlike the novel, is limited to Mundt's single moments — "einzelne Momente" (1842, 113-14).

Otto Lange describes the novella as a child born in southern latitudes, where it originally was a short, erotic tale ("eine kleine Erzählung von erotischem Charakter"). In modern times this genre, which he considers to be a poem, has expanded in length and has become indistinguishable from the novel. Lange considers it fortunate, however, that

Goethe has left posterity with an outstanding example of this genre, a poem ("ein Gedicht") that serves as a prototype — "Maaßstab für das ... was eine eigentliche Novelle genannt zu werden verdient" (1844, 115). This yardstick, although unspecified, presumably is Goethe's *Novelle* of 1828.

Poetic Realism

In his literary history of Romanticism Hermann Hettner differentiates, as have many commentators, between the novel and the novella by scope: the former portrays the totality of the world and the latter — here Hettner seems to rely almost exclusively upon Tieck — is limited to a single "Vorfall" which is set "in's hellste Licht" and illuminated from all sides. Commensurate with its etymology, the genre emphasizes the vagaries of chance, unprecedented events, and surprisingly new relationships. The unexpected twists and turns that attend the novelty of such a single event are comparable with the Aristotelian "Peripetie" and distinguish the novella from all other narratives. Without actually using the terms, Hettner undoubtedly had Tieck's "Mittelpunkt/Wendepunkt" in mind (1850, 116).

Joseph Freiherr von Eichendorff, in yet another literary history, also credits Tieck for being the first German writer to master the art of the novella. Tieck accomplished this feat in the early 1820s, shortly after abandoning Romanticism, by modelling his works upon those of Cervantes. Yet, Eichendorff criticizes the works of both novellists — he faults Cervantes for preciosity and Tieck for writing only occasional novellas ("Zwecknovellen"). Eichendorff joins a large company of critics by defining the novella in terms of size and describes it as portraying one piquant scene ("aus dem Gesammtleben irgend eine einzelne pikante Szene"). Tieck's novellas, however, tend to be dialogues of art criticism ("dialogisirte Kunstkritiken"), a development Eichendorff deplores as unhealthy — "der umgekehrte Weg der gesunden Dichtung" (1851, 117-18).

Early in his career as a writer, Theodor Storm cites Gervinus' popular and influential literary history and singles out the passage where Gervinus, using Reinbeck's term, refers to the novella as a single "Situation" or "Moment" of poetic interest. In that sense, Storm notes, his own prose works are novellas for they owe their brevity to his very

conscious attempt to portray only the truly poetic — "das wirklich Poetische" (1851, 118-19).

In a brief foreword to a volume of his collected novellas that appeared in 1854, Tieck, who had died in 1853, refers all critics or readers
who might be interested in the form of the novella to his remarks in the
preface to his work of 1829 (see the discussion in the previous chapter).
Tieck apparently had much less confidence in his earlier analysis than
his above suggestion implies. Rudolf Köpke, in conversations with Tieck
between 1849-1853, reports him as saying that it is difficult to define the
novella ("es ist nicht leicht zu sagen, was eigentlich die Novelle sei, und
wie sie sich von den verwandten Gattungen, Roman und Erzählung,
unterscheide"). Upon analyzing his own works, Tieck remarks that a
number of his novellas have a point ("eine Spitze"), yet others do not.
Tieck therefore concludes that it is hard to find a common denominator
("einen allgemeinen Begriff") which adequately describes all novellas.
Judging from the context of Tieck's remarks, it remains unclear whether
the above "Spitze" in any way is related to his earlier "Mittelpunkt" or
"Wendepunkt" or to Mundt's "Pointe" (1855, 78).

Moriz Carriere, in yet another history of literature, offers what now
can be considered a traditional compilation of characteristics of the novella: it is related to the novel much like a poetic narrative is related to
the epic, and it deals with a single situation that is either freely invented
or based upon historical fact. Since its very name implies novelty, the
genre concentrates upon unusual events, unique characters, or upon the
twists of mood and fate — "Wendungen des Gemüths und Schicksals"
(1854, 121).

Friedrich Theodor Vischer employs a different simile, albeit a very
familiar idea, when he postulates that the novella is related to the novel
like a single ray of light is related to a broad beam ("wie ein Strahl zu
einer Lichtmasse"). The novel involves an all-encompassing portrayal of
world conditions through a series of "Situationen." The novella concentrates upon portraying only one segment or slice of life. He calls attention to the thematic singularity of the novella by stating that the genre
deals with one human life, one "Situation," one human experience, one
crisis, or one twist of fate. Vischer then traces the origins of the novella
to Boccaccio, whom he simultaneously blames and praises for discovering and for revealing to the world that human beings are mortal. Unlike
the *Schwank* and the anecdote, which in the main are humorous, the no-

vella provides an insight into the serious depths of life and inclines, therefore, with regularity toward the tragic (1857, 122).

Rudolph Gottschall characterizes the genre as a prose narrative of one "Begebenheit" that excludes the magical elements of the fairy tale ("das Wunderbare des Märchens"). Using Aristotelian terms, Gottschall notes that this type of narrative, like the drama, progresses rapidly toward a crisis and tends to tie and unravel only one knot. The novella originated in Italy and Spain and was transplanted into Germany by the Romantics, especially by Tieck. The proliferation of novellas in journals and newspapers suggests that the current state of novellistic affairs is in a period of decline — "belletristische Verflachung" (1858, 125-26).

In his book on aesthetics, Friedrich Beck takes a new tack in differentiating between the novel and the novella: the former derives its content from the era of the heroic sagas ("aus der alten Heldenzeit"), whereas the latter deals with events of consequence that occur in the present, hence its name. The poet, by a few but broad and powerful strokes, portrays a contemporary situation in which individuals are engaged in action (1862, 126).

Wilhelm Heinrich Riehl notes in the foreword to his collection of narratives, *Geschichten aus alter Zeit* (1863), that he could as easily have used the more elevated term "Novelle," but chose, instead, the German word for story ("Geschichte"). Riehl prefers the German term because it implies to him that action dominates ("daß ... etwas geschehe, daß nicht die Reflexion, sondern die Tat den Knoten schlinge und löse"). The true story teller, Riehl argues, emphasizes the firm, pure line of action ("die feste, reine Linie der Handlung") and only hints at other matters (127).

Ludwig Eckardt traces the antecedents of the novella to the anecdote, an unknown story ("unbekannte Geschichte") originally told for the sake of its witty, concluding "Pointe." This type of conclusion continues to characterize the novella in modern times. The novel portrays a whole life, the novella depicts only a slice of life until it encounters either an external or an internal turning point. The limited length of the novella inclines it toward symbolism and rapid narrative progression. The narrative stance of the novelist is objective, that of the novellist subjective (1865, 139-40).

In 1868 Gutzkow refocuses his attention upon the theory of the novella. He postulates that *Roman, Novelle*, and *Erzählung* all undertake the portrayal of the human condition ("Menschenschicksalen"). The

novel does so in broad-scale, universal terms, whereas the novella limits itself to particulars. The mainspring that drives the action of the novella is chance ("Zufall"). The *Erzählung*, the simplest of the three narrative forms, excludes both the universal as well as the particular and depends, instead, on its internal, self-contained premises ("Voraussetzungen") — premises that Gutzkow does not specify. He does specify, however, that the *Erzählung* resembles the drama. The novella stands highest within the hierarchy of prose narrative forms because the writer fashions events in such a way that they appear as chance to the affected character, but as fate to everyone else. The novellist thus faces a daunting task: he must make sense out of what initially seems to be nonsense (94-95).

Hermann Oesterley believes that the novel and novella developed simultaneously and, with the exception of scope, are identical. The novel presents an all-encompassing portrait, the novella only a segment ("Ausschnitt"). In order to develop this excerpt into a well-crafted work of art, the novella strives toward a centerpoint ("Mittelpunkt" or "Schwerpunkt") and narrates only one "Begebenheit" that involves a so-cial conflict (1870, 140-41).

In 1871 Paul Heyse and Hermann Kurz published what was to be-come the very famous *Deutscher Novellenschatz*. In the foreword, Heyse provides a brief history and analysis of the novella. Goethe had originally introduced the genre into Germany and Kleist had provided a number of splendid examples. But it was Ludwig Tieck who first brought the no-vella to national attention by sundering it from the fantasy world of the Romantics and by attempting to restore it to its rightful place, the realm of reality. This process took several decades. The novella did not come into its own until the romantic spell was completely broken by the dawning of the age of "Realismus." The return of society at large to a realistic Weltanschauung also led the narrative arts to seek out the trail of reality originally blazed by Goethe. Hardly had literature again been set upon the right path when it was endangered by the ever-increasing needs of newspapers and magazines. This insatiable journalistic demand led to over-production and all literature, including the novella, suffered by becoming hackneyed.

Heyse distinguishes between the old-style and the modern novella. The former consists of a simple report of a remarkable event or an imaginative adventure story. The modern novella, by contrast, portrays the deepest and most morally significant questions of life. Heyse then

differentiates between the novel and the novella by scope rather than by length. The novel is a complicated construct of interlocking circles that represents human lives and attempts to depict a whole culture or society. The novella is a concentrated and intensified portrayal of one such circle, of one conflict or "Schicksals-Idee," of only one human being in action.

Heyse reveals that he and Kurz chose the narratives for their *Novellenschatz* by using the criterion of distinctiveness. The basic plot ("Grundmotiv") of a novella should not only be unique, but also should be such that it lends itself to a brief summary that stands out in strong relief or silhouette. The latter characteristic, Heyse believes, is so important that it can be used as a gauge for determining the suitability of the plot for a novella. Heyse singles out as an outstanding example Boccaccio's ninth novella of the fifth day, the story of Federigo degli Alberighi and his falcon. This story contains all the hallmarks of a novella since it portrays the lives of two people through an external twist of fate that develops the characters more deeply ("durch eine äußere Zufallswendung, die aber die Charaktere tiefer entwickelt"). The falcon, moreover, renders this tale so singular that it remains indelibly imprinted in the memory of the reader. Heyse ends by suggesting to novella writers that it would do no harm to identify the location of the "falcon," the specific thing that differentiates their story from a thousand other ones — "wo 'der Falke' sei, das Spezifische, das diese Geschichte von tausend anderen unterscheidet" (141-49). This portion of Heyse's analysis became famous as the "Falkentheorie," gained wide acceptance, and was interpreted to mean that a novella should contain a concrete, unifying symbol (see, for example, François 1891, 268).

Almost two decades after first attempting to define the novella, Friedrich Theodor Vischer returns to the topic by first describing his own work, *Auch Einer* (not published until 1878). Vischer explains that originally he intended to write only a short *capriccio*, but the work grew to the point where it became difficult to categorize — too long for a *capriccio*, yet too short for a novel. Vischer advocates that if *Auch Einer* must be classified, it should fall under the rubric novella. He emphasizes that it be so labelled not on account of its length, but on account of its portrayal of one narrow band of life ("einen schmäleren Ausschnitt aus dem Leben"). The broad canvas of a novel, by contrast, depicts a whole life. Vischer also differentiates between the two genres much as had

Mundt in 1828: he too describes the structure of the novel as linear and that of the novella as radiating around a "Centrum" (1874, 124).

Wilhelm Heinrich Riehl provides a tongue-in-cheek account of how he accidentally had fallen in with a company of "Poeten" and unwittingly had written novellas without knowing what a novella was. This lack of knowledge did not prove to be a handicap because many a celebrated no-vellist labors under identical circumstances. In his own novellistic efforts, Riehl reports, he had forgotten to narrate and had instead concentrated on character portrayal. Fortunately, his friend Heyse came along to shed light upon his darkness and to initiate him into the mysteries of the no-vella: the novella is nothing more than the portrayal of a psychological conflict that is solved by a story told in the economical, concise form of a narrative lecture. Despite this injunction for economy, many authors turned profligate by writing far too many novellas (1874, 127-28).

In the same year, Gottfried Keller writes that the modern penchant for speculating about the novella is totally unwarranted. Current efforts to establish the form of the novella through *a priori* speculation remind him of alchemists seeking the philosopher's stone ("Goldmacherelixier"). Keller disdains all theory and states that the writer should simply do his best and, with his next effort, should strive to do better (157). Only a year later, however, Keller inadvertently reveals that he too harbors a no-vella theory of sorts. He writes Friedrich Theodor Vischer that one of his Seldwyla *Geschichten* (Keller used the word *Novelle* sparingly to char-acterize his own works) is a short novel. This development evolved be-cause much of the material was presented through summary and deduction. Such a narrative approach, Keller notes, is typical for the novel, but not for the novella, which requires an approach that focuses on anecdotal action — "anekdotisch geschehend" (1875, 157).

In 1875 Heyse writes Theodor Storm that he has just examined his novella anthology ("Schatzgräberei") and has inspected each novella for the presence of its "Falken." He confesses that he takes it amiss when he fails to find a novellistic motif with a problem or a psychological colli-sion and is unable to suppress a secret yearning for a "Mittelpunkt" that organizes the work (149).

Friedrich Spielhagen acknowledges that the attempt to differentiate between novella and novel has caused many critics headaches. He feels confident that he will not be gainsaid when he describes the novella as dealing with fully-developed or fixed characters. The novella merely de-

scribes or reveals the nature of these characters and brings them into a conflict that it then resolves. This resolution is so consistent with the nature of the characters that the ending is predetermined. Older novellas emphasize the intertwining of conditions and relationships, modern novellas emphasize the uniqueness of the characters. In both cases the novella has a small cast of characters, highlights only one event or action, and comes to a rapid, direct conclusion. The novel, in addition to its breadth of subject matter, portrays a large cast of characters and details their development, environment, and education. The novelist therefore pursues his goals at a leisurely pace along meandering pathways.

Despite these clear and distinct differences between the genres, both the layman and the experienced aesthetician at times confuse the two. Spielhagen attributes such confusion to the peculiarity of the contemporary novella. Modern man no longer can tell a tale with the direct simplicity of a Boccaccio. Boccaccio saw but one dimension, one color, one remarkable event that took place among a few people and simply converted this material into a novella. The modern writer, however, sees multiple dimensions, a rainbow of colors, and before he is even aware of it, has unwittingly transformed the remarkable event of what should have been a novella into a novel by stressing surroundings and the genesis of the characters (1876, 160-62).

Theodor Storm reports in 1881 that Georg Ebers had remarked in a newspaper that a serious writer should allow himself the recreational luxury of writing such a trifle as a novella only after he had completed a true work of art, a three-volume novel (Ebers's original remarks seem to have been lost, see the Storm-Keller *Briefwechsel* 1877-1887, 75-76). An incensed Storm responded with a short apologetic of the novella that he intended to publish as a preface to an upcoming, Christmas edition of his works. In terms that seem partially borrowed from Heyse, Storm avers that the modern novelle is a serious art form and no longer simply the brief, gripping account of an unusual event with a surprising "Wendepunkt." Like its sister, the drama, the modern novella can deal with the most profound and significant questions of life. Just like the drama, the novella requires a conflict at midpoint that organizes the whole work. Both genres also require a tautness of style that excludes all inessentials. For these reasons the novella is the strictest and most demanding of the prose genres (119-20).

As he later wrote Gottfried Keller, Storm decided against publishing this "Preface" because Paul Heyse advised against doing so. Keller, in agreement with Heyse, replies with an analogue, telling Storm that a dinner guest should not, along with the main dish, also be presented with the recipe. Keller then restates the position he had formulated in 1874: he considers *a priori* theories and rules inappropriate for all forms of art, but especially for the novella since this genre is still in its formative stages — "das Werden der Novelle ... ist ja noch immer im Fluß" (*Briefwechsel*, 80). Two years later, upon describing his latest novella, *Zur Chronik von Grieshuus*, Storm reveals in a letter to Keller that he is not in total agreement with Heyse's theories, for in this work he simply sets the falcon free — "[ich laße] den Boccaccioschen Falken unbekümmert fliegen" (*Briefwechsel*, 123).

Six years after differentiating between the novella and the novel, Friedrich Spielhagen returns to the topic. He remarks that in Germany the two genres, as recognized in theory and observed in practice, are sharply differentiated. Thus, when a German author of consequence, a Paul Heyse or a Gustav Freytag, writes either a novella or a novel, he proceeds in the fashion of an architect first to lay a proper foundation, suitable, as the situation requires, for either a palace or villa. Such is not the case in France, where an aesthetic laxness prevails in both theory and practice. The novella, he insists, deals with a small number of fixed characters in conflict. The main task of the novellist is to work out this conflict and to depict the catastrophe as briefly as possible.

The modern novella, Spielhagen concedes, has a propensity to portray the most complicated of human situations and conflicts and tends to tarry among details. Such lingering often expands a novella into a novel. As a corrective, Spielhagen advocates a return to fundamentals by applying and adhering to Goethe's definition. A novella thus should subordinate all other concerns in order to concentrate upon portraying one unique "Begebenheit." The novel, on the other hand, should attempt to portray the whole human condition through exhaustive detail. Upon comparing the two narrative genres to the drama, Spielhagen concludes that the differences are sufficiently clear to allow for the formulation of strict rules. One rule dictates that no motif can serve simultaneously for both a novel and a drama. Therefore, no novel can be transformed into a drama. A novella motif, however, is almost always dramatic. Thus every novella can be transformed into a drama. These rules, while not in-

scribed upon stone tablets, are nevertheless valid. Such a conclusion, Spielhagen avows, is supported by many an "unerhörte Begebenheit" involving a small number of characters that has been transformed into drama (1882, 162-66).

Theodor Fontane reports that Rudolf Lindau, during the course of a visit, criticized modern German novellas because they failed to adhere to novellistic principles as revealed to him by Ivan Turgenev twenty-five years earlier. Lindau found contemporary novellas deficient because they lacked veracity, objectivity, reality ("Wahrheit, Objektivität, Realität") and then listed a number of poor novella writers. Fontane, although he fails to reproduce this list, does note that he could not bring himself to disagree with Lindau's assessment. Both men did agree, however, that four contemporary writers, Keller, Meyer, Storm, and Anzengruber, were very much the exceptional novellists of the day (1883, 170-71).

In 1885 Wilhelm Heinrich Riehl returned to the topic of the novella, this time by writing a satirical essay in which he compares the novella with the sonata. Both genres, he notes, are of Italian origin and both terms lack meaning. The two terms were imported into Germany during earlier times, but have now come to dominate the contemporary German art scene in the form of treasures, a "Novellenschatz" as well as a "Sonatenschatz." The genre is considered by many Germans as ultramodern, yet ancient Egyptian, Chinese, Roman and medieval poets also wrote novellas. Music, too, is considered a modern art form, yet the ancient Greeks plagued themselves with noises only they called music. Both the sonata and the novella should be heard only by small audiences.

Riehl interweaves a number of serious theoretical, historical, and analytical observations into his satire, but destroys the impact of every such remark by following it with a humorous *non sequitur*. In his conclusion, Riehl informs the reader that he should consider the material he has just read as the outline of a novella. He offers to bequeath this outline to any reader interested in transforming it into a novella. The raw material for this genre is so ubiquitous, he observes, that anyone can reach out and grasp it (128-39).

Conrad Ferdinand Meyer echoes, apparently unwittingly, Friedrich Schlegel's theory that the hallmark of the novella is a historical event that the author transmits through a narrative stance that is simultaneously objective and subjective. Meyer writes Felix Bovet in 1888 that he prefers the historical novella to the "Zeitroman" because this genre

allows him to lodge, in disguised form, "mes expériences et mes sentiments personnels." This type of novella, moreover, provides "une forme
très objective et éminemment artistique, je suis au dedans tout individuel
et subjectif." Meyer then provides an example of his subjective involvement in *Die Versuchung des Pescara*: "Dans tous les personnages du
Pescara, même dans ce vilain Morone, il y a du C. F. M." (1908, 138-39).
Four years earlier, in a letter to Paul Heyse, Meyer had expressed his
fondness for the frame because this device helped him achieve objectivity: "Ich halte mir den Gegenstand gerne ... so weit als möglich vom
Auge" (1908, II, 340).

Precursors of the Modern Age

With the migration of Naturalism into Germany in the 1880s, the
novella gradually became for the new generation of writers a *passé*,
epigonic genre. By the 1890s terms such as *Kurzgeschichte, Erzählung,
Skizze,* and *Geschichte* began to gain popularity (Nehring 1981, 384-85).
Gerhart Hauptmann, considered by many critics the first German artist
to adopt Naturalism, subtitled *Bahnwärter Thiel* (1888) a "Novellistische
Studie." In view of these changes, Friedrich Spielhagen returns to, and
attempts to shore up, the theory and genre of the novella. In 1895 he
insists, just as he had in 1882, that the "Signatur der Novelle" revolves
around Goethe's definition. The novella has a small cast of fixed characters who, in their brief involvement with one another during the course
of only "eine Begebenheit," unfold rather than develop. In reaction to the
vogue for new genre labels, Spielhagen describes the sketch ("Skizze") as
a complicated, unfocused idea. The novella, by contrast, is a clear and
well-established form that narrates one remarkable event. Great artists
— Kleist, Goethe, Tieck, Brentano, Storm, Keller, Heyse, and many
others — had developed the genre so that it resembles the last, striking
act of a drama. The novella so closely resembles the drama that the two
genres are often distinguishable only through the presence or absence of
dialog (1895, 167-68).

Paul Heyse writes in his memoirs that writers of his generation had
not inherited the novella as a finished art form from their literary forbears. Even Goethe, Germany's greatest writer, had not involved himself
seriously with this genre and had buried most of his novellas in novels,
where they became lost. His one independent example, *Novelle*, suggests

Goethe believed the genre portrays the unprecedented ("das Wunderbare, Unerhörte, wenigstens Einzigartige"). Wieland's narratives also are
problematical since they skirt the borderline between novels and moral
sketches. Tieck, by following the precepts of Boccaccio and Cervantes,
created the modern German novella. Tieck's works, along with those of
his successors, comprise the modern German *Novellenschatz*. Yet many of
Tieck's works are flawed by irony, the nemesis of Romanticism, and
therefore lack the freshness and vitality that characterize the novellas in
The Decameron and the *Novelas ejemplares*. Modern times have produced
two types of novellas — those that merely entertain and those that qualify as serious art. The former, as they proliferate in newspapers and journals, amount only to social chatter. The latter qualify as artistic creations
because they portray a significant aspect of human life that involves a
spiritual or ethical conflict. This conflict is restricted to an unusual incident that reveals a new aspect of human nature. Masters of the artistic
novella include Mérimée, de Musset, de Maupassant, Turgenev, and
Keller. Heyse urges that talented young writers, much like gifted young
composers, should study with a master, for both art forms possess
transmittable techniques. One such technique for the novella involves
the requirement for a clear silhouette or "Falken," as in the story from
The Decameron. Another technique, already mentioned, requires the novella to resolve a spiritual problem within a severely circumscribed compass. Heyse concludes his novellistic prescriptions with the disclaimer
that an individual lacking in talent will be unable to profit from this advice. Yet, these prescriptions, Heyse believes, can have the same prophy-
lactic and curative effects in the realm of novellistic aesthetics as do the
pharmaceutical ones in medicine (1900, 150-57).

   In 1901 Paul Ernst observes that the theories of Naturalism have led
to a great deal of artistic confusion. Ernst cites as an acute example the
notion of *milieu*. Originally an element of the novel of Naturalism, this
feature recently has been inflicted upon the drama, where it has caused
much aesthetic mischief. In similar fashion, the novella, too, has suffered
at the hands of Naturalists. This genre, which like the drama concentrates only upon essentials, has been confused with such pseudo-genres
as *Skizze* and *Studie*, both of which rightfully belong in the realm of
painting. To illustrate his point, Ernst retells Giovanni Sercambi's story
of the prodigal prince of Constantinople. In his analysis Ernst points out
that an unusual incident prompts the prodigal to make an almost instan-

taneous decision that radically alters the course of his whole life. A Naturalist would have provided numerous, minute details and given a thousand contributing reasons that would finally have led to an agonized decision. But in this true example of the novella, the author is concerned only with essentials that he presents in an artistic shorthand.

Ernst also provides a modern example of the genre, C. F. Meyer's *Die Versuchung des Pescara*. In this novella Pescara stands before a fateful decision: for the price of a betrayal, he can have the crown of Italy. By comparison, Sercambi's novella is childish, for not only does Meyer's work have much greater depth and breadth, it also offers a number of sharply drawn characters, a hint of local color and landscape, and even a description of the times. Amidst this wealth of information, the hand of the master novellist never falters, for Meyer limits himself to providing only indispensable information. Ernst then classifies novellas into three categories: those that deal with a decisive, fateful moment; those that deal with humorous, often erotic subjects; and those that depend on a witty or sharp retort.

Ernst believes that the genre is in decline and attributes this dissolution to the spiritual relativism of the current age that is hostile to every artistic form that demands a beginning and an end and a cause and an effect. He notes that the novella suffered a similar fate when the Weltanschauung of Renaissance Italy was transformed by the Church and the infusion of Spanish literary ideals (1901, 68-76). Three years later Ernst notes that the novella and the tragedy entail forms so strict he terms them eternal ("ewig"). The novel, which he believes is not a full-fledged art form ("Halbkunst"), lacks necessity, restraint, and form (1904, 21).

A year later Heinrich Hart grumbles that many modern authors continue to distinguish between the novel and the novella only by length. Such writers label as novellas works that any knowledgeable person would call a sketch, study, or novel. He recommends that a Bureau of Literature be established and given the very easy task of classifying works by genre. The novel, Hart maintains, portrays a comprehensive, intricate web of action and characterization encompassing either a whole human life or era. In structure the novel resembles a configuration of concentric circles; thematically it treats the commonplace and the typical. The novella, however, portrays a single, unified action that illuminates one moment. In structure the novella resembles only one circle; thematically it treats the atypical. Hart classifies novellas into two types:

extended anecdotes, as written by Boccaccio and Maupassant, and the German novella, which deals with significant ethical, social, or psychological problems as written by more modern authors, beginning with Tieck. Hart reiterates that length is an inadequate criterion for distinguishing between the novel and the novella (1905, 181-82).

Georg Lukács differentiates between the genres along lines reminiscent of Hart, Ernst, Heyse, and others. The novel depicts the totality of an individual human life against the backdrop of the whole world in all its richness. The novella also depicts an individual human life, but only through one fateful hour ("Schicksalstunde") that is so significant and decisive that by comparison all other facets and experiences of life pale into insignificance (1911, 183-84).

In 1912 Paul Arnold attempts to delineate Goethe's theory of the novella by analyzing the epigrammatic definition of 1827, "eine sich ereignete unerhörte Begebenheit." With the singular term *eine*, Goethe emphasizes that the novella deals only with one event ("Begebenheit"), in opposition to the novel, which deals with several. *Begebenheit* is not limited to mean one event, but rather a psychological conflict and the accompanying sequence of events that leads to its resolution. This sequence should have, in the baroness's words from *Unterhaltungen*, the unity of a poem. Since Goethe characterized an invented story as *sich ereignet*, this term means that the events described by the novella have already occurred. The element *unerhört* signifies that the event falls outside the realm of the commonplace and is something unique — "etwas Besonderes, Sonderbares" (1251-54).

The following year Arnold classifies novellas into two categories. The older, objective novella, as written by Goethe, exhibits unity of action by conforming to the requirement of narrating "eine sich ereignete unerhörte Begebenheit." Such a novella achieves unity by presenting a conflict and resolving it through a sequence of objectively narrated events (the action). The modern, subjective novella, as written by Theodor Storm, achieves unity by subordinating action to the development of a dominant mood ("Stimmung"). This mood is not inherent in the material itself, but lies in incipient form within the emotions of the reader. The writer channels his efforts toward creating an atmosphere that will evoke the desired mood. Arnold believes that with the recent creation of the subjective novella, the genre has developed, fulfilled, and exhausted its potential. Every attempt to exceed or transcend the simplicity of the

objective or subjective novella would destroy the "Novellenform" (1913, 1676-79).

Hermann Herrigel in 1913 notes that the novella constitutes a closed, circular narrative form, whereas the novel lacks such unity. The novella, therefore, constitutes an art form and the novel does not. The genres can also be distinguished by the Lebensanschauung of the author. The novellist, a Romantic, seeks the "Pointe" and casts his material into a distinct form; the novelist, an Impressionist, seeks the historically factual and does not face the restrictions imposed by form. The novella traces its origins from the joke, through the anecdote, fable, and parable, to the naive novella of *The Decameron*. These older narrative forms are characterized by a simple "Pointe." By comparison, the "Pointe" in the modern novella is sophisticated. The theme of the novella, like that of an adventure, is bound neither to time nor to an historical event. The early novel was an expanded novella that also contained a "Pointe." The discoveries of modern science have led to radically different perceptions of reality. Human life no longer is considered infinite and transcendental, but temporal and understandable only in terms of the fleeting moment. The modern novel reflects this new, impressionistic view by depicting the rapidly changing psychological dynamics of life. The modern novel is a *Zeitroman* that writes the history of contemporary life (1913, 81-86).

Robert Musil, a novellist of stature, characterizes the novella and novel in terms similar to ones developed earlier by Ernst, Heyse, Hart, and Lukács. In almost total opposition to Herrigel, Musil notes that a spiritually intense experience of momentary duration results in a novella; a similar experience of extended duration results in a novel. Musil compares the inspiration for a novella to an unexpected, lightning-like flash of intuition that illuminates and reveals the world in its true colors, thereby changing the writer's whole Lebensanschauung. Musil stipulates only one formal condition for the novella, that of brevity (1914, 184-86).

4: Between the Great Wars (1915-1945)

DURING THE 120 years between the publication of Goethe's *Unterhaltungen* and Musil's "Die Novelle als Problem," artists dominated the attempt to fashion a theory of the German novella. This theory, as the two previous chapters show, reveals a broad array of opinions. An attempt at classification reveals that one group of writers at times seems to forget that the formulation of theory involves a process whereby general principles are derived from the observation of phenomena. When such lapses occur, these authors tend to forget that the phenomenon under study is a human construct and describe the novella not only as if it had descended from Mount Parnassus with a life of its own, but also arrogate it prescriptive aesthetic autonomy. The ideas of such theoreticians often lack persuasive force because they tend, as Gottfried Keller pointed out, to approach the novella on an *a priori* basis. Another band of the theory spectrum involves those critics who satirize the genre. Such satires, while often amusing in their criticism and mockery, neither describe the novella nor offer an explanation of why such an enterprise may be unnecessary, impossible, or foolish. Such approaches do suggest, however, that the novella may be a genre that lacks a distinctive, universally accepted form.

A third category is represented by those critics who over the course of twelve decades iterate that a novella — to list a sampling of oft-repeated characteristics — is a prose narrative that originated with the anecdote, portrays one realistic *Situation* or *Begebenheit*, resembles one episode of a novel, portrays one segment of life, has a *Wendepunkt*, has a close kinship to the drama, and is shorter than the novel. Another set of critics makes what seem at best questionable claims: the novella, for example, is a poem, is to be differentiated from the drama by the absence of dialog, is poetry descending toward prose, is an account of a contemporary event, or is written by an author who embraces a romantic Weltanschauung. Many of the opinions alluded to above were delivered in the form of brief and what at times seem almost casually considered assertions.

Yet another band of the theory spectrum is represented by those authors who devote close attention to the topic and attempt to characterize the novella through extended analyses. Such authors include, to name the most famous, Goethe, the brothers Schlegel, Tieck, Mundt, Gutz-

kow, Heyse, Spielhagen, and Ernst. A last band of the opinion spectrum to be singled out, the efforts of scholars and literary historians, often reflects an uncritical acceptance of ideas expressed by the artists. Such attempts are of limited usefulness because they lack adequate development or objective analyses. Examples within this category include Gervinus, Hettner, Eichendorff in the role of literary historian, Carriere, and Biese.

After the turn of the century the discussion about the novella undergoes a change: artists fall silent and scholars begin to dominate the discourse. This change also signals a directional shift: the artists attempted to characterize the genre in a straightforward, direct fashion; the scholars often attempt to describe the novella by delineating and evaluating the theories of the artists within the context of their works. This shift marks the advent of modern literary study (*Literaturwissenschaft*, often in the form of *Geistesgeschichte*) and simultaneously heralds the birth of an academic discipline.

McBurney Mitchell, one of the first American representatives of the new *Wissenschaft* to approach novella theory, analyzes Goethe's definition of 1827 against the backdrop of the era and of Goethe's whole novellistic oeuvre. He finds the individual elements of this epigram, expressed in much-expanded form, in works ranging from *Unterhaltungen* to *Novelle* and, on this basis, concludes that the phrase "eine sich ereignete unerhörte Begebenheit" is the "quintessential result" of a thirty-year investigation that culminates in "the first definition of a form" (1915a, 215-36).

In a monograph devoted exclusively to genre theory, Mitchell also traces and analyzes the theory of the novella between 1798 (the Schlegels) and 1912 (Heyse). Although he deals with many of the theoreticians mentioned in the previous two chapters, he singles out the Schlegels, Goethe, Tieck, Mundt, Spielhagen, and Heyse for having made especially significant contributions to the theory of the novella.

Mitchell believes the Schlegels pioneered novella theory and credits them with isolating such novellistic features as paradox, realism, turning points, concentration upon one singular or novel event, and convertibility to a drama (1915b, 8-21). Goethe, Mitchell notes, characterized the genre as a prose narrative of a single, unique event that occurs in the realm of commonplace reality and at times incorporates the element of chance. The structure of such a narrative should approach the unity of a poem. The definition of 1827, he repeats, is "the quintessential result" of

a thirty-year investigation (23-33). Tieck emphasized that the novella features a single, unique event with a turning point that leads the action into an unexpected direction and to an unpredictable, yet natural conclusion. This *Wendepunkt* serves double duty: it is an element that renders both the genre and every individual example thereof unique (33-38). Mundt, Mitchell notes, emphasized that the novella portrays fixed characters and that its structure resembles a circle drawn around a center (38-44). Spielhagen, whose ideas Mitchell considers as derivative of the Schlegels, Tieck, and Mundt, characterized the genre by its fixed characters and by its capability to be dramatized (20-22 and 103-104).

Lastly, Mitchell comments on Heyse, whom he greatly admires for enriching German letters with novella masterpieces and a superb theory. Mitchell believes that Heyse, with his ideas of "silhouette and falcon," characterizes the novella with such aptness that his theory is the only one among the many to achieve "general acceptance in all quarters." This theory is sufficiently broad to encompass and characterize both the Romance as well as the German novellas. Heyse, moreover, also incorporates and reflects many elements of earlier theories — including, among others, those of Hettner, Mundt, Goethe, and Tieck. In his conclusion, Mitchell tempers his praise by observing Heyse "borrowed what he needed from his predecessors" and that his theory, therefore, "is thoroughly eclectic." Heyse's contribution thus did not lie so much within the realm of originality as it did in his ability to select, to abstract, and to summarize essentials (76-100 and 104-107).

In the same year Mitchell sets Heyse on the pinnacle of novella theory, Oskar Walzel, whom many literary historians consider the founder of the new *Literaturwissenschaft* (see Pabst, 1949, 256), fires a broadside against the prevailing theories of the novella. Walzel begins by pointing out that Spielhagen had ascertained that the novella deals with fixed characters. Hebbel, however, arrived at the opposite conclusion because in the novellas of one author, Tieck, the characters develop — "Tieck teilt ... der Novelle die werdenden Charaktere zu." The history of novella theory, Walzel observes, is replete not only with such antinomies, but also with other easily-refuted assertions. As an example of the latter, Walzel cites Vischer's characterization of the novel as presenting world conditions ("Weltzustände") and of the novella as presenting only an excerpt from them ("Ausschnitt aus ihnen"). Vischer's theory falls short not only because novels do not portray world conditions, but also because no

narrative form could possibly transmit such conditions adequately or accurately (1915, 161-63).

Walzel then undertakes a selective survey of German novella theory. He begins with *Unterhaltungen* and dismisses as a "Novellenprogramm Goethes" all theoretical discussions contained therein because they emanate in the frame ("aus der Lage der Rahmenerzählung") and because the word *Novelle* fails to appear in either the text or in the Goethe-Schiller correspondence at the time of composition. He examines Goethe's epigram of 1827 in context and, after intimating that Eckermann was an unreliable source, agrees with Feuchtersleben that with this ambiguous phrase Goethe attempted to characterize only the story he entitled "Novelle." Walzel then turns to the theories of the Schlegels and Tieck and finds them derivative: the Schlegels borrowed many of their ideas from Goethe's *Unterhaltungen*, whereas Tieck, who with his theory attempted to justify only his own works, borrowed his idea of the *Wendepunkt* from A. W. Schlegel. Walzel next criticizes Heyse for saying so little that was new about the genre. He also characterizes Storm's defense of the novella against Ebers's attack as impoverished and considers it fortunate that it remained unpublished. Walzel concludes his survey by noting that much of Ernst's theory is simply an amalgam of older observations that Ernst has meshed into a logical whole (170-83).

Although Walzel's stance about the prevailing theories of the novella is highly critical, he singles out three characteristics or elements as applicable to the genre. The first, sociability ("Geselligkeit"), was developed principally by Goethe and suggests that the novella, as noted by the baroness in *Unterhaltungen*, can play a significant role in harmonious social intercourse (Walzel earlier had discounted the remarks of the baroness). The second, developed by Friedrich Schlegel, is irony, which Walzel interprets to be a device the novellist employs to gain distance between the events and the reader. An excellent example of such distancing can be seen in C. F. Meyer's *Die Hochzeit des Mönchs*, a novella into which Dante spontaneously incorporates members of his audience. The last element, mentioned only casually by Ernst, involves the original, oral recounting of the novella. Walzel believes that if a novellist were to reintroduce this form of narrative transmission, he would accomplish for the novella exactly what staging does for drama (171-84).

In 1916 Georg Lukács returns to genre theory and describes the shorter epic forms in terms borrowed from earlier novella theories. Such

narratives deal with the workings of chance. The narrator, in his subjectivity, carves out of the infinitely many world events one unusual human
experience ("ein Lebensstück"). The novella portrays a single remarkable
event ("Merkwürdigkeit" or "Begebenheit"), gives eternal form to a
mood ("Stimmung"), and provides an unveiled glimpse of the senselessness of life (90-92).

After the hiatus imposed by the First World War and its aftermath,
scholars returned to the theory of the novella. In 1921 Paul Arnold analyzes Tieck's theory of the novella by explicating the *Wendepunkt* in light
of Goethe's "Ferdinand" and Tieck's own *Die wilde Engländerin*. In both
stories the remarkable event ("das Wunderbare") that accompanies reversal manifests itself externally — the chance opening of the desk top and
the accidental tearing of the dress. Arnold advocates that reversal should
not be interpreted as a strictly external event, but should be expanded to
encompass the internal, spiritual change — Ferdinand's repentance and
Florentine's change of heart. Arnold then argues that the novellistic
category of "das Wunderbare" is an element Tieck transferred from the
fairy tale to the novella and that it marked the shift from the realm of
reality to the realm of fantasy (260-66).

Two years later, Arnold also analyzes Storm's works and theory in
conformity with the classifications he had developed in 1913: the objective novella, which emphasizes the unity of action, and the subjective novella, which stresses the unity of mood ("Stimmung"). Storm's early
novellas are subjective because he limited their content to lyrical episodes that contributed to the evocation of mood ("Gesamtstimmung").
In 1872, with *Draußen im Heidedorf*, Storm changed directions because
he wanted to write a novella that was not dominated by mood ("ohne
den Dunstkreis einer bestimmten 'Stimmung'"). From this point onward
Storm also embraced action, which Arnold defines as the conflict and its
resolution ("der Konflikt mit seiner Lösung"). Arnold notes that in his
later novellas, as splendidly illustrated in *Der Schimmelreiter*, Storm incorporated both unities (1923, 285-88).

Hans Heinrich Borcherdt, in his history of the German novel and
novella, attempts in the foreword to distinguish between the two genres.
Using Goethe as a springboard, he observes that the novel is a subjective
epic, whereas a novella is "eine sich ereignete unerhörte Begebenheit."
The novel, through a series of episodes, concentrates upon describing
one human being within the context of his environment. By emphasizing

psychological motivation, this genre strives for the unity of development. The novella concentrates upon one event (Tieck's "Vorfall" and Goethe's "Begebenheit"). By emphasizing the workings of chance ("Zufall"), this genre strives to develop the unity of the event. Both the novelist and the novellist regard life as tragic because they are painfully aware of the immense gap between the real and the ideal. The former approaches his work subjectively, the latter objectively (the novellist does, however, impart his subjectivity in the frame). The novel exhibits an open form, the novella a closed one (1926, 1-8).

In 1928 an exponent of *Geistesgeschichte*, Bernhard Bruch, compares the tragedy with the modern German novella. Both genres have strict formal requirements since the one aims at peripeteia and the other at the "Pointe." The genres also are subject to formal constraints that for the drama are imposed by the stage and for the novella by the frame (whether a frame actually exists is immaterial). The drama is the objective portrayal of the development and resolution of a contemporary conflict. The novella is a subjective depiction of an event from the past. The subjective stance of the novellist is restricted by time and the need to portray events so that they appear to be objective. Time, in Bruch's view, has an architectonic function that acquires crucial formal significance: "*die Zeit selbst* ist die Form, in der die Novelle sich vollzieht" (118-21).

The protagonist of the drama is an individual who, in the exercise of his free will, actively contributes to forging his fate. The protagonist of the novella is an individual who, lacking free will, falls unwitting victim to a fatal event. The protagonist's passivity precludes the novella from being tragic, although the word, for lack of a better one, often is used to characterize the novella. The tragedy portrays a conflict between objective, universally valid ideals. The hero succumbs by adhering to one principle, thereby falling victim to the other. The novella lacks such a conflict because it portrays the machinations of transcendental chance as they configure to destroy one predestined individual (122-27).

The very goals of peripeteia and "Pointe," as well as the attainment of these goals, differ radically. The tragedy unfolds in a parabolic form and, through discovery, culminates in reversal — the hero's recognition of his fault and his death. The novella proceeds directly towards its predetermined, catastrophic ending — the "Pointe." The novellistic *Wendepunkt* is merely a twist of fortune and is not accompanied by a radical change

("Wandlung") as is the dramatic peripeteia. The novella does not allow for curvature of its linear progression to the concluding "Pointe." This "Pointe" portrays through one central event the fate of one individual. The "Pointe" does not, however, explain why fate visited the catastrophe upon the individual. The novella thus exudes an aura of fatalism and ends, ultimately, in ambiguity. Bruch ends his comparison by concluding that the two genres stand in a paradoxical relationship. The novella is very closely related to drama and, as Storm observed, is indeed its epic sister. Simultaneously, however, it is also its exact opposite — "das genaue Gegenbild der wirklichen Tragödie" (128-36).

In the introduction to a German translation of *The Decameron*, André Jolles defines the novella as the narration of a significant, seemingly true "Begebenheit." The event is emphasized to such an extent that it acquires greater importance than do the people to whom it occurs. Both Goethe's *Werther* and Mérimée's *Carmen*, for example, depict how two men perish because of love. *Werther* emphasizes the man, *Carmen* the perishing. This priority of event over character distinguishes the novella from the novel (1928, 114).

In a preliminary study to a larger undertaking that failed to materialize, a comprehensive study of the history of the German novella, Arnold Hirsch in 1928 attempts to arrive at a clear understanding of the genre. Wishing to avoid the pitfalls of generating a novella theory on an *a priori* basis, Hirsch approaches the topic by first tracing the history of the word *Novelle* in Germany from its initial appearance in 1472 to roughly 1820, when the term gained currency (13-22). Adopting a skeptical stance similar to Walzel's, Hirsch reviews the history of German novella theory beginning with the Schlegels and ending with Paul Ernst (22-72).

Upon concluding his survey, Hirsch observes that every theory analyzed has its limitations. Despite these limitations, several of these theories develop points that seem applicable to the genre. In a rhetorical quandary, he asks: which theory encompasses the genre ("Welche Theorie erfaßt das Wesen der Gattung")? In search of an answer, Hirsch applies various epistemological systems, including Aristotelian logic, the strict sociological approach advocated by Max Weber, and the scientific method as outlined by Heinrich Rickert and Ernst Cassirer. Yet all these methods, Hirsch concludes, lack applicability in the arts — "in den Wissenschaften, die sich mit Kunstwerken befassen" (73-85).

Hirsch then turns to the three basic literary genres and their corresponding categories of human experience or interpretation: the lyric, in which the poet's subjectivity nullifies the objective world; the drama, in which the objective world cancels the poet's subjectivity; and the epic, in which a poet's subjectivity stands in opposition to the objective world (88-90). In order to isolate the "Idealtyp" of the novella, an epic genre, Hirsch analyzes the narrative stance in Boccaccio's *Decameron*, Aeneas Silvius's "Eurialus und Lucretia," Goethe's "Novelle," Kleist's "Die Marquise von O ..." and "Das Erdbeben in Chili," Arnim's "Isabella von Aegypten" and "Der tolle Invalide auf [dem] Fort Ratonneau," and Mann's "Der Tod in Venedig" (93-145).

At the end of these analyses, Hirsch notes that the novella is the portrayal of an objective action ("Handlung"), divided into parts or segments. The poet exercises his subjectivity by arranging these parts in accordance with his plan to form an artistic unity. In his summary of the "Idealtyp" novella, Hirsch observes that the poet, in order to achieve his artistic purposes, stylizes and thereby consciously destroys the natural, objective fullness of the world ("*Fülle* des Weltbildes"). The novel and the *Erzählung* both attempt to portray the world in this fullness, the former in broad-scale terms, the latter through a small, representative sector. The novella, by contrast, presents only one unique or remarkable ("unerhört") situation that falls outside the normal world processes. Despite having earlier considered Goethe's definition as overvalued ("überschätzt") and also having cautioned against its adoption, (40-41), Hirsch now emphasizes that the remarkable event ("diese Wahl des Unerhörten und Merkwürdigen") has almost always been cited as the decisive criterion for the genre. Hirsch's final answer to his rhetorical question seems to be based upon the ideas of Goethe and Friedrich Schlegel: the novella is a subjective, artistically stylized formulation ("Formgebung") of the (objective) world that is limited to one "Situation" describing unusual events — "Geschehnisse" (145-47).

The following year Hermann Pongs describes the novella as a daring venture of the spirit ("Wagnis des Geistes") in which the artist transforms a trifle such as an anecdote, *Schwank*, or "sich ereignete unerhörte Begebenheit" into an intensely symbolistic art form. Boccaccio, who founded the social novella ("die Gesellschaftsnovelle"), indelibly stamped the genre by employing a frame. This device transmits the spirit of the artist, which is expressed, as Friedrich Schlegel observed, by an overt

objectivity and a covert subjectivity that leans strongly toward symbolism. Many of Boccaccio's narratives are anecdotes or *Schwänke*. The novella differs from these narratives in that it revolves around one central point or thing that has great symbolic potential, as does, for example, the falcon in Boccaccio's novella (1929, 97-98).

Pongs notes that Heyse's commentary about the silhouette and the falcon has had a great impact upon German novella theory and practice. Heyse over-emphasized the material aspect of the falcon and this view led critics to ascribe to the novella a concrete symbol ("Dingsymbol") as an external, formal feature. Pongs does not argue with this view, but emphasizes that such an interpretation fails to appreciate the internal, more significant intangible that the falcon represents — Federigo's unconditional love. Federigo kills the falcon, but his love continues to live and remains constant to the end. This simple *Dingsymbol*, in its wider application, is the very heart of the novella, for it has a wide-ranging, complex set of functions. In addition to representing Federigo's love, the falcon also forms the midpoint of the novella, shows the irony of chance (Federigo unwittingly gives Giovanna exactly what she came for), reveals Federigo's noble spirit, and leads to Giovanna's change of heart. The falcon thus reflects almost every aspect of the novella and provides, in addition to the external, also an internal structural form: the *Dingsymbol* fuses the theme of unconditional love with the "unerhörte Begebenheit" of the lady Giovanna's visit to the earlier spurned Federigo (99-101).

Pongs examines two modern novellas, Heyse's *Zwei Gefangene* and Franck's *Südseeinsel*, and notes that they display only external *Dingsymbole*. These symbols — Pongs also refers to them as "Falkenfassade" or metaphors — lack the all-pervasiveness of the Boccaccian falcon since they neither inform the whole novella nor unify the intangible with the "unerhörte Begebenheit." Yet, other novellas, beginning with the fate novellas of the early nineteenth century, exhibit the boldness Pongs requires of the novella (101-105).

In *Das Erdbeben in Chili* Kleist dares to pit the solitary individual against the world, thereby revealing the powers of fate. This novella begins with the "unerhörte Begebenheit," the catastrophe of the earthquake, which at the end is counter-balanced with the catastrophic deaths of Josephe and Jeronimo. The falcon or *Dingsymbol*, the illegitimate child, in one way or another informs the novella from beginning to end, just as did the falcon in Boccaccio's novella. Conceived by chance

("Zufall") in the beginning, Phillip survives his parents at the end. This survival, Pongs believes, both symbolizes and explains all the events of the novella. The child, a symbol of creation, represents the unlimited grace of God. Guilt-ridden humankind, incapable of divine grace, establishes rigid customs that lead to the senseless deaths of the parents. The child's survival symbolizes the reestablishment of God's eternal grace. At the end Don Fernando is seized by this spirit and feels "als müßte er sich freuen." Pongs believes that in this novella Kleist has elevated the *Dingsymbol* to its highest possible level and has, thereby, exhausted its potential (105-107).

Pongs concludes his essay by analyzing Kleist's *Die Marquise von O...*, which begins with the "unerhörte Begebenheit" of the marchesa's newspaper announcement. This novella lacks a falcon, but does contain a signifier. This "Symbolon," the count's dream of throwing mud at the swan, lacks the concreteness of an external falcon and is thus a metaphor. This metaphor, like the internal function of the *Dingsymbol*, unifies and reflects the whole action of the novella ("nimmt das Ganze der Novelle ... zusammen"). Pongs observes that the "Falkensymbol" no longer seems an adequate vehicle for expressing either the depths or the intense subjectivity that constitute the inner structure and thematic concerns of the modern novella. This inadequacy, already visible in Kleist's time, explains the limitations of the "Fassadenovellen" of Heyse and Franck. Pongs then observes that a more thorough, historical study of the foundations of the nineteenth-century novella needs to be undertaken (107-109).

In 1929 Adolf von Grolman writes an essay entitled "Die strenge 'Novellenform' und die Problematik ihrer Zertrümmerung." The title is misleading since Grolman fails to delineate the form of the novella, strict or not. He notes that the original Renaissance novella comprises a form of social intercourse used by high society as pedagogic entertainment. The demise of the aristocracy in 1789 led to the disintegration and destruction of the genre. Goethe, in his "Erzählungen deutscher Ausgewanderten," managed to preserve a few remnants of the form, but the novella perished under the onslaughts of modern political, formal, economic, social, and technological developments. Grolman believes that the genre is more suitable for the southern than the nordic temperament and that it rightfully belongs in a Florentine arbor or arcade (155-65).

Hermann Pongs follows his seminal essay of 1929 with a seventy-three page effort that analyzes the foundations of the nineteenth-century novella (1930). In eight sub-chapters he traces the development of the novella from Boccaccio to late German Romanticism. In this essay, however, his main concern lies with the interpretation of individual works rather than with the derivation or development of genre theory. In his remarks on Boccaccio (110-18), Pongs repeats his earlier conclusions and categorizes the stories of *The Decameron* as social novellas. After examining the *Novelas ejemplares* (118-24), Pongs concludes that they differ substantially from *The Decameron*: Boccaccio's works exhibit the unity of the "Pointe," whereas Cervantes's works exhibit unity of character. Pongs next turns to Goethe's *Unterhaltungen* (124-134), a work he holds in low esteem because he views it as a failed attempt to return to Boccaccio's social novella. None of Goethe's narratives exhibits the unity of a Boccaccian falcon novella. The early Romantic novellas (135-49) emphasize the category of the wondrous ("das Wunderbare"). Pongs observes that Tieck's works of this period are examples of the fate novella ("Schicksalsnovelle"), a genre in which an individual acts in accordance with subconscious dictates and becomes the victim of inexorable, monstrous fate. Pongs believes that in the early works of E. T. A. Hoffmann, many of which are art novellas ("Kunstnovellen"), the protagonist's search for the ultimate in art leads to an unbounded intensification of the wondrous.

Kleist (150-66), the equal of Boccaccio and Cervantes, creates, as Pongs noted in his earlier essay, a new form of the fate novella, "die tragische Schicksalsnovelle." Goethe's novel *Die Wahlverwandtschaften* (166-70) belongs in the history of the novella because it emphasizes the unique individual. This work, Pongs believes, bridges the gap between the earlier forms of the German novella and the later, psychological novellas of the nineteenth century. Pongs labels Hoffmann's later narratives (170-79) mood novellas ("Stimmungsnovellen"). These works continue to deal with the wondrous, but emphasize the occult as it manifests itself in ghosts, black magic, and the realm of the uncanny. In his last sub-chapter, Pongs deals with the late Romantic psychological novella. Tieck, by equating the novellistic "Pointe" with his *Wendepunkt*, partially opened the door for this type of novella by noting that the reversal, although total, is a natural (in opposition to wondrous) consequence of circumstance and character. Pongs finds it ironic that Tieck, early in his

career, lifted the category of the wondrous out of the cradle for baptism yet, in his later career, helped weave its shroud. Goethe's 1827 definition of the novella, with the terms "unerhört" and "Begebenheit," incorporated both the Romantic (the wondrous) and Romance (the falcon) views of the novella and opened wide the door for all manner of novellistic possibilities, but especially for the development of the psychological novella (179-83).

André Jolles ascribes the invention of the novella to Boccaccio and that of the fairy tale to Gian Francesco Straparola. He traces the development of the latter genre through Giambattista Basile, Charles Perrault, and Jean de La Fontaine. The eighteenth century witnessed an explosion in the number of such tales, which in Germany reached their apex with Wieland. The Romantics carried this genre (albeit in a different form) well into the nineteenth century. Jolles differentiates between the two genres. The novella, he repeats from his essay of 1928, is the narration of a significant event that seems to have occurred and that stresses the priority of event over character. The fairy tale is the narration of a non-significant event that does not emphasize actual occurrences, but concerns itself rather with the wondrous. Contrary to prevailing opinion, both genres constitute art forms. The novella inclines thematically toward the true and the natural; the fairy tale also inclines toward the true and natural, but combines these aspects with elements of the wonderful (1930, 167-73).

In 1931 Pongs once again returns to the topic, this time to analyze the possibilities of the tragic in the novella. He notes that Kleist first expanded the theme of the genre by plumbing the depths of the soul. In this process Kleist simultaneously preserved the distinctive Romance form while increasing the magnitude of its symbolic potential. Pongs disagrees with Bruch's declaration that the modern novella is incapable of portraying the tragic because the hero, lacking free will, simply falls victim to a fatal event without facing conflicting ideals. Pongs also disagrees with Bruch's observation that the novella is tied to the past. The novellist, unlike the dramatist who is bound to the stage, is completely free to pursue any topic (including the tragic) during the time (including the present and the future) and at the place of his choice. Kleist, in his novellas, exercised this freedom by transforming Boccaccio's social novella and Cervantes's character novella into a genre that portrayed the individual as he is pitted, in his solitariness, against the in-built, tragic

elements of the universe (185-87). Pongs devotes fifty-nine pages of his essay to describing the tragic elements in eight German novellas, beginning with Kleist's *Die Verlobung in St. Domingo* (1810) and ending with Hans Grimm's *Der Richter in der Karu* (1930). At the end of his analysis, Pongs concludes that both the Romance and the German forms of the novella suffer a grave injustice if an attempt is made to define them with the same set of criteria. Schlegel's characterization of the genre as a story outside of history that incorporates irony, Lukács's description that it portrays the senselessness of life, and Bruch's anti-tragic sentiments, while perhaps applicable to the Romance novellas, simply fail to describe the German ones. The form has evolved from the playful, light social entertainment of the Renaissance to the serious, modern German "Problem- und Schicksalsnovelle," a genre that can bear even the heavy weight of tragedy (248-50).

E. K. Bennett in 1934 publishes a monograph on the German novella. In the first chapter, "The Novelle as a Literary Genre," Bennett summarizes theory by noting that the genre incorporates characteristics isolated by theoreticians from the Schlegels to Ernst. Thus the novella, to list only a few characteristics, is a prose epic that emphasizes one singular, chance event in a realistic fashion. From a formal viewpoint, the novella incorporates a turning point and a striking element that often features a concrete object with great symbolic significance (1-19).

In the main body of his text, Bennett interprets a large number of German novellas either within the context of historical periods or the classifications developed by Pongs and, to a lesser extent, by Bruch, Hirsch, and Grolman. The history of the German novella begins with Goethe's *Unterhaltungen*, a work modelled on *The Decameron*, but departing from the original by emphasizing a moral element (20-36). In the next chapter, Bennett concludes that Kleist preserved the external form of the genre, but discarded the social aspect by expanding the content to include the most complex and difficult metaphysical questions (37-46). The next phase of novellistic development, the Romantic novella, radically changed both form and content. This manifestation of the novella lost "the simplicity and severity" of the Romance form and the content changed from unusual events of the everyday world to the supernatural and fantastic (47-76). The "discursive novella" of the late Tieck and the authors of "das junge Deutschland" concentrated their themes upon tendentious topics of the real world and failed, therefore, to

make a lasting impact. Bennett credits Gotthelf and Auerbach (both authors wrote "Dorfnovellen") with returning the novella from the realm of fantasia to that of the mundane (77-123).

The finest flowering of the German novella took place during the period of Poetic Realism (1840-1890) with authors like Annette von Droste-Hülshoff, Otto Ludwig, Adalbert Stifter, Franz Grillparzer, Eduard Mörike, Theodor Storm, and Gottfried Keller. Bennett interprets the term "Poetic Realism," coined by Otto Ludwig, to mean a "complete description of reality, the attribute 'poetic' signifying that ... it accords to [life] positive value." The subject matter of these novellas often involves topics of bourgeois concern. The German novella, best exemplified by Droste-Hülshoff and Keller, reached its pinnacle because it incorporated all the formal features developed by Goethe, Kleist, and the Romantics: "realism enriched by poetical depth and symbolical significance." After interpreting several novellas of the authors mentioned above, Bennett concludes with the works of Keller. In the hands of this author, the German novella "reaches a maximum, beyond which no development is possible" because Keller incorporates many of the novellistic features developed by theoreticians from Goethe onward (124-92).

Upon encountering the divergent opinions of Bruch and Pongs about the novella and tragedy, Bennett turns to Schopenhauer. This philosopher noted that tragic situations are brought about by three causes: fate, a villain, or the force of circumstance. The latter situation is most applicable to modern life. Bennett believes that, owing to its optimistic and positive valuation of life, the era of Poetic Realism was incapable of producing a full-fledged tragedy. Yet, the pessimistic tragic impulse could not be entirely suppressed and found its best expression in three novellas: Wilhelm Raabe's *Des Reiches Krone*, Stifter's *Abdias*, and Storm's *Der Schimmelreiter* (193-205).

The appearance of the psychological novella, whose chief exponents are Paul Heyse and Conrad Ferdinand Meyer, signals the dissolution of the bourgeoisie ("Bürgertum"). These two patricians, preoccupied with an individualistic, psychological approach, no longer represent either "Bürgertum" or its ideals. This development, along with Keller's fulfillment and exhaustion of all novellistic possibilities, led to the disintegration of not only the novella of Poetic Realism, but of the genre itself. The process of extinction was hastened by the advent of psychoanalysis, that most intense of individual, psychological approaches, and is best ex-

emplified in the novellas of Arthur Schnitzler. Bennett concludes his monograph by tolling the bell for the novella and by announcing the coronation of the short story — "die Kurzgeschichte" (206-53).

In 1934 Robert Petsch describes the novella as a narrative of medium length and locates the genre between short and long narrative types. The verse novella ("Der arme Heinrich," for example) originated in the Middle Ages, whereas the prose form was invented by Boccaccio and Cervantes. The genre displays a striking beginning, an internal development that progresses rapidly from one sharply profiled peak to the next, and a short, intensely charged ending pregnant with meaning. The novella deals with an unusual event that takes place within the realm of the normal-possible and features one or more turning points that may be associated with a falcon, a highly expressive symbol (184-90).

Johannes Klein attempts both to define and to provide a history of the genre within the confines of a short essay. The founder of the novella, Boccaccio, portrayed an event from life and turned it into an art form. Boccaccio wrote for social purposes and his novellas often contain a moral, but Boccaccio himself remained amoral. Cervantes's novellas expanded the scope of the genre by increasing the magnitude of the central event and by incorporating moral questions. Upon adoption in Germany, the novella had to lose both social and moral aspects in order to reflect the power of fate as it manifested itself in the unusual events that took place on a daily basis during the French Revolution and the Napoleonic wars. The modern novella has both an internal and an external form. The internal form, ultimately, is life itself. The external form of the novella involves three elements: the central event, Goethe's "unerhörte Begebenheit;" the leitmotif, Heyse's falcon, which may not always be present; and the idea, Heyse's requirement that the plot should lend itself to brief summary (1936, 195-200).

Klein then lists the differences between a number of genres and the novella. The novel develops and reveals the fates of several characters through a series of events, thereby reflecting the world. The novella only reveals the fate of one individual through one event, thereby reflecting a segment of the world. The novel reveals what a human being is, the novella reveals what happens to him. And, as a last representative example, the novel seeks the laws of the universe and portrays the fate of people, the novella seeks a chance occurrence and leaves the fate of the individual open. The novella differs from the *Erzählung* in that the former

changes the natural sequence of events, whereas the latter does not. The novella inclines toward the heroic and constantly displays prominent formal features, for example, a midpoint. The *Erzählung* inclines toward the idyllic and displays no constant formal features. The novella also differs from the anecdote. The two genres are similar in that they emphasize an event at midpoint, but differ in that the anecdote depicts one moment, whereas the novella depicts several (201-205).

Klein also compares the novella with the ballad and finds several similarities. Both genres stress a midpoint and emphasize this feature through leitmotifs. They are dissimilar in that the ballad sings of the illusions of life, whereas the novella tells of the delusions of life. The novella and the drama, as the Romantics and Theodor Storm noted, stand in close kinship. Yet, they differ in three substantial ways: the drama shows necessity, the novella need; the drama portrays the fate of the hero as representative, the novella as isolated; and the drama operates according to the precepts of justice, whereas in the novella every aspect, including justice, is subordinated to action. Klein then provides a thumbnail sketch of the history of the novella from Goethe to Ernst by classifying the genre in agreement with the sub-genres (i.e., "Characternovelle," "Schicksalsnovelle," "romantische Novelle,") developed by Pongs (206-20).

Erich Härlin, in an impressionistic essay on the form of the novella, notes that the genre originated with the anecdote, an interesting story. The novella, an intensified anecdote, is a highly interesting story that with the brilliance of a flash of lightning illuminates one incident or event, one feature, or one perspective and thereby reveals the essence of existence. The genre appeals more to the reader's intellect than it does to his emotions. The novella contains a "Pointe" or "Spitze" and narrates its event with such vividness that the reader believes himself engaged in the action. This incident is of such great existential concern that the affairs of the readers ("meine Sache ... *unsere* Sache") are being narrated. Härlin next compares the *Erzählung* with the novella and finds that the former, much like a human body without a skeleton, is devoid of form. He then notes that the novella is a short genre that portrays an abrupt, radical change in the life of a human being. This change often remains unexplained and may, in fact, be inexplicable. In conclusion, Härlin maintains that the genre portrays a certain attitude, relationship, or Lebensanschauung (1937, 7-18).

Georg Lukács, in an essay devoted primarily to the social and political aspects of Gottfried Keller's novellistic oeuvre, also comments peripherally on the theory of the novella. Lukács differentiates between the classical (Boccaccian) novella and the modern one. Both forms concentrate upon depicting social reality by a remarkable, central event. The older novella portrayed, in an objective and artistically lean fashion, the disintegration of feudal society. The modern novella deals with bourgeois society and its attendant complex of character individualization, capitalistic division of labor, and the growing gulf between public and private life. Tieck's *Wendepunkt*, as it applies to the modern novella, shows how a very remarkable, highly individualistic event becomes typical for all of society. Lukács illustrates this interpretation through Keller's *Romeo und Julia auf dem Dorfe*. The feud between Manz and Marti is unique for the two participants and both men are ultimately ruined because of their stubbornness. Yet, as Keller points out, such ruin is commonplace in the society of his day. In this way, Lukács observes, the turning point shows a dialectical shift — what for the individual is very atypical has become typical for society at large (1939, 222-25).

The reversal between the typical and atypical, along with the concentration upon the unique event, distinguish the novella from the novel. Keller chose the novella because this form, more so than the novel or the drama, offered him the best pedagogical device for educating the individual for citizenship ("Erziehung zum Staatsbürger") in modern Swiss society. Lukács also differentiates between the novella and drama. The drama directly reflects the totality of life through one event. The novella portrays only an excerpt or segment of life ("Lebens*ausschnitt*"), allows for chance, and shows individual circumstances. Keller's novellas, by concentrating upon one remarkable event, mirror the social laws of his society. In this way Keller simultaneously adheres to the "laws" of the classical novella while also creating the novella anew (226-44).

In 1939 Pongs once again revisits the theory of the novella, this time to investigate the topic of the daimonic ("das Dämonische"). The category of the daimonic posits the existence, alongside the natural world, of a supernatural one. The daimonic is ambiguous since it encompasses both the over- and underworlds with their attendant manifestations of the sublime and the horrible, of the divine and the demonic, and of light and darkness. Goethe, who experienced the daimonic in both its positive and negative forces, believed it was an inexplicable power over which

man had no control. Pongs postulates that the Romantics, as revealed in so many of their works, replaced the category of the tragic with the ambiguous powers of the daimonic. Even Goethe, whom Pongs calls the great pagan, felt compelled in his old age to call upon the holy powers of light in order to counter the evil powers of darkness (251-54).

Pongs analyzes three German novellas that concern themselves with the daimonic. In Büchner's *Lenz* the forces of darkness battle those of light within the confines of the protagonist's soul. During the course of the struggle, one force or the other gains momentary dominance. This temporary advantage is reflected in the novella by a vacillation from threatening nature to the idyllic parsonage, insanity to sanity, night to day, atheism to piety, spiritual agony to ecstasy, and fulfillment to emptiness. Since Lenz ultimately succumbs to the powers of the abyss, there is no central, all-encompassing *Dingsymbol* (254-65).

Pongs notes that Mörike, in *Mozart auf der Reise nach Prag*, saw the composer in the same light as had Goethe when, in admiration, he had exclaimed that it was not Mozart, but the daimon that controlled his genius, who had composed *Don Juan*. Yet, at the very pinnacle of creative achievement and fulfillment, Mozart is assailed by a daimon from the nether world. This assault suggests that the powers of light, having exhausted Mozart's creative potential, have abandoned him. Mozart's predicament is reflected by the *Dingsymbol* — the ripe pomegranate that Mozart, in casual, almost inadvertent fashion, picks and cuts apart. Both the pomegranate and Mozart have ripened, thereby fulfilling their purposes. Mörike's novella, Pongs believes, reveals the schism between the dark and light sides of life and underscores the tragic dimension of existence by signalling that fulfillment and completion mean death (265-74).

Pongs believes that in Gotthelf's *Die schwarze Spinne* the daimonic powers, here rooted in myth and manifested in the divine and the demonic, engage in cosmic war. Almost every element that is a part of the world — including, for example, plants, animals, the human community, and even the earth itself — either becomes an active combatant or in some way reflects this titanic struggle. The main battle ground of this war, as is to be expected, is once again located in the human breast. The power of darkness, concentrated in the all-pervasive *Dingsymbol* of the spider, originally was a human being. The power of light, as symbolized by the Christian spirit of transcendental love and of self-sacrifice, ulti-

mately wins. Yet, as the window post so ominously shows, the demonic is ever-present and chafes to be liberated (275-86).

Pongs believes that the tragic and daimonic dimensions are ineluctable elements of existence since they are woven into the fabric of the universe or the human psyche. The daimonic thus manifests itself with much regularity in the novella: it is the plague in *The Decameron*, the French Revolution in *Unterhaltungen*, the realm of the wonderful and supernatural for the Romantics, and, to list two examples from Kleist, the earthquake in *Das Erdbeben* and the daimon of justice and injustice in *Kohlhaas*. Pongs postulates that the tragic and the daimonic are related. The daimonic often appears in an uncertain twilight zone between good and evil (for example, the devil in Gotthelf's novella presents himself as friendly and helpful). The tragic, which requires a choice between two opposing values, often is a response in face of the ambiguous chaos of the daimonic. When the individual chooses one course of action over another, the unchosen course exacts its price. The individual may well impose order upon chaos, but at the cost of his life — thus the first mother, Christian, and the priest in Gotthelf's novella all must die (286-91).

Pongs concludes his ten-year investigation of the novella by analyzing mankind's condition in the universe which, he reiterates, is subject to the unpredictable assaults of the daimonic. Yet, since the tragic is also an innate element of the universe, mankind is endowed with the freedom to choose between values. The tragic is thus a guarantee ("eine Bürgschaft") of the existence of God. This guarantee is revealed by the symbol, a beacon which serves to assure mankind that in its struggle against the forces of darkness, the powers of light will ultimately prevail. The symbol also transforms what seems to be a chance occurrence into a universally valid event and imparts it with meaning. The symbol thus partially illuminates and reveals, but never totally explains, the mystery of human existence (295-96).

5: Planting the Seeds of Doubt (1946-1959)

S CHOLARLY ACTIVITY INVOLVING the novella, once again severely curtailed by world war, resumed after 1945. In one of the first post-war efforts, Bayard Quincy Morgan attempts to differentiate among three forms of prose narratives — the short story, the novelette, and the novel. Using a practical, almost mechanical approach, Morgan distinguishes by length, reading time, content, and degree of development. The short story, by definition an economical form, severely limits the number of characters and events and deals with both in a concise fashion. This genre, the speedboat of fiction, races to its objective which, once attained, may lack importance. The novelette, owing to its greater length, has fewer restrictions about the number of characters or incidents and can deal with both in larger numbers as well as in greater detail than can the short story. The novel, a full-fledged ship, has none of these restrictions. This genre, in subject matter, can provide an account that at times has the impact of a real, "crucial life experience" and, in the process, often circumnavigates the globe at a leisurely pace.

Morgan locates the novelette between the short story and the novel. The novelette, between 40 to 90 rather than between 10 to 1,000 pages in length (these numbers are suggestive, not prescriptive), has the space not only for more characters and incidents, but also for more detailed development and exploration of motivation and of states of mind than does the short story. The novelette, although more circumscribed than the novel, retains sufficient capacity to deal with the life of an individual, a whole age, or even a dynasty. The short story normally is read in one breath, the novel in many sittings, and the novelette in one sitting. Many critics of German literature have remarked upon the similarities between the novelette and the drama. Morgan notes that life is arranged in a rhythm of three- to four-hour periods. Such a period, too long a span for reading a short story and too short for a novel, falls within the time-frame of the novelette and the drama. Both genres are of sufficient length to pursue topics in depth, yet are short enough to be grasped in one sitting, thereby impressing themselves deeply upon the consciousness of the reader (1946, 34-39).

Walter Pabst, in a *Forschungsbericht* of both German and Romance novella studies, observes that the turn of the century witnessed a shift in

scholarly approach. Before this shift, scholars attempted to identify the original sources of plots and episodes found in the works of famous authors. These scholars drew few conclusions and often contented themselves with observing that authors like Boccaccio, Shakespeare, or Goethe lacked originality in plot invention because they borrowed material from earlier sources. Yet the identification of a source as "Mots, Dits, Lais, Fabliaux" often led to speculation about the form of these genres, which, in turn, led to speculation about the form of the novella. Two authors, Paul Ernst, in a series of studies published as *Der Weg zur Form* (1906), and Oskar Walzel, in his essay "Die Kunstform der Novelle" (1915), initiated studies of the novella form (1949, 249-53).

Pabst classifies scholars of the novella into two schools, the radicals and the moderates. The radicals, Lukács, Bruch, Grolman, and Klein, believe in the existence of an ideal novella type and seek to characterize it (259-63). The moderates, Hirsch, Petsch, and Pongs, neither believe in, nor do they attempt to establish, strict novellistic norms or "laws" (263-71). Pabst then analyzes the Romance scholarship on the novella and notes that during the period under study (1920-1940), not one Romance scholar made an attempt to define the novella. After citing Hellmuth Petriconi's belief that the novel, in essence, is not a genre ("keine Kunstform"), Pabst ends his study by asking whether this conclusion is not equally applicable to the novella (273-93). Four years later, as noted in the earlier discussion of the Romance novellas, Pabst answers his question by stating there is no such genre as the novella: "es gibt weder 'die romanische Urform' der Novelle noch 'die Novelle' überhaupt. Es gibt nur Novellen" (1953, 245).

In another *Forschungsbericht* (this one aimed at pedagogues), Heinz Otto Burger first provides a thumbnail sketch of the theory and criticism of the novella. After tracing the etymology of the word back to the Justinian Code, he ascribes the invention of the genre to Boccaccio. The novella spread from Italy to the other Romance countries and finally migrated to Germany with Goethe's *Unterhaltungen* (1951, 294-98). Burger comments upon the novella theories of the brothers Schlegel, Tieck, and Goethe and then turns to the flowering of the genre in the hands of Kleist, Droste, Stifter, Keller, Heyse, Storm, Raabe, and Meyer. Burger also discusses the theories of Vischer, Heyse, and Storm (298-304) and then focuses his attention on such modern critics as Ernst, Walzel, Hirsch, Grolman, Pongs, and Petsch (304-307). Burger con-

cludes that the novella is an independent genre that has evolved over the course of centuries. The original form is determined by two features: the unique event and the society to which it is told. Goethe's definition that the genre constitutes a novel event that took place is thus applicable to both the older and the modern novella. Other constituent parts of the modern genre include a falcon, a *Wendepunkt*, and a strong propensity toward symbolism (308-310).

Bernhard von Arx, in a book-length study, analyzes the novellistic practice and theory of the Goethe era. This study, which grew out of Arx's participation in Emil Staiger's 1946-1947 Seminar on the novella, begins with the report that during the seminar many theories and definitions of the genre had been examined. Since the secondary literature was at best inconclusive, the seminar participants were confused about what constituted a novella. In summarizing the work of the seminar, Staiger noted that only one non-controversial statement could be made: a novella was a narrative of medium length. This description, which serves as the focus of Arx's investigation, fixes the location of the novella in the space between the very short and the very long narrative. Arx, unaware of Morgan's essay, calls this space the maneuvering room ("Spielraum") of the novella. Arx intends to explore this space, but has no interest in pursuing a study of the formal features of the genre (1953, 7-10).

After pointing to the existence of a large body of medium-length eighteenth-century narratives, Arx states that Goethe, with his *Unterhaltungen*, continued the tradition of the Renaissance novella established by Boccaccio. Upon examining Goethe's theoretical statements in *Unterhaltungen*, the correspondence, the conversations, as well as other places, Arx concludes that Goethe's various utterances do not add up to a novella theory. Even the definition of 1827 must be considered a spontaneous expression because Goethe did not know what a novella was — "was eine Novelle sei, ist Goethe im Grunde selber unklar" (15-22). Upon examining Goethe's novellistic oeuvre, Arx concludes that since Goethe incorporated every novella save one into either a framework or a novel, he placed no great value upon a single example. The exception, *Novelle*, reflects the very old Goethe's attempt to summarize his vast experience and knowledge into one work that exhibited an artistic unity that was as palpably organic as a flowering plant (23-63).

In two chapters devoted to Kleist, Arx first discusses that author's Weltanschauung, which was dominated by his need to reveal, again and again, the cruel injustices that God inflicted upon humankind. Arx then compares the attitudes of Goethe and Kleist toward the novella. Goethe basically rejected the narrative of medium length because it was too short a form to accommodate his cosmic interests. Kleist, however, was forced to choose the novella because, having only one theme, he was unable to fulfill the requirements of a genre of greater compass. Goethe narrated novel events in order to entertain his readers. Kleist, in his monomaniacal compulsion to rail against God, had only one theme and ignored all others (67-85).

In a chapter devoted to the Romantics and the novella, Arx draws the same conclusions as he had for Kleist. The Romantics, inspired by Goethe's novels (especially *Wilhelm Meister*), attempted to portray the totality of the universe through the novel. Yet failure upon failure attests to their inability to write a satisfactory example of this genre. The novel, Arx maintains, remained an object of wishful thinking ("Wunschtraum") and constituted for the Romantics one of many attempts to attain the unattainable. Arx attributes this inability to three causes: lack of patience to produce such a lengthy and intricately complex work as a novel, youthful inexperience, and, as a concomitant manifestation, a fragmented, rather than unified personality. These reasons led to the production of many fragments and novellas. The novella best suited the Romantics since it allowed them to present one highly unusual event that afforded a brief glance into infinity (89-97).

Arx illustrates this thesis in separate analyses of the works and personalities of Ludwig Tieck, Clemens Brentano, Achim von Arnim, and E. T. A. Hoffmann. Tieck, who began his career by writing short pieces for Nicolai's *Straussfedern*, botched all attempts at lengthy prose works (*Lovell, Sternbald, Aufruhr, Accorombona*). Tieck did not find his true *métier* until 1819 when, in mid-career, he abandoned Romanticism and turned to the novella, eventually producing thirty-eight examples of this genre. The *Wendepunkt*, Arx postulates, is merely a remnant of Romanticism, for it allowed Tieck to incorporate the miraculous elements of the fairy tale into the realistic novella. In his old age, however, Tieck abandoned all formal requirements for the novella, including even the *Wendepunkt* (98-113).

Arx notes that Brentano feared everyday reality and sought refuge in the world of dreams and in the supernatural ("das Wunderbare"). Brentano's escapism is reflected by his favorite genre, the fairy tale. Arx differentiates between this genre and the novella by the presence or absence of logic, causality, and the laws of nature: the more prevalent these features, the more likely that the work is a novella; the less prominent, and the more that fantasy dominates, the more likely that the work is a fairy tale. Brentano's one novella, *Kasperl und Annerl*, lacks unity because this work combines elements of both genres. The first part, the realistic story of Kasperl, is tedious because the author himself lacked interest in the mundane. The second part, the story of Annerl, captures the reader's attention because the supernatural seems to dominate the action and to cancel the realistic aspects of this story (114-28).

Arnim, in Arx's view barely a Romantic, had a very firm grasp of reality. Unlike those Romantics whose psyches were dominated by one, all-consuming idea, Arnim had a broader Weltanschauung and was, therefore, capable of creating satisfactory, lengthy prose narratives. Yet two traits, a tremendous impatience and a proclivity to attack the natural order of worldly affairs, prevented Arnim from being a successful novelist. Arnim's true *métier* was the novella, the recounting of a remarkable event that takes place in a multi-faceted world. Arnim's greatest success in this genre was *Der Tolle Invalide*, a story that treated the most remarkable event in the lives of Francour and Rosalie and, once recounted, lacked further interest for the author (129-49).

Arx regards E. T. A. Hoffmann as the prototypical Romantic who was obsessed by one thought — the cosmic struggle between the forces of good and evil. Whereas Kleist is possessed by the idea of an unjust God, Hoffmann is possessed by the thought of a God who, although capable of granting man's wishes, refuses to do so. Man's soul, in Hoffmann's view, is the battleground upon which the forces of God and the Devil engage in perpetual battle. Although man can embrace the good and eschew the evil, the victory is never permanent. Hoffmann therefore continually revisits this battleground in medium-length narratives that range between the fairy tale and the novella. Hoffmann also regularly slipped the bonds of reality through wine. Such escapes proved to be only illusory, for the next morning grim reality, augmented by a hangover, reasserted itself. The only way out was re-intoxication. Hoffmann's works, many written while under the influence, reflect the author's need

to escape from a philistine world. It is hardly surprising, claims Arx, that Hoffmann's genre of choice was the fairy tale novella ("Märchennovelle"), for this genre best allowed him to portray his fragmented world view (150-70).

Arx concludes his monograph by emphasizing that the novella, by no means a foreshortened novel, is a legitimate form in its own right. The individual author chooses one genre over another in correspondence with his view of how the world is constructed. A Goethe, with his expansive, multi-faceted Weltanschauung, chooses the breadth and depth of the novel to express himself. A Romantic, with his one-dimensional view, chooses the novella because, lacking patience, he believes that he has found the key that unlocks the door to the meaning of life and that he can present his exciting discovery through one unique event. Arx, who places the novella between the short and long prose narrative, also differentiates between the novella and the anecdote. These narratives are alike in that they overestimate the value and significance of the individual event. They differ in that the anecdote is mere gossip about one individual, whereas the novella seeks to transcend the individual and attempts to penetrate the mysteries of the universe (173-76).

In the year following Arx's book, Johannes Klein publishes his monumental, almost 700-page *Geschichte der deutschen Novelle*. This work, Klein notes in the foreword, was essentially completed roughly two decades earlier, but not published at that time for political reasons. In the introduction, devoted to the theory of the genre, Klein repeats (at times verbatim) many of the ideas he had developed in his article of 1936. In his expansions, he also compares the novella to such genres as the *Schwank*, the legend, the fairy tale, and the short story. The novella is an artistic form, the *Schwank* is a humorous, artless tale. The novella, a realistic genre, stops at the threshold of the supernatural. Both the legend and the fairy tale cross this threshold, the former for religious reasons and the latter to revel in the realm of fantasy (1954, 12-16).

Klein devotes his lengthiest theoretical excursus to differentiating between the novella and its "illegitimate" Anglo-Saxon child, the short story. The novella originated during the Renaissance, an age when style dominated art and manifested itself in form. The short story originated in an epoch during which style, hence also form, had disintegrated. The novella is the art form of an era in which the world and life made sense; the short story is the narrative medium of a time during which both the

purpose of life and the world came under such sharp questioning that the Zeitgeist at times bordered on despair. Klein also differentiates by narrative technique. The ending of the short story is visible from the very beginning, that of the novella is unpredictable. The novella tends to develop character (albeit in a limited sense), the short story shuns such development. The novella concentrates upon describing tragic and catastrophic events; the short story intensifies the senseless horror of such events. The novella ends with an unexpressed but intimated question, the short story ends with a resounding "No" (16-25).

Klein classifies novellas into three basic types: the epic, the dramatic, and the lyric. A novella can be tragic or humorous, with the action driven by character or fate. The novella has either a closed or an open form, with the former resolving all questions and the latter leaving a number of questions unanswered. One other structural element regularly associated with novellas is the frame, a device which can take two forms — it can be an insignificant feature that serves only to connect a series of novellas, or it can acquire independent significance that augments the story. Klein concludes his introduction with a brief analysis of the history of the genre (30-59). He devotes the vast bulk of his book to twenty-eight chapters in which he analyzes hundreds of novellas by over sixty authors.

In 1954 Joseph Kunz publishes a lengthy article on the novella in Wolfgang Stammler's *Deutsche Philologie im Aufriß*. Although the major thrust of the essay lies in providing a historical synopsis of individual authors and their works, Kunz also traces a thematic thread through the various developmental phases of the German novella. Goethe, the originator of the German genre, wrote during the French Revolution, an era in which the forces of chaos were unleashed. The outbreak of the daimonic threatened to destroy the well-ordered, rational universe and rendered life uncertain. One of Goethe's responses to these unpredictable forces involved the employment of the novella as a medium for expressing the conflict between the rational and irrational. Romanticism, the next phase of the novella, so intensified the power of the irrational that it came to dominate the era and found its best expression in terms of the occult and the supernatural. Many authors viewed the world as controlled by supernatural forces and believed that the individual, now totally isolated (in Goethe's world the individual functioned within society), stood fully exposed to their malevolence (1795-1809). The

works of the young Tieck and Hoffmann show the individual perishing under such onslaughts. The works of Arnim and Eichendorff reveal that these dark forces can be fought and even defeated. Kleist, who was not a Romantic, also shows the isolated individual facing the natural (as opposed to the supernatural) powers of the world and, by an exercise of will, defies the powers of this abyss.

The next, more realistic phase of novellistic development showed a diminution, but not an elimination, of the irrational. This phase, initiated by the older Tieck, can best be characterized by that author's interpretation of "das Wunderbare," which constituted a synthesis of the real world with that of the Romantic irrational. Tieck's emphasis upon the mundane — "Wendung zum Alltäglichen" — is attended by an accentuation of chance ("Zufall"), a less virulent form of the irrational than the ravaging Romantic one (1809-39). The novellistic phase that followed, Kunz calls it "Hochrealismus," placed an even greater emphasis upon everyday occurrences than did the previous stage. Yet, even in this period, elements of the irrational persist in vestigial form, for the individual continues to be isolated and alienated (1839-80). Kunz concludes his survey by describing the novella of the twentieth century and notes that despite such literary movements as Naturalism, Impressionism, and Expressionism, the individual, as depicted in the novella, continues to be assailed by forces that originate from the realm of the mysterious and the irrational (1881-90).

The year 1954 proved productive for novella studies, for, in addition to the above works, Walter Silz published a book, *Realism and Reality: Studies in the German Novelle of Poetic Realism*, that in approach was to serve as a model for later publications. In the introduction he highlights the theory of the novella and characterizes the nature of Poetic Realism. Utilizing an incremental approach, Silz defines the genre as an amalgam of characteristics identified, among others, by Goethe, Friedrich Schlegel, Tieck, Heyse, Storm, Spielhagen, and Vischer (1-9).

Silz believes that since the novella has a natural affinity for realism, it had its finest developmental phase between roughly 1830 and 1890, the age of Poetic Realism. This age followed on the heels of Classicism and Romanticism, with the former stressing the ideal and the latter the fantastic. Social, political, economic, scientific, and other developments, commencing in roughly 1830, contributed to the formation of a new spirit that stressed an objective, realistic appraisal of the world. Silz be-

lieves that this new spirit found its voice in Poetic Realism, a literary middleground between Romanticism and Naturalism. The poetic realist depicts the world in an objective fashion. This portrayal is not a historical, sociological, or scientific account, it is rather a unified work of art whose shape is determined by the dynamic that arises between the author's creative sensibility and selectivity. Quoting Otto Ludwig, Silz argues that the novella of Poetic Realism does not attempt to portray "raw nature," but through selection and poetization strives for an "artistic reproduction of reality" (9-16).

Silz devotes the remainder of his book to interpreting nine novellas. Part of his commentary for each narrative includes an analysis and an identification of formal novella characteristics. Silz regards *Die Judenbuche*, to choose only one example, a masterpiece of the genre because it has a prominent central event, an "idea," a falcon, a silhouette, at least one leitmotif, a *Wendepunkt*, and a small cast of fixed characters (36-51). Silz, however, does not believe that the genre was ever confined to the strait jacket of theory, for he points out that over the course of six decades individual authors of Poetic Realism expanded the depth, breadth, and length of the novella. Droste's *Judenbuche* and Storm's *Schimmelreiter* extended its scope from the description of one central event to that of a whole lifetime, a task normally reserved for novels. Grillparzer's *Der arme Spielmann* expanded the novella into "a vessel of psychological revelation" (67) and, as a last example, Meyer's *Der Heilige* endowed the genre with a "new capacity: that of giving ... the picture of a whole age" (95). At the end of his study, Silz deprecates theory in favor of artistic primacy by insisting that "great literature is made by poets, not by theorists" (152).

Fritz Lockemann, after noting that scholars have tended to neglect the frame in the novella, provides a short typology of this device. There are two forms of the frame, the cyclical and single. The cyclical frame, normally cast in the third person narrative voice, has a specific intent (Scheherazade, for example, tells stories to stay alive). The single frame, usually cast in the first person, functions as a legitimizing device to lend the narrator and his tale verisimilitude. The frame can either be closed or open. The closed frame creates the illusion that the narrator is a participant in a social circle that is telling stories. The open frame creates the illusion that the reader is listening to a narrator who is divorced from the events he narrates. The frame also can be a combination of the open

and the closed: the narrator is both a member of a social circle and tells a story in which he is a participant (1955-56, 335-37).

Lockemann postulates that the frame functions as a shield to ward off chaos. In *The Decameron*, the frame characters tell stories in response to the external dangers of the plague. In *Unterhaltungen*, the frame undergoes a permutation. Once again, the frame characters flee external danger, here the French Revolution, but discover that chaos has insinuated itself into their midst (the political argument). Goethe, as did Boccaccio, employs stories in order to fend off chaos and to restore social harmony. In the earliest, usually cyclically framed novellas, chaos threatened either society at large or a smaller social unit. Beginning with the nineteenth century, however, the individual is seen as becoming more and more alienated from society. This isolation is reflected in the novella that now stands independently and, when framed, leads to intricate and complicated interrelationships between the frame and the story itself. Lockemann then analyzes several novellas in which the frames are used to combat chaos (338-50).

In an afterword, written in 1965, Lockemann stands by his now decade-old conclusions. The fundamental structure of the novella, he emphasizes, is a tension-filled narrative in search of a resolution. This resolution, which is initiated by the *Wendepunkt*, is often achieved with the aid of the frame. The one feature that distinguishes the novella from the *Erzählung* of medium length (Lockemann seems to have Arx's definition in mind) is that the novella is intent upon achieving greater poetic quality (350-51).

In 1956 Nino Erné publishes an unusual monograph, *Kunst der Novelle*, that consists of essays, dialogues, and lectures purportedly written by a study group that included a professor, a librarian, an actress, a poet, a dancer, a student, a French Chevalier, and Erné himself. Although Erné's work is not written in the style of a scholarly disquisition, many allusions reveal his familiarity with novella theory and criticism. After tracing the origins of the novella to the Italian Renaissance, Erné describes the genre as the narration of a novel event. In comments characterizing prose narratives, Erné observes that the fairy tale opens with the formulaic "once upon a time" and treats events from the mythological past. The *Erzählung* takes place in a more recent, yet still distant past. The novella occurs in the present. In musical terms the fairy tale begins with a dreamy and haunting pianissimo, the *Erzählung* with a moderate

andante, and the novella with a full-chorded fortissimo ("voller Ak-
kord"). Upon analyzing the beginning of eleven different novellas, Erné
devises a scale that is bounded at one end by the dramatic opening in
which the author yanks open the curtain and the reader finds himself a
witness to an event in full progress. The other, anecdotal boundary begins with the revelation that something has already happened and the
reader is witness to the denouement. Beginnings falling between the
dramatic and anecdotal are possible, yet they usually involve the frame
rather than the story itself (7-29).

In a lecture supposedly delivered by the professor, Erné argues that
the frame antedates stories and goes back to the days of cave men telling
each other tales. Boccaccio transformed this primeval narrative situation
into a composition of classical symmetry. Since Boccaccio's main interest
involved stories, the frame is simply an ordering device (ten stories to be
told in ten days) that is independent of the narratives. Erné analyzes the
frames in novellas by Meyer, Turgenev, and Conrad and concludes that
the social, cyclical cornice of Boccaccio has virtually disappeared. Erné
argues that in modern times the frame is justified only when it either
mirrors or bears a strong relationship to the story itself (30-43).

In the next chapter, devoted mainly to the function of the narrator in
the frame, the professor repeats that the nineteenth-century novellist had
lost all interest in the Boccaccian frame. This development led Mérimée
to invent a new form, the perspectival frame ("[der] perspektivische
Rahmen"), which he first employed in *Vénus d'Ille*, fully developed in
Carmen, and varied masterfully in *Lokis*. In *Carmen* the strands of the
frame and of the main narrative are so closely interwoven that they present one inseparable tapestry. Mérimée also uses the narrator of the frame
as a counterpoint to the events of the main narrative, thereby increasing
the tension of the story line (44-52).

The actress then dissects *Vénus d'Ille* in order to identify the
"Kristallisationspunkt," the point of the story that functions like a metaphorical hub from which all narrative spokes radiate. This hub, the
statue of Venus, is the center from which all action emanates in concentric circles. The actress concludes by praising this work as the ideal novella, for it incorporates all essential features of the genre, including a
double narrative plane ("der doppelte Boden"). This two-fold plane
consists of presenting information in such a fashion that two equally

plausible explanations — one mundane, the other miraculous or occult — can be advanced in explanation of the mysterious events (53-61).

In a lengthy dialogue the various characters, mainly the professor and the librarian, exchange opinions about the nature and function of this double narrative plane. After setting aside the totally fantastic narrative (for example, the fairy tale), the group agrees that the novella seems to have an affinity for the supernatural. This phenomenon, especially prevalent in the works of the Romantics, is most visible in Hoffmann, who created works in which the protagonists took wing to fly above pedestrian reality. At the end of such works, a number of explanations are possible — they were wine-induced visions or nightmares, they were the ramblings of an insane mind, or they were inexplicable manifestations of the supernatural (62-84).

In a chapter entitled "Pointierung," Erné explains that the group had examined Goethe's famous definition of 1827 from many points of view and, after also having seen it supported by the theories of the brothers Schlegel and Tieck, had decided that the "unerhörte Begebenheit" constituted the center of novellistic gravity. The word *unerhört* can be traced to the Greek anecdote, which originally meant a matter that was not known or had not gained currency. Erné classifies the "Pointe" into five categories. The anecdote, which constitutes the raw material of the novella, contains the simplest "Pointe" — often only a witty rejoinder. Such a witticism may tickle the reader's sense of humor, but it fails to touch his heart or spirit. The second type of "Pointe," to be found in the classical novella, is more complex than the one in the anecdote because it is lengthier, barbed, or multi-faceted. A third manifestation of this phenomenon involves the modern novella of decadence where the story-line is interrupted or fragmented. Such a novella contains a situation in which, like the self-inflicted sting of a scorpion, the "Pointe" becomes an instrument of social self-destruction. In lyrical novellas (as opposed to dramatic ones) the "Pointe" may be so well hidden that it becomes nigh invisible. Every novella, nevertheless, has a "Pointe" and Erné exhorts his readers to look for its hiding place. The final form, labelled "Salto mortale," involves a situation where the author seems to take great pains to prepare the way for a "Pointe" which, ironically, he never allows to develop. This type of "Pointe," Erné concedes, may be more applicable to the short story than to the novella (85-97).

Erné seems to be at a loss when it comes to the contemporary novella since he accords this topic tripartite treatment. In the first part he rejects the notion that the novella perished under the onslaught of the short story. The novella, after all, is a *European* phenomenon and represents the most compact and concentrated narrative art form. The modern form of this narrative, sometimes called the short story, was created by writers like Maupassant, Chekhov, and Pirandello. These narratives actually are slender novellas. The novella started life as a very short form, expanded in length to as many as a hundred pages in the nineteenth century, and now, in the twentieth century, is shrinking back to original size. A strong novella current continues to flow even in contemporary times and can be seen in such examples as Sartre's "The Wall," Faulkner's "A Rose for Emily," and Hemingway's *The Old Man and the Sea* (98-103).

In the second sub-chapter the poet accuses Erné of waving a magic wand in order to charm away the contemporary short story. Maupassant, Chekhov, and Pirandello's works are not novellas, but short stories, because these narratives lack such novellistic features as a "Pointe," dramatic tension, or a turning point. O. Henry, generally considered the father of the American short story, actually wrote short novellas since all of his narratives exhibit a "Pointe." The poet believes that Hemingway's *49 Stories* clinch his argument. Much as did the narratives of Boccaccio and Mérimée upon original appearance, so too do Hemingway's stories reveal a new narrative form, that of the short story. This form, a child born of the union of despair and Nihilism, seeks to flee from its *Weltangst* through bull-fighting, big-game hunting, alcohol, and war. The short story, as exemplified by "A Clean, Well-Lighted Place," with its existential anthem to "nada," is a fragile genre that is incapable of carrying such novellistic burdens as a turning point, something surprising, a "Pointe," or the wondrous (104-109).

In the third sub-chapter, the poet describes the situation of the German soldiers and artists who, upon returning from the horrors of war, encountered only rubble and chaos. These artists, lacking essentials such as bread, warmth, and a bed, were unable to cultivate an appreciation for such novellistic nuances as the wondrous, fate, or the "Pointe" because the world for them had turned pointless. Forced to re-create their lives as well as all values, these writers also re-created the narrative form in accord with their own needs. This form, the rubble story ("Trüm-

mergeschichte"), as mastered by Wolfgang Borchert, best voiced the experiences, conditions, and concerns of a whole generation. This generation lacked the time and the inclination to devote to novels and chose the short story because one brief glance sufficed to reveal clearly the naked faces of existence and of death (109-14).

Erné reports in the last chapter that the professor died shortly after the study group had broken up. Late in life he had seemed convinced that the death of the novella was inevitable. Erné attributes this demise to the lack of the one prerequisite condition — a social group, preferably led by a woman, that is listening to and evaluating a narrative brief enough to be recounted in one evening. Such social circles have gone the way of the novella. Erné believes, however, that one day they will regroup and that when this comes to pass, a new bird will take wing (115-21).

Benno von Wiese publishes the first of two volumes on the German novella in 1956. Although Wiese's principal interest lies in the interpretation of novellas, he, like Walter Silz, also comments on the theory of the genre. After citing the results of such critics as Petsch, Pongs, Pabst, Arx, Klein, and Kunz, Wiese observes that the status of the novella as a genre is very uncertain. He is not prepared, as are Pabst and Arx, to abandon the genre. Wiese believes the novella exists ("dennoch gibt es die Gattung 'Novelle'") and that it is anchored to the rock of Goethe's definition. The novella deals with one event ("mit der *einen Begebenheit*") that is usually treated concisely in a subjective, artistic fashion. Wiese does suggest, however, that the term *novellistisches Erzählen* (novellistic narration) be employed in order to escape the large volume of theoretical freight that tradition has loaded upon the term *Novelle* (11-15).

After examining elements of novella theories by the brothers Schlegel, Tieck, Vischer, Heyse, Storm, Ernst, and others, Wiese postulates that such features as "Symbol," "Wendepunkt," "Falke," "Leitmotiv," and "Silhouette" are either subsumptions or indirect expressions of Goethe's single, extraordinary event. One problematic area with this minimum definition, Wiese concedes, arises with the "Charakternovelle." Yet, even in Kleist's *Michael Kohlhaas*, often cited as the example *par excellence* of this sub-genre, the presumption that character is decisive proves to be incorrect, for ultimately action dominates. Wiese concludes by observing that the genre of the novella should not be considered a pigeon hole into which only certain items are to be deposited.

It should, instead, be viewed as a living organism that survived only by developing and by adapting to changing times and conditions (16-32).

Fritz Lockemann returns to the topic of the frame in 1957, this time in book-length form. He devotes the introduction to theoretical aspects of the novella and the main body to individual authors and their works. After assessing the criticism of Arx, Klein, Grolman, Kunz, Pongs, and Wiese, Lockemann postulates that from its very inception with Goethe's *Unterhaltungen*, the German novella has been stamped by the formal feature of the frame. He reiterates his earlier typology (the cyclical, single, open, closed, or combination frame) and continues to maintain that the frame functions as an instrument of order to shield against the attacks of chaos (7-14).

The frame, even if missing, is an integral part of the genre because it portrays the most fundamental novellistic situation — a narrator and a listener. The other crucial element is a tension-filled plot that consists of a single event and exhibits a "Pointe." The "Pointe" (at times called a "Wendepunkt" or a "Kristallisationspunkt") and the frame are both intimately related to chaos. The novella, consequently, often exhibits two turning points: the first when chaos defeats order and the second when chaos yields the field to order. These reversals, which increase the tension of the plot, are structural elements of the novella and differentiate this genre from the anecdote and the short story. The latter two genres exhibit only one turning point that serves to resolve rather than to augment tension. Those narratives in which chaos dominates at the end are anti-novellas — "Gegennovellen" (14-16).

Lockemann acknowledges that the urge to impose order upon chaos is a significant motivator in both art and life. This urge is emphasized in the novella to such a point that it becomes the object of artistic representation. Form (the *Dingsymbol*) and content ("die unerhörte Begebenheit") unite at the *Wendepunkt* to reflect the totality of the novella. The novella is thus an artistic construct comprised of three basic elements — frame, chaos or order, and turning point — that writers reconfigure in ever-changing constellations. These elements amount to "laws" ("Strukturgesetz" and "Gattungsgesetz") that govern the novella (19-22). Lockemann devotes the remainder of his book to showing these laws in operation during the historical unfolding of the German novella from Goethe to Werner Bergengruen.

In 1958 Lutz Mackensen concludes that recent scholarly attempts to define the novella all ended in a blind alley. A few studies (principally by Arx and several Anglo-American attempts to define the short story) have even led to the absurdity of creating literary yardsticks to take the measure of prose narratives by length. Despite these failures, there nevertheless remains a difference between a *Novelle*, an *Erzählung*, and a *Geschichte*. The antecedents of the novella can be traced to the thirteenth-century Florentine emphasis upon "*bel parlare*," an elegant style of speaking that emphasized pointed syntax and striking turns of phrase. This style, first seen in its literary manifestation in *Il Novellino*, was later adapted by Boccaccio. The Italian novellists did not emphasize content (which often amounted to borrowings of well-known stories), but a sophisticated style that aimed to amuse and to entertain. This emphasis upon verbal accomplishment as a social grace migrated to the other Romance countries and, four centuries later, even appeared in the title and works of Goethe's *Unterhaltungen* (the term means either "conversation" or "amusement"). Yet, by the time Goethe adapted the novella into a modern setting, the requisite social circle in which such elegant discourse thrived had all but disappeared (391-402).

The novella underwent a radical transformation at the hands of Kleist: it no longer emphasized light-hearted social banter, but topics of the greatest philosophical, religious, and ethical significance. This transformation was accompanied by attempts to define the novella. Efforts by Goethe, the Schlegels, Tieck, Mundt, Laube, and Heyse merely beclouded the issue because they attempted to describe or to prescribe content. Mackensen seeks to restore clarity by turning to the first grand master of the novella. Boccaccio's tales, mostly reworkings of older stories, became new by virtue of compliance with the stylistic stance espoused by *bel parlare*. Mackensen analyzes *The Decameron* and sees therein primary as well as secondary novella characteristics. Included among the former are a cool, amoral narrative approach, a unifying frame, a tendency toward symbolism, and an inclination toward verisimilar stories. Secondary characteristics include oral transmission, brevity, emphasis upon entertainment, and a closed form. By a closed form Mackensen means that once told, a novella does not reach beyond itself and does not excite further discussion or interpretation. Since a novella is actuality a narrative stance ("Erzählart") rather than a genre or form, all

attempts to ascribe formal features must end in a list that will never add up (403-10).

Harry Steinhauer, more than two decades after the original publication of *Die deutsche Novelle* (1936), revises his textbook and, this time, addresses the theory of the novella. Citing Walter Pabst's conclusions for the Romance novella, Steinhauer announces that he too is skeptical of all theory devoted to the German genre since it often is "outworn, one-sided, or downright erroneous." Included in this criticism are, among other features, Goethe's unprecedented event, Tieck's turning point, and Heyse's falcon and silhouette. The "most perspicacious" observation about the novella, that it is "a story of medium length," has been made by Emil Staiger. This definition allows for characterizations based on size and, in keeping with this principle, Steinhauer devises a scale on which the novel, novella, short story, and anecdote exhibit, in comparative terms, increasingly more narrative compression. After noting that the novellistic house has many mansions, Steinhauer counsels that "it would be well to avoid dogmatic statements ..." (1958, 14-18).

Theodore Ziolkowski devotes a portion of his interpretation of *Un-terhaltungen* to Goethe's novella theory and practice. Upon comparing Goethe's and Boccaccio's frameworks, he observes that the latter, since it is totally divorced from the narratives, constitutes a wooden, "tedious interruption" and reveals that Boccaccio was interested only in stories. Goethe's frame, by contrast "natural and spontaneous," shows that his interest in the events and characters of the frame equalled his interest in the stories themselves. Goethe's conflation suggests that he considered the novella to be a medium that simultaneously functioned both as entertainment and as ballast for maintaining social equilibrium — a function that is reflected by the very title "Unterhaltungen."

Although Goethe fails to use the term *Novelle*, the remarks of the chaplain and the baroness apply to the genre. The chaplain's comments reveal that he is mainly interested in content, specifically the impact a significant event may have upon the life of an individual. The baroness, on the other hand, is interested in form. Her remarks about *Arabian Nights* are critical of stories that lack a clear beginning, middle, and end, whereas her injunction to the chaplain regarding the type of story he is to tell amount to a call for "classical unity and moderation" (1958, 59-64).

In an essay entitled "Streit um die Novelle," Johannes Klein grouses that scholars have failed to agree with his thesis that the novella is a primeval art form ("Urform des Erzählens") engendered by life itself. A case in point is Benno von Wiese, who fails to mention this thesis, yet seems to agree with the first half when he observes that novellistic narration antedates the genre itself. Moreover, since the novella narrates and elevates an event that is singular and real ("einmalig und wahr") to an art form by symbolism, Wiese also seems to agree with the second half of the thesis that life and art are intimately related. Klein then criticizes Wiese's skeptical critical positions regarding the theory of the genre and, simultaneously, also pays several half-hearted compliments to Wiese's interpretations. Klein concludes his essay by observing that artists, when creating their works, seldom pay much attention to the efforts of their fellow artists. This practice, while justified in the world of art, is questionable in the world of scholarship. Although Klein's article contributes very little to the theory of the novella, it does show the beginning of a tendency for scholars to disagree with each other in increasingly sharp terms (1959, 169-71).

Rafael Koskimies, in his study of the European novella, notes that the practitioners of the genre at times also contribute to theory. This dual role often leads to attempts to define or to stake out the territory of the "true" novella and several writers even attempt to adhere to these theoretical principles in their works. More often, however, the novellists concern themselves less with theory and more with technique — practical matters such as the discovery of trade secrets or how to write more effectively. Koskimies lists and analyzes several elements that are often cited as formal structural features of the novella. One feature of the early (classical) novella, the frame and the resulting multiple narrators, can hardly be considered a necessary structural element of the genre since many novellas stand independently. The frame is thus merely a technique that writers use to forestall the reader's boredom by presenting him with different narrative voices. Other classical elements, for example *bel parlare* and the novelty of motifs, also prove problematical. The former was part of the creative process that led to the emergence of Italian as a written language, whereas the latter is hardly applicable since many novella themes can be traced to older sources (1959, 411-18).

More modern elements of the theory, such as Goethe's definition or Heyse's "Falkentheorie," are equally problematical. Goethe's definition is

rather thin and inapplicable even to his own novellas in *Wilhelm Meister*. Heyse's falcon, which soars in a few German novellas, cannot be sighted in many French ones. Yet the falcon appears in many *contes* and in almost every anecdotal narrative by O. Henry. Koskimies lists other elements of the theory (the kinship of the genre with the drama, the *Wendepunkt*, and a dramatic beginning, to name only a few) and notes that they too turn out to be problematical when rigorously applied either to many German or to other European examples of the genre. Koskimies concludes his essay by emphasizing that the impact of a great work of art does not depend upon its compliance with a set of aesthetic regulations. It depends, rather, on the artist's acuity of vision and ability to give shape to what he sees when he looks into the depths of the human heart. In the narrative art forms he does so in a language that is uniquely his own — a language that trembles and resonates in accord with the pain and joy of the human condition (419-38).

Walter Silz in 1959 provides a brief but cogent analysis of the German novella from its inception to modern times. The Romance form of the word can mean either a short narrative or something that is novel. Goethe, credited with introducing the genre into Germany, in practice and theory did more to recapitulate the Romance past than he did to lay the foundations for the German genre. That task was left to Kleist. The novella for this author represented a genre capable of expressing the deepest concerns of modern, isolated man facing a hostile universe. Kleist's contribution to the novella went unappreciated for more than a century. The Zeitgeist of the epoch, Romanticism, found its best artistic expression in the fairy tale. Silz disallows such hybrids as "Märchennovelle," "Legendennovelle," or "Romannovelle" and insists that the theoreticians and practitioners of the nineteenth century formed and cast the novella as a distinct genre. Hallmarks of this form include realism, an organizing central event or conflict, concise and selective portrayal of both characters and natural features, and a focal point that involves a crisis in the life of an atypical human being (82-87).

The novella differs from its ancestor, the anecdote. The anecdote, which (to use Goethe's words) is the narration of a novel event that occurred, is best suited to be a newspaper article. Just as a fact is not truth, an anecdote is not a novella. A narrative becomes a novella only when it transforms a unique event into an artistic, often symbolic account that reveals a truth about the human condition. The short story provides the

modern, hurried reader a narrative with exciting effects and a surprising ending (all in one, quick gulp). Yet this form, a close relative of journalism, lacks the poetic weight and value of the novella. Much closer relatives of the novella are the drama and the ballad. The novella shares with the former genre a central conflict and catastrophe and with the latter a supple form that transmits (often through symbols) a highly concentrated story that turns around a central event (87-90).

Much as he had done in his book of 1954, Silz summarizes the ideas of the nineteenth-century theoreticians and also describes Poetic Realism. This epoch, sandwiched between Romanticism and Naturalism, developed the novella as the dominant literary form. In content, to paraphrase Heyse, the novella expanded from the remarkable event to encompass everything that concerned the human heart. The advent of Naturalism, Impressionism, and Expressionism signalled the end for the novella as a dominant genre. The Poetic Realists had attempted to superimpose artistic form and structure upon the "reality" of the people and events they portrayed. The Naturalists did not go beyond describing sordid reality. The Expressionists, when not actively hostile, showed a sullen indifference to reality. Silz concludes that the German novella reveals a metamorphosis of German thought and letters that has led from the real to the surreal. Thus, upon reading Kafka, the reader encounters an author who portrays an acutely real world that, paradoxically, is devoid of all reality (91-99).

6: Doubt Established (1960-1970)

A FEW NINETEENTH-CENTURY commentators (Bouterwerk, W. Meyer, Rumohr, Riehl, Keller) were quite skeptical about defining the novella, yet their opinions went largely unheeded. Most critics assumed there was such a genre and attempted to chart its waters. The post-war era, as inaugurated by the skepticism of Pabst and Arx, witnessed several reactions. Klein, Burger, Lockemann, and Erné remain unmoved and insist the novella is a distinct genre. Silz and Wiese also believe there is such a form (albeit an elastic one), but distance themselves from rigid prescription. A third group, Mackensen, Steinhauer, and Koskimies, call for the revaluation of all novellistic values. From this point onward, most critics, regardless of the opinion with which they align themselves, feel constrained in their navigations to take into account this once-small trickle that has acquired the force of a current.

Influential essays by Manfred Schunicht and Fritz Martini reflect this development. After taking note of Pabst's work, Schunicht states that many terms bandied about in the criticism of the novella are based on misunderstandings. Such are the cases for Tieck's turning point and Heyse's falcon. At the end of the eighteenth century the term *Wendepunkt* became popular for describing a life crisis. Tieck underwent such an ordeal in 1802 when he lost the ability to differentiate between reality and imagination. He found relief upon falling under the influence of Solger, who postulated that Hegel's concept of the absolute manifested itself in the finite world in the form of "Punktualität." Tieck thought this term referred to the instant when the subjective and the objective fuse and relabelled it the *Wendepunkt*. Schunicht views this term as so uniquely personal to Tieck that he calls for its exclusion from the nomenclature of novella theory (1960, 439-52).

Upon selecting stories for *Novellenschatz*, Heyse chose a memorable plot as his main criterion and cited the story of Federigo and his falcon as an example. Pongs misinterpreted Heyse's criterion as a *Dingsymbol*. Since Heyse only meant that a novella should be memorable, Schunicht calls on critics to follow Federigo's example by slaughtering this vexatious bird, but exhorts them to refrain from dishing it up in future novella criticism (452-59).

Schunicht believes it is impossible to differentiate among prose narratives on the basis of form. Yet, the novella can be characterized from three viewpoints: the function of the narrator, the situation of the reader, and the structure of reality. The novella aims at duplicating the perspective of a reporter who provides an objective account of an event he has witnessed. This perspective, facilitated by a narrator in the frame, creates the illusion that the reader, too, is a witness to real events. This narrative stance leads to what Schunicht calls the bilateral structure of the novella — the dichotomy between the objective and the subjective. Since the novella is an artistic creation, the author strives to attain two goals seldom found in reality, the unity of shape and the finality of a satisfactory ending. He achieves these goals by being selective and by introducing implausible events. This process leads to the dilemma where an event seems both real and implausible. The novellist solves this problem by introducing the element of chance. Since the reader shares the narrator's perspective, he remains confident in his illusion and accepts chance as real. Schunicht emphasizes that his observations apply only to novellas of the nineteenth century. Modern novellas differ from older ones because the perspectival partnership between narrator and reader has been dissolved. The reader now stands alone in mystified contemplation of an incomprehensible reality (459-68).

Schunicht's rejection of the *Wendepunkt*, in view of his own emphasis on the role of chance in the novella, is puzzling. Tieck provides an example from *Unterhaltungen* of how chance (the discovery that the locked desk top can be sprung) leads directly to a turning point (Ferdinand becomes a thief). Schunicht, with his biographical emphasis, fails even to mention Tieck's commentary in this area and declares Tieck's notion of the turning point inapplicable to the novellas of other authors (450-51). Also unexplained is what seems to be a delayed reaction. Schunicht states that Tieck had his crisis in 1802 and became acquainted with Solger in 1811; yet, he did not formulate his ideas about the *Wendepunkt* until 1829.

Fritz Martini also rejects the conclusions of Pabst and Arx because narrative types such as *Erzählung*, *Novelle*, *Roman*, and *Kurzgeschichte* represent distinct forms. Martini views the novella as a dynamic genre that has changed over the course of time and emphasizes that his remarks are confined to the novella of Poetic Realism. Since authors of this period wrote highly individualistic works and aesthetic opinions, at-

tempts to formulate a firm definition of the novella are fruitless. It is possible, however, to describe the background that helped give the novella of the era its distinctive shape (1960, 353-58).

Martini reacts to several commentators, agreeing with Heyse, for example, that the novella, once confined to the narration of an unusual or humorous event, has been transformed into a form so protean that it can treat any human concern, including portraiture of character. This mutability has increased the tension between the objective and the subjective aspects of the novella. The modern novellist imparts his subjectivity by aiming for a high degree of artistry in his account of a "real" but unusual event or character. This technique, facilitated by a narrator who insists that the story he is telling took place, leads to a paradox — the greater the objectivity on one level, the greater the subjectivity potential on the other (361-69).

Martini then distinguishes between *Erzählung* and novella. The former portrays its subject matter in chronological, causal, and expository fashion. The latter exhibits leaps and gaps in narrative sequence and emphasizes contrasts and symbols. The theme of the novella often is irrational or incalculable and tends to unfold rather than to develop. The plot is thus open rather than closed. Structural elements often found in the novella include *Leitmotive*, *Dingsymbole*, and a frame that includes a narrator who tells a story from memory (370-77).

The Zeitgeist of the era, which was informed by a strong sense of determinism, is mirrored in novellas by protagonists who find themselves trapped in such dire predicaments they welcome death. This determinism also reflects another significant feature of the novella, its incorporation and transformation of tragedy. The hapless individual stands not only helpless as fate enacts itself, he is unable to fathom its workings. Such lack of understanding extends to the narrator in the frame, who can present only a limited, hence fragmented, account. Such fragmentation, in turn, portrays the fractured Weltanschauung of the epoch (382-89).

Katharina Mommsen, in a book-length study of Goethe and *Arabian Nights*, believes that the chaplain in *Unterhaltungen* (not the baroness, who is critical of *Arabian Nights*) best reflects Goethe's views on the short narrative. Goethe distinguished carefully between the tightly structured novel and the loosely structured frame narrative. Goethe, much like Scheherazade, scattered stories and fairy tales into this frame

and consciously avoided unity (1960, 58-64). Two years later, upon editing a volume of Goethe's novellas, Mommsen repeats these conclusions and emphasizes that for Goethe the novella functioned as entertainment and diversion in face of threatening political and daimonic forces (1962, 188-90).

Stephen Spender, in his introduction to an anthology of German stories, remarks that the short story normally presents "a segment" of experience, but that the German variety tends to reflect "a whole view of life." The typical story tells no "more about a character than is necessary," but with German examples "the tendency is the reverse." The German story depicts "very real circumstances," but this reality amounts to the surreal, because "the German story is ... fairy tale, legend, parable." Lack of space, Spender explains, prevented him from including stories by Eichendorff, Mörike, Novalis, and Brentano. He was able to include "three very long stories" by Büchner ("Lenz"), Kleist ("The Earthquake in Chile"), and Kafka ("In the Penal Colony"). Spender regrets excluding Goethe's "novella" *Werther*, but has found room for Stifter's "short novel" *Brigitta* (1960, 9-14). These pronouncements illustrate that confusion about prose genres is not the exclusive domain of German critics, but extends to a British critic and poet of the stature of Spender.

Joachim Müller, citing Goethe's belief that elements of the epic, the lyric, and the drama often appear together in even the shortest poem, finds it only natural that difficulties arise when attempts are made to demarcate between sub-genres such as novella and *Erzählung*. Regarded as interchangeable in the past, these terms in recent decades have acquired qualitative nuances. The term *Erzählung* now carries the implication that it is a lesser narrative form than the novella because it fails to adhere to high, formal standards. Müller regards the two genres as separate, but equal, and considers all attempts to establish a hierarchy unwarranted. The novella is the account of a sharply profiled, tension-filled central event that emphasizes a "Pointe." It unfolds at a rapid pace, displays surprising plot twists, and tends to be a tightly organized, well-balanced, and closed form. The *Erzählung* features a tension-free, decentralized event that unfolds at a leisurely pace and is treated in an oblique fashion. The *Erzählung*, more loosely organized than the novella, emphasizes an implicit question rather than an explicit answer and tends, therefore, to be an open-ended form (1961, 470-79).

Hermann Pongs returns to novella theory in 1961, seeking this time the common ground in which the various forms of the novella are rooted. Pongs believes this ground to be Goethe's definition of "eine sich ereignete unerhörte Begebenheit." This description posits the dynamic tension generated when the commonplace is juxtaposed with the unusual. Simultaneously, the definition either accommodates or incorporates many of the elements developed by later critics and theoreticians. Examples include, among others, the turning point, the falcon, the daimonic, chaos versus order, the central event, and the closed form. Finding such fertile, common ground is especially important since many recent critics have declared the novella dead (3-7). Pongs attempts to prove in the remainder of his slender volume that the novellas of Friedrich Franz von Unruh render this declaration premature and exaggerated (7-43).

Henry Remak considers it ironic that in the very decade one group of critics is declaring the novella dead, another group is showing a lively interest in its form. After identifying himself as a member of the latter group, Remak avows that no literary pharmacy can fill the prescription for a good novella. Since a work of art is a meld of both the typical and the individual, it should be possible to identify typical formal features. These features include Goethe's definition, an affinity for the catastrophe, and the *Dingsymbol*. After explicating these elements, Remak applies them to three novellas by Gottfried Keller and concludes that Keller, despite his highly skeptical theoretical stance, instinctively recognized and incorporated the essential formal components of the genre into his oeuvre (1962, 424-38).

Six years after anchoring his views of the novella to the rock of Goethe's definition, Benno von Wiese observes that modern critics have discovered that such formal elements as *Wendepunkt* and *Falken* are inapplicable to the genre. These discoveries prompt Wiese to reemphasize the term "novellistic narration" and to attempt to define the maneuvering room ("Spielraum") of the genre. Wiese again describes the novella as concentrating upon one novel, yet true event. Such dualism (Schunicht called it the bilateral structure) leads to the narrative tension of the genre (1962, 9-15). This tension is expressed and augmented by three characteristics often associated with the novella — irony, chance, and signification ("*Ironie*," "*Zufall*," and "*Zeichen*"). Irony, which can wear many masks, usually represents the narrator's subjective attempt to distance

himself from the material he is presenting. Chance, often intertwined with irony, becomes a significant element of a short narrative because it allows for surprising turns of plot (18-21). Since the novella is of such limited compass, it presents its material by means of leaps and contrasts rather than by smooth transitions. To compensate for this narrative abridgement, the novella often employs signifiers that are laden with meaning (21-24). It seems that as Wiese attempts to banish such full-blooded features as *Wendepunkt, Falken*, and *Dingsymbol* through the front door, he allows their shadowy versions to slip in through the back door.

In a lengthy history of the German novella, Hellmuth Himmel provides an excellent, in-depth account of the development of the genre from its oriental antecedents to Goethe's *Unterhaltungen* (9-29). Upon turning to theory, he dismisses many prevailing notions. He opines, for example, that neither the discussions in *Unterhaltungen* nor Goethe's definition of 1827 contribute to the theory of the novella. In similar fashion, he also discards Heyse's theory as unclear and lacking in originality. Only the pronouncements of the Schlegels, Tieck, and Mundt are worthy of consideration — "damit [ist] die Theorie der Novelle abgeschlossen." Of the ideas developed by these critics, Himmel finds of interest only those aspects that deal with the *Wendepunkt* (1963, 29-41). He divides the main body of his book into nine chapters, arranged chronologically by literary period, and devotes his principal attention to analyzing the novellas of more than 250 authors. In execution of this massive undertaking, Himmel often identifies the *Wendepunkt* of a given narrative, but makes only infrequent attempts to describe other characteristics. Like many critics, Himmel too considers the novella, if not already dead, then at least gasping for its last breath.

In 1963 Benno von Wiese, in the novella volume of the *Sammlung Metzler*, provides an excellent orientation to the theory and criticism of the genre as well as an extensive bibliography. Wiese describes the genre by summarizing and synthesizing the ideas of theoreticians from Wieland to Heyse. After citing the lack of unanimity in opinion, he again pleads for adoption of the term "novellistic narration" (1-13). Wiese also distills influential scholarly findings from Friedrich Schlegel to Fritz Martini (13-27). He devotes the next four chapters to providing a history of the novella that begins with the oriental antecedents and ends with Fontane (33-71). In the final chapter, where he describes the mod-

ern short prose narrative, Wiese, too, observes a dissolution of the novella. He attributes this phenomenon to three causes: the expansion and the contraction of the genre into the realms of the novel and the anecdote, the influence of foreign writers such as Maupassant and Pirandello, and the development, explosive growth, and influence of the Anglo-American short story. The disintegration of the genre can best be seen in Günter Grass's *Katz und Maus* which, although sub-titled "Eine Novelle," is only a fragment or an ironically narrated short novel. The contemporary short prose scene, created by such authors as Heinrich Böll, Ilse Aichinger, and Wolfdietrich Schnurre, is dominated by the Anglo-American-inspired short story. This genre, which is even more difficult to define than the novella, exhibits a number of tendencies: it is open in form, stresses atmosphere rather than action, poses questions rather than presents solutions, lies between the novella and the anecdote or sketch in length, and allows the author the greatest possible formal freedom. This genre may also be best suited to portray the incomprehensibility, fragmentation, and horror of the modern world (74-81).

Gerhart Fricke delineates what he regards as Goethe's pedagogical intentions for the novellas of *Unterhaltungen*. The chaplain, by first telling a pointless ghost story, captures the group's interest and helps restore social harmony. After three similar stories of equal quality are told, the refugees (as well as the readers of *Die Horen*) have been sufficiently schooled in listening to poor stories to be more appreciative of better ones. There is thus a clear progression from the first four very poor stories to the much better ones that are told later and that comply with the baroness's high formal standards (1964, 277-90).

In 1964-1965 Karl K. Polheim publishes a monograph-length *Forschungsbericht* on the criticism of novella theory. German artists and critics have been pondering the nature of the genre for almost two centuries, but the first two post-war decades have witnessed a mushrooming of interest. Polheim classifies recent critics into three groups: the first provides strict definitions of the novella, the second declares it dead, and the third seeks new foundations or directions. He assigns all critics into either the normative or the historical schools of thought. The former seek to identify characteristics common to all novellas — often they seek the proto-form ("Urform") — whereas the latter attempt to describe the developmental phases of the genre from its inception to modern times (1-8).

Polheim then creates a square of criticism into which he places four commentators, the normative Arx and Klein and the historical Pabst and Martini. Each critic represents the most radical position of his respective school. Arx claims that the novella has no formal features, while Klein insists upon a prototype ("Urform"). Pabst believes that there is no such genre as the novella, while Martini insists that at least one historical phase of the novella exhibits a number of common features. Polheim believes that these critics prove to be excellent representatives of their schools since all other opinions fall between the extremes they posit (9-32). In later chapters Polheim analyzes the criticism of the previous two decades under such categories as the historical development of novella theory from the Middle Ages to the end of the nineteenth century (32-64), new attempts at theory (64-86), and attempts to join novella theory to interpretation (86-100).

In his final chapter Polheim observes that critics of the normative school, upon singling out such hallmarks as the unprecedented event, turning point, falcon, leitmotif, and chance, fail to make a case since they neither confirm the presence of these features in novellas nor their absence from other genres. The historically oriented critics, while expressing wide-ranging opinions, have shown that novellas of a given period can be loosely characterized. Yet, since it is impossible to draw parallels between the novellas of the various periods, not one of these characteristics can be elevated to a norm. Polheim concludes his *Forschungsbericht* with a tautology that states that a novella is an artistic narrative: "Eine Novelle ist eine künstlerische gestaltete Erzählung." Conversely, "eine künstlerische gestaltete Erzählung ist eine Novelle." A novella, when unshackled from its normative chains, stands on equal footing with an *Erzählung* (101-109).

In 1965 Johannes Klein writes an essay on the novella for the *Reallexikon*. In keeping with the encyclopedic nature of the volume, Klein provides a short history of the genre as well as a summary of theory. As on previous occasions, he insists that the novella is a narrative "Urform" that from its very beginnings dealt with an unusual, but real event. With the passage of time the novella preserved this original feature, but added such artistic characteristics as *Wendepunkt, Leitmotiv,* and *Dingsymbol.* Klein then distinguishes between the novella and other forms much as he had in 1954 (686-92).

Henry Remak, in an essay devoted to symbolism and the novella, defines three related but separate categories: a metaphor is an "analogy of apparently disparate empirical phenomena;" an allegory is a "disguise of one thing as another;" and a symbol is a "concrete object" that, when organically integrated into a novella, acquires a "more universal dimension" than it intrinsically possesses. These symbolic forms display varying degrees of aesthetic success. The allegory is least effective because it leans toward artificiality. The metaphor is an improvement over the allegory because it shows the poet's creativity. The symbol is the "most productive" of the three because it makes the reader a "cocreator" (1965, 37-38).

Remak analyzes symbolism in three novellas: C. F. Meyer's *Pescara*, Keller's *Romeo und Julia*, and Storm's *Schimmelreiter*. He considers Meyer's work to be "artificially inseminated" with five allegorical paintings. Upon examining their functions, Remak regards these paintings as clumsy, transparently manipulative insertions. Such allegorical "oversaturation" leads to a mediocre novella. The other two novellas, while not devoid of allegory, employ it sparingly, but effectively — as with the color red in Keller's novella and the ash tree in Storm's. These allegories remain peripheral and are overshadowed by powerful, organic symbols that seem encapsulations of the entire story — field and stream in *Romeo und Julia*, and horse, sea, and dike in *Schimmelreiter*. Remak analyzes a number of other novellas and advances a two-pronged theory: the greater the presence of allegory, the poorer the novella; conversely, the stronger the symbol, the better the novella. Remak emphasizes, however, that the presence or absence of these devices serves as neither signpost nor guarantor of quality in a novella (41-62).

In another essay devoted to the formal aspects of the novella, Remak lauds Tieck for emphasizing (and thereby establishing) the *Wendepunkt* as a significant idea in the critical rhetoric of the novella. Yet, both Tieck's analysis and the secondary literature lack clarity when it comes to establishing either the number or the exact location of such points. An analysis of several novellas reveals to Remak that the genre contains two such points. The first and decidedly secondary one ("der *auslösende* Wendepunkt") simply initiates the external action and is normally found early in the novella. The second, primary one ("der *auflösende* Wendepunkt") depicts an internal decision that leads to a surprising yet natural resolution and is normally to be found near the end. Remak observes that in the best novellas, the "auflösende" point tends to combine

external and internal aspects — a decision is made and quickly carried out. Such a *Wendepunkt*, often at the end of the novella, resolves the novellistic problem (1965, 45-48).

The anecdote, Remak notes, prominently features a "Pointe." The novella, having inherited this feature from its ancestor, often ends with a striking, ironic, and unique twist. Such an ending stands in strong relief to the objectively narrated main body of the novella. The novellist uses this device to impart his own (correct) opinion, which is at variance with a generally accepted (incorrect) judgment as stated in the novella. At times the "Pointe" is accentuated and reveals a metaphysical dimension. In such an instance, the "Pointe" stands in a strong ironic or paradoxical relationship to some generally accepted judgment. This relationship prompts the reader to re-evaluate not only the whole story, but at times, even his own philosophy of life, and forces him to develop a judgment of his own (50-54).

Kenneth Negus believes that Heyse's views about the novella have been almost universally "misread and distorted." The famous *Falkentheorie*, for example, is actually more an invention of Heyse's readers than of Heyse himself. Since Heyse included all types of stories in his *Novellenschatz*, he viewed the genre in "broad and loose" terms. After analyzing passages from Heyse's foreword, Negus comes to the same conclusion as had Schunicht: Heyse was merely stating his preference for an exciting story line. Heyse listed four features of the novella: the basic motif, the silhouette, condensability, and falcon — "(1) *Grundmotiv*; (2) *Silhouette*; (3) *Inhalt in wenigen Zeilen*; (4) *Falke*." The last three features serve as subordinated "elaborations" of the first. Thus the falcon, far from being a significant element of Heyse's novella theory, is only a "*metaphorical embellishment, and a badly designed one at that!*" Negus categorizes as a "most serious" error any attempt to elevate Heyse's falcon to a *Dingsymbol*. This error, first committed by Pongs, came about because that critic arrived at valid conclusions about the significance of symbols (even *Dingsymbole*) in a number of novellas, but his point of departure, Heyse's falcon, was based on a misconstruction (1965, 174-81).

Heyse did, however, have a number of ideas about the novella (Negus seems loath to label them a "theory"), with the most fundamental being the *Grundmotiv*. This motif, normally unrelated to the main symbol (if there is one), consists of a pithy plot summary. The *Grundmotiv* of *Michael Kohlhaas*, as stated by Kleist, involves the story of a virtuous man

who becomes a robber and murderer. In *Romeo und Julia*, this motif, as formulated by Keller, involves the ancient theme of lovers from feuding families. These *Grundmotive* do not even hint at a *Dingsymbol*, although each novella prominently features such a symbol: the one in the form of the horses and the other in the form of the disputed field. Heyse's theory, if it may be so called, could be roughly summarized as follows: the novella is a realistic genre that stresses a highly individualistic theme expressed as an isolated, but "sharply defined *Grundmotiv*" (181- 87).

Josef Kunz in 1966 publishes *Die deutsche Novelle zwischen Klassik und Romantik*. He notes that scholarly discoveries of the last decade have led him to welcome the opportunity to rewrite his history of the German novella that first appeared in 1954. Kunz seems to dissociate himself from his earlier views, noting that virtually everything that appears in the current volume is new. He implies that Pabst's conclusion dooms efforts to establish a unified theory for the novella. Kunz intends to delineate chronologically the scope of the German novella tradition from the time it forsook its Romance antecedents and underwent a transformation into ever-new forms (7-11). In the text Kunz provides plot summaries, analyses, and interpretations of the novellas of Goethe, Wieland, the Romantics, and Kleist, but seems to have become theory-shy. Thus, in his discussion of Goethe, he observes only briefly that the definition of 1827 is almost universally accepted and cited (41). Upon discussing Tieck, Kunz fails even to mention that this author had made any observations germane to theory (61-72).

Hans Malmede sets two goals in his monograph, *Wege zur Novelle* (1966): he will first attempt to determine why all scholarly efforts to define the novella have failed and then to establish a valid procedure for further investigation. Malmede emphasizes that he intends to proceed in a rigorously logical manner (9-11).

After analyzing the ideas developed by Pabst, Grolmann, Arx, Lockemann, Bruch, Kunz, and Hirsch, Malmede notes that all seven critics have failed spectacularly to produce a viable theory (13-78). Arx, to single out one critic as a representative example of the group, begins his study by commenting upon the lack of consensus that envelops the theory of the novella. He then proposes one undisputed criterion, that of medium length. Arx realizes that this definition is so imprecise that it is meaningless. He attempts, therefore, to approach the problem from another angle — he argues that if we were able to understand the person-

ality of the novellists, we would understand something about the narrative of medium length. Malmede points out that Arx's attempt is foredoomed because he confuses quantity (medium length) with quality (the author's personality). Arx next interprets several novellas from the Age of Goethe. In so doing, he compounds his original error by approaching this task with the preconceived notion that he will evaluate Goethe positively and all other authors negatively. He thus argues that the great breadth and depth of Goethe's interests require the large scope of a novel for expression because they cannot be adequately expressed within the confines of a narrative of medium length as can the interests of the Romantics. Arx torpedoes his own argument when he claims that in *Novelle* Goethe not only succeeded in compressing his grand, cosmic view into the concentrated form of a narrative of medium length, but achieved nigh-perfect unity while so doing (34-38).

In the second part of his study, Malmede analyzes the ideas developed by Walzel, Klein, Petsch, Pongs, and Wiese. These critics, while also failing to establish an acceptable theory of the novella, have succeeded in illuminating one or more facets of the genre. Walzel mentions several times that a handful of critics emphasized formal aspects of the novella, but did not concern themselves with content. Walzel here makes a significant point, but fails to pursue it (80-83). Klein describes the novella from the point of view of content ("*ein* auffälliges Ereignis") as well as form ("Mittelpunkt" or "Wendepunkt"), yet he, too, fails to develop these characteristics (84-94). Petsch describes both form and content, but presents his ideas in such an entangled, haphazard fashion that they do not form a cohesive theory (95-101). Pongs, in four essays devoted to the symbol, neither defines the symbol nor does he establish that a symbol is an indispensable structural element of the novella. His idea of the *Dingsymbol*, which Malmede considers an error, has caused much grief in later novella theory. Pongs does establish, however, that the novella has two forms: the "Falkennovelle," which has a central motif (symbol) and the "Charakternovelle," which lacks a central motif. Pongs makes another mistake by further dividing the genre and by ascribing such disparate characteristics to the resulting sub-genres that he unwittingly proves that the novella can be characterized neither by form nor by content (103-13). Wiese also fails in his multiple efforts to capture the outlines of the novella. His substitution of *novellistic narration* for "Novelle" is so poorly conceived that it fails even to state the dimensions of the prob-

lem, much less to solve it. Wiese does, however, mention Goethe's definition of 1827 with regularity, but fails to develop its implications (114-31).

Malmede summarizes with the observation that all attempts to develop a theory of the novella along formal lines have failed because there is no such thing as form — "eine an sich bestehende Form, eine Form von sich selbst, gibt es nicht." Similarly, all attempts to define the novella from the viewpoint of content have also failed because content is protean (148-50). Malmede then attempts to formulate a theory of the genre wherein he incorporates elements from the critics he considers partially successful. He begins by returning to Boccaccio, for whom a narrative was a novella, fable, parable, or history. The element common to all these narrative types is the singularity of the event — Goethe's "*eine* sich ereignete unerhörte *Begebenheit* [emphasis added]." Malmede next differentiates between the novella and the *Erzählung* by recasting Goethe's definition: a novella is an event that causes one to take notice ("eine zum Aufmerken veranlassende Begebenheit"), whereas an *Erzählung* is merely unspecified narration. Malmede continues to characterize the novella by noting that it must adhere to the laws of story telling which, in brief, demand that the event be told in a sensible or intelligible fashion. For this to happen, the narration of an event will include characters and incidents that precede as well as those that follow its occurrence. The novella presents a single-stranded theme, has a midpoint (which need not be in the middle), and, unlike the novel, eschews secondary episodes or themes. These characteristics contribute to the brevity of the novella. Malmede views the novella as a very accommodating narrative form that allows not only for an immense range in content, but also, among many possibilities, for motifs to be converted to symbols and for characters to overshadow the event (147-56). Malmede, who started his study in iconoclastic fashion, comes to conclusions that replicate elements of standard German novella theory. His effort resembles, in some ways, an attempt to get from one sidewalk to the other by circumnavigating the globe rather than by crossing the street.

Gerald Gillespie, in one of the earliest Anglo-American oriented studies of the novella, remarks that Spain, Italy, France, and Germany lay claim to three types of realistic prose narratives. In these countries the novella lies between the short narrative (*cuento*, *racconto*, *conte*, and *Erzählung*) and the long (*novela*, *romanzo*, *roman*, and *Roman*). English lit-

erary criticism, which employs two of the above narrative types (short story and novel), lacks an equivalent term for the narrative of medium length and employs, instead, the awkward term "short novel." After undertaking a brief survey of German novella theory, Gillespie points to a "noticeable gap in English terminology" for describing prose narratives (1967, 117-26). Gillespie then analyzes *The Old Man and the Sea* and concludes that Hemingway's "short novel" exhibits such novellistic characteristics as dramatic structure and tension, an "unheard-of event," a turning point, and a main symbol. In similar fashion, Gillespie also comments briefly on medium-length narratives by Joseph Conrad, Henry James, Thomas Mann, William Faulkner, André Gide, and Guy de Maupassant. Gillespie believes that the works by these authors constitute ample reason for English critics to fill the gap in genre terminology by adopting the term *novella* (225-29).

Josef Kunz, who in 1966 reacted to Pabst and Arx by side-stepping theory, in 1968 publishes an invaluable anthology that spans 150 years of German novella theory and criticism. In the introduction Kunz overcomes his aversion to theory by describing four characteristics of the Romance "Idealtypus" of the novella: novelty, realism, social concerns, and a narrative intention of entertainment. Goethe, who incorporated these features in his *Unterhaltungen*, added the element "unerhört." The addition of this element, as emphasized by artists and critics alike, elevated the novella from mere entertainment to the status of a serious art form that could deal with fate. The older Romance novella exhibits two primary formal features: a bifurcated narrative approach and an artistic economy that concentrates upon one central event. Secondary formal features include such elements as "Pointe," symbol, and chance (1-12).

The German novella, which incorporates the above characteristics, underwent a process of transformation during which it developed its own, additional features. Most prominent among these are the turning point, conflict, and either the total loss or the radical change of the frame. These features, especially the loss of frame, have led to a complication of the genre — the formerly one-stranded theme has been expanded into multiple episodes that are reminiscent of the novel. Other changes include the resemblance of the novella to the drama, the incorporation of tragic elements, and the possibility of also emphasizing character. Since these changes serve as the basis for intense critical debate, almost no feature of the modern novella remains undisputed. Kunz em-

phasizes, however, that one feature finds almost universal acceptance — the novella deals with an event. Thus, although he still believes that Walter Pabst's observations have rendered all attempts to define the novella problematical, Kunz now considers it possible to categorize and to distinguish the novella from other genres. Much of Kunz's analysis seems to be a summary of ideas from theoreticians and critics he anthologizes (13-23).

A. Peter Foulkes and Edgar Lohner, following the precept of Steinhauer, also introduce novella theory into the American classroom with their textbook, *Deutsche Novellen von Tieck bis Hauptmann* (1969). After warning students to approach theory with caution and urging them to concentrate upon the works, they define the genre as portraying "a single 'novel' occurrence." This event often involves a turning point, a "significant and pregnant point in time" that illustrates the "capriciousness of fate" as it impinges upon the life of the individual. After tracing the history of the genre and providing a short survey of theory, the two critics isolate as a common element from these theories one "central conflict" or one "crucial event." The finest examples of the genre appeared during the age of Poetic Realism. Naturalism has brought on such a "bewildering complexity of theme and form" that it has become "almost impossible to offer any significant definition" (1-14).

In an essay devoted to the frame of *Unterhaltungen*, Joachim Müller in 1969 argues that many critics err when they assume that the work amounts to no more than a casual effort to replicate the Romance novella collections. *Unterhaltungen* represents Goethe's serious attempt to come to grips with the French Revolution. Goethe adapted the framework from *The Decameron* and *The Heptameron* because he saw parallels between the social disjointment caused by the plague and the flood and the revolution that exploded in France (152-63). This turmoil, in both its political and social manifestations, erupts with the argument between the privy councillor and Karl (Müller calls this event the "unerhörte Begebenheit" of the frame). After the enraged councillor leaves, the baroness is able to restore harmony by declaring general amnesty and by urging the group to pursue harmless, non-political interests. Müller emphasizes that the decision to tell stories in the Romance works was prompted by the need for entertainment or diversion. In Goethe's work, the first four novellas are told for the same reasons. But, as the later statements of both the baroness and the chaplain attest, the last two no-

vellas and "Das Märchen" are told in keeping with Goethe's belief that the novella also can be used for pedagogical and social purposes — "ein lehrreiches, nützliches und geselligkeitsstiftendes Gefäß für ein unerhörtes Ereignis" (163-73).

Josef Kunz in 1970 brings out the second volume of his history of the German novella, *Die deutsche Novelle im 19. Jahrhundert*. Kunz characterizes the novella of Realism from both thematic and formal viewpoints. Of the former, he notes that Realism implies an emphasis on mundane reality. Yet, many authors of the period deal with such Romantic themes as the artist in society, the "Doppelgänger," and elements from fairy tales. The novellas of Romanticism can be differentiated from those of Realism. The Romantics glorified beauty, but the Realists, ever mistrustful of categories, show much doubt and skepticism toward beauty. This attitude reveals itself in its extreme manifestation in novellas that express such pessimism that they choke off even the will to live. Kunz lists, as his last thematic characteristic of the novella, an epigonic attitude. The authors of the period express appreciation for the ideals of bygone days, but lack the will or the ability to re-create them (7-10).

Upon turning to formal considerations, Kunz describes a shift in emphasis: the older novella inclines toward depiction of event, the newer one toward portraiture of character — often the whole life of the character. This shift is accompanied by a tendency toward self-conscious reflection and introspection. This phenomenon is aided by the introduction of a narrator who, in addition to playing a role in the events he narrates, often intensifies the inclination toward reflection by telling of events that have already taken place. Such retrospection leads to the creation of a mood whereby the events radiate an aura of inevitability. The novella also reveals, as observed by Goethe, a conflict between the restrained and the unregulated. Kunz believes that the novella underwent changes by growing from the narration of a single event to a genre that encompasses fate, the whole life of a character, and multiple episodes. This growth has made it difficult to differentiate between the novella and the novel (10-14).

In a development reminiscent of Arx's participation in Staiger's seminar, Donald LoCicero was inspired by a graduate course to write a dissertation, *Novellentheorie: The Practicality of the Theoretical* (1965), under the direction of Kenneth Negus. In 1970 he publishes the work. After selectively reviewing the secondary literature, LoCicero concludes

that no definition has met with universal acceptance. In hopes of alleviating this dilemma, he determines to examine major elements of German novella theory as developed by Goethe, Tieck, and Heyse (13-26).

LoCicero believes, despite Helmuth Himmel's opinion to the contrary, that Goethe attempted to define the novella when he pronounced it to be "eine sich ereignete unerhörte Begebenheit." After applying this definition to Goethe's narratives in *Unterhaltungen* and to "Nachbarskinder" and *Novelle*, LoCicero concludes that Goethe's practice was at variance with his theory (27-45). Since Tieck's opinions come remarkably close to replicating those of Goethe and A. W. Schlegel, LoCicero concludes that this author's unique contribution to theory consists of his emphasis upon one *Wendepunkt*. The turning point, along with the notion that a novella is both wondrous and commonplace, (which is only a recasting of Goethe's definition), constitute for Tieck the principal criteria of the genre. After examining and rejecting Schunicht's conclusions about the psychological implications of the turning point, LoCicero applies the theory to three of Tieck's own novellas, *Die Verlobung, Der Gelehrte,* and *Der fünfzehnte November*. Much as he did with Goethe, LoCicero concludes that Tieck's theory lacks applicability to his own works (46-65). Heyse's theory of the novella, as outlined in *Novellenschatz* and *Jugenderinnerungen*, in many respects is derived from Tieck and Goethe. After analyzing Heyse's comments and the observations of such critics as Mitchell, Bennett, Himmel, Silz, and Schunicht, LoCicero arrives at the same conclusion as does his dissertation director — the "Falkentheorie" is more a product of scholarly misunderstanding than of Heyse's invention. All Heyse meant to say is that a good novella should exhibit, as does Boccaccio's narrative, a strong and individualistic character (66-83).

Since theoreticians and scholars agree that the novella deals with a remarkable event, LoCicero reasons that any work lacking such an event should be excluded from the genre. Conversely, any theory that de-emphasizes the novelty of event would be inimical to the genre. Adalbert Stifter advocates precisely such a reversal in his foreword to *Bunte Steine* when he formulates "das sanfte Gesetz" and insists that simple, mundane events constitute the most important aspects of life. Yet, each of Stifter's six narratives in *Bunte Steine* deals with an extraordinary event (84-108). LoCicero reacts to this lack of congruence between theory and practice by cautioning against the adoption of rigid theory (109-14).

Karl Konrad Polheim follows his *Forschungsbericht* with an anthology that presents the theories of authors from the nineteenth century and thereby complements Kunz's anthology that emphasizes scholarly efforts of the twentieth century. As companion volumes, these two works form an invaluable compendium of German novella theory and criticism. In his foreword Polheim merely takes note of the wide divergence of opinion to be found in nineteenth-century theory (1970, XIII-XVI).

In 1970 James Trainer and Brian Rowley publish separate essays on the *Märchen* and the *Novelle* of the Romantic period. Both critics use Goethe as a springboard. Trainer believes that Goethe, with his "Märchen" from *Unterhaltungen,* liberated the realm of imagination from Gottsched's literary prescription for strict verisimilitude. Simultaneously, Goethe elevated the fairy tale from the province of folk literature to the *Kunstmärchen,* that popular, but short-lived art form of early Romanticism (97-99). Beginning where Trainer ends, Rowley comments upon the difficulties of differentiating between the fairy tale (the genre of the supernatural) and the novella (the genre of *"das Unerhörte"*). Uncomfortable with the terms *Märchennovelle* and *Novellenmärchen,* Rowley nevertheless believes that the narratives of the Romantic period exhibit, in rough chronological sequence, a progression toward realism. The fanciful fairy tale first gives way to the novella that contains realistic features, but is still dominated by fantasy. This type of narrative is supplanted by one that reverses the pattern — a novella that contains fantastic features, but is dominated by reality. This shift, Rowley cautions, is neither smooth nor clearly visible (121-24).

In 1970 Rolf Schröder publishes his reworked dissertation (written under the direction of Friedrich Sengle) on the hitherto much-neglected Biedermeier novella. After reviewing the secondary literature, Schröder remarks that, having learned the lesson taught by Pabst, he intends to approach the narrative of medium length in a non-normative, historical fashion (1-12). He begins his study of the novella by commenting upon the elderly Tieck. After taking note of Tieck's psychological problems, Schröder attributes their resolution more to Tieck's relocation in 1819 to Dresden than to Solger's Hegelian influence. In Dresden Tieck was able to accept reality and even found a modicum of happiness. His newly-found equanimity, in combination with the growing popularity of literary almanacs ("Taschenbücher") and the consolidation of a middle class that valued conversational skills, inspired Tieck to create a new form, the

"Diskussionsnovelle." The "Taschenbücher" provided a market for this genre, whereas the emphasis upon conversation provided the form (four-fifths of a typical Tieckian novella consists of dialogue). Although Tieck vacillated between the fantastic and the prosaic in his work, he accentuated the latter. Schröder dismisses Tieck's theoretical remarks of 1829 because Tieck himself paid scant attention to the *Wendepunkt* and used the terms *Geschichte, Novelle, Anekdote, Erzählung,* and *Roman* interchangeably (13-52).

In a chapter aptly entitled "Novellenwut" (novella mania), Schröder reports that the German literary market was flooded by more than 500 novellistic scribblers ("Vielschreiber"), with a few writing more than 100 novellas. Such proliferation supports Mundt's contention that the novella was indeed a German house pet. One unfortunate aspect of this popularity, however, was that novellas by Droste-Hülshoff, Stifter, Hebbel, and Ludwig were lost among the lesser works written by Gersdorff, Hanke, Jacobs, and Prätzel (53-73). After confirming Hirsch's claim that the term *Novelle* gained currency only after 1820, Schröder devotes a chapter to cataloguing the hundreds of synonymous terms (all manner of "Geschichten," "Erzählungen," "Anekdoten," "Bilder," "Skizzen," to cite but a few) that were employed during the Biedermeier period. Once established, the term acquired such modifiers as "Märchen-," "Idyll-," "Kulturgeschichtliche Novelle" (74-92). Because the novella was viewed as hack work ("trivialliterarische Ware"), it was deemed unworthy of serious attention (93-118). Yet, since recognized authors (Goethe, Tieck, Grillparzer) wrote novellas, several critics (Solger, Marggraff, Alexis, Ast, Mundt) made a few desultory attempts to formulate a theory by discussing such categories as scope, event, and reflection. These attempts produced disparate results. In scope, for example, a novella could range from two newspaper lines to a multi-volume effort of a thousand and more pages (119-51).

Schröder examines the novellas of the period in order to ascertain whether the genre, as countless theoreticians have observed, is a realistic one. Considering this claim justified, he comments upon the concerted effort to diminish fantasy ("das Romanhafte") in order to focus more intensely upon everyday reality (152-76). This tendency manifests itself in a number of ways. Many authors claim, for example, that the events in their novellas took place. Other authors emphasize realism by specializing in geographical regions. Another group prominently features well-

known historical events. Still another group features eccentric heroes ("Sonderlinge") whom they subject to sharp psychological analysis. Schröder singles out, as a last example, authors who specialize in portraying what he calls the Werthers of the nineteenth century, characters who reveal both admirable and negative qualities (177-210).

In his conclusion Schröder restates his anti-normative stance by emphasizing that the Biedermeier novella displayed an astonishing range of length. This development leads Schröder to conclude that, in their attempts to characterize the novella, theoreticians of the period were influenced more by the medium (prose) than by such a normative consideration as length. The novella, if it must be described, can best be characterized by its strong leaning toward realism. Citing Heinrich Laube, Schröder claims that the most remarkable feature of the genre involves the choice of protagonist. The Biedermeier novella, by choosing as its protagonist a character neither good enough to be a hero nor bad enough to be a villain, reveals a democratic tendency, for it emancipates a large part of humanity by declaring it a fit subject for art (211-37).

Harry Steinhauer in 1970 quickly reestablishes his credentials as a skeptic when he observes that "the enormous mountain of German criticism has been labouring for two generations and has not even brought forth a mouse." He excoriates critics for presenting "contradictory," "obscure," "shallow," and "absurd" results that he summarizes in a list of twenty-nine items. Steinhauer classifies the errors of critics into four categories: mistaking the whole for the part, mistaking the part for the whole, succumbing to national (German) myopia, and fixating upon Boccaccio. An historical overview of the genre reveals to Steinhauer that the novella has undergone a developmental process since its beginnings with Boccaccio. Individual phases include elevation from entertainment to art, broadening of theme and mood, emphasis upon social gamesmanship, and change in length that shows an increase in Germany and France and a decrease in Great Britain and the United States. During early development the novella became an object of much carping, moralistic attack, while during the later phases it became a subject of niggling literary criticism and theory (154-63).

Steinhauer classifies modern critics as either rigorists or latitudinarians. The rigorists (Grolman, Klein, Lockemann) adopt a strict "normative stance" and insist upon the existence of an *Urform* or "ideal model of a novella." The latitudinarians (Pabst, Staiger, Goethe), believe

that the novella amounts to nothing more than "an exciting story." Although Steinhauer's sympathies lie with the latitudinarians, he is unwilling to accept either Pabst's anarchy or Staiger's imprecision and assays his own definition. The novella, "a narrative of medium length," is situated "between the novel and the short story" and is "told for the purpose of instruction and/or entertainment." This genre uses "any literary device that enhances the aesthetic experience." Ever fearful of rigid prescription, Steinhauer calls for a flexible interpretation of even this definition. He concludes his essay by exhorting critics to direct their attention to areas that show more promise than does the pursuit of such a will-o'-the-wisp as the *Urnovelle* (163-74).

7: Modern Criticism (1971-1980)

THE CONSOLIDATION OF two camps, characterized as normative and historical by Polheim, and as rigorist and latitudinarian by Steinhauer, shows that the current of skepticism alluded to in the previous chapter has acquired the force of a riptide. Yet, the skeptical Steinhauer, while warming himself at latitudinarian fires, fails to pitch his tent in their camp. His position seems more in line with another school, that of the moderates as defined by Pabst in his *Forschungsbericht* of 1949. This group, identified in the last chapter by the position represented by Silz and Wiese, also presents a range of opinions, but differs from the other two in that it postulates, in undogmatic fashion, that there is such a genre as the novella and that it tends to have one or more recognizable features.

In the introduction of *Die Novelle* (1971), Frank Ryder steps forward as a moderate. Keenly aware of the problems recently uncovered in novella criticism, he nevertheless affirms the existence of the genre. He acknowledges that the novella may not be *"definable,"* but it can "be *characterized"* by the notion of "family resemblance." When applied to narratives, this idea reveals a pattern of common features. Since there are no established rules, and since very few (if any) novellas exhibit all such characteristics, subjective judgments must play a significant role. Ryder identifies several characteristics which, when found in sufficient numbers, point to the narrative constellation "novella." This genre tends to portray a single, central event that involves a small number of fixed characters. This extraordinary, yet verisimilar event is accorded priority over the characters. The novella also features a *Wendepunkt*, which Ryder defines as the "segmentation of the narrative line, with sudden changes in direction." A concomitant of such a reversal is a "non-linear" approach to narration. When there are two turning points, the first triggers the action and the second resolves it. The novella often portrays an intrusion of the chaotic or the irrational into a well-ordered existence. Since the novella undertakes the task of the novel within the compass of a short story or *Erzählung*, it reveals a dense, compact structure and relies heavily upon symbolism and a terse, dramatic narrative style (xiii-xxviii). Ryder's essay represents an excellent summary and introduction to standard German novella theory.

Alois Wierlacher, the only critic to devote more than cursory attention to Georg Reinbeck's theory of the novella, traces this early critic's ideas back to eighteenth-century drama theory. The drama emphasized, as Lessing and others observed, interesting events ("Begebenheiten" or "Ereignisse"). This description, along with Wieland's definition, led Reinbeck in 1817 to define the novella as a short novel. Upon becoming aware of Denis Diderot's "Entretiens sur les fils naturel," where that author emphasized that the drama concentrates upon one main event, Reinbeck in 1841 calls his original opinion a mistake. He recasts his definition in conformity with Diderot, declaring that by concentrating upon a single event, the novella resembles the drama. After connecting Reinbeck's ideas with Storm's view that the novella is a sister of the drama, Wierlacher concludes that Reinbeck, not Friedrich Theodor Vischer, should be credited with recognizing the kinship of novella and drama (1971, 440-47).

In 1972 Henry Remak comments on the structural element of the frame. Remak's point of departure is Wolfgang Kayser's analysis of the prototypical narrative situation that consists of a story, an audience, and a narrator. Although Kayser never mentions the genre by name, all his illustrations come from either single novellas or large novella collections. Tracing the origin of the frame to oral literary traditions, Remak notes that when a story teller spins his yarn, the audience has a two-dimensional experience: it empathizes with the tale itself, which took place in the past; yet, it is also acutely aware of the narrator, who is part of the immediate present. If the story is sufficiently long, the narrator will color and enhance by employing any number of devices (for example, dramatic pauses or interjections of his own opinion). Since he often tells of raw or ugly actions or situations, the narrator tames or civilizes his material in order to make it presentable and inoffensive to his audience. These aspects of the earliest narrative situation continue to live on in the novella. Remak postulates that the novella attempts to combine dramatic content with an epic mode of transmission. This development, too, is rooted in oral tradition. The frame thus has two functions: it palliates raw content, and it transforms the dramatic dimensions of this content into epic ones.

The novella metamorphosed with the passage of time: the audience changed from a stylized collective to one individual (the reader), and the narrator changed from an objective reporter to a subjective artist. These

transformations are visible in the evolution of the genre. In *The Decam-eron*, the ten narrators, who also comprise the audience, remain undiffer-entiated and tell their stories in a stylized, homogenized fashion. Goethe's *Unterhaltungen* reveals heterogeneity since both the narrators as well as the stories they tell are individuated. Despite some social disrup-tions, Goethe's work retains stylized features since there is a strong em-phasis on social customs and mores. In yet another development, the narrator in Brentano's *Kasperl und Annerl* not only participates in the ac-tion, he becomes one of the most interesting characters in the novella. These changes have led to great narrative flexibility. The author can re-count the story in either an objective or subjective fashion and then counterbalance this approach with its opposite in the frame. In the best novellas, the frame strengthens the story proper ("Binnenerzählung"). Yet, the frame also poses a possible danger since it can destroy propor-tions, compete with the story itself, blur the clarity of structural lines, and ruin the compact, concentrated form that is essential to the novella (246-50).

Remak applies his theory by evaluating the success of several frames. In *Elsi von der Tanne*, Wilhelm Raabe fails in his attempt to graft the frame onto the main narrative, but in *Die Schwarze Spinne*, Gotthelf fuses the two components masterfully. Since the genre deals with an event that is both novel and real ("unerhört" as well as "sich ereignet"), it at times strays into the realm of the implausible. The frame provides the author with a device for gaining verisimilitude, for the frame narrator can insist that he personally witnessed the event. On this basis, Remak believes that Storm's integration of frame and main narrative in *Der Schimmelreiter* represents a tour de force. Yet, even here, Remak wonders whether it was necessary for the narrator to encounter the ghost rider on the dike (250-55).

After commenting on the dearth of formal approaches, Remak clas-sifies recent novella studies into one of three categories: the theoretical, which tends to ignore works; the ideological, which traces motifs through a number of novellas without drawing structural conclusions; and the "work immanent," which interprets single novellas, but ignores theory. Remak describes the frame in its six different forms: it stands in-dependent of the main narrative; it merges into the main narrative; it presents a subjectively inclined but uninvolved narrator; it reveals a nar-rator who is uncertain of his material; it exhibits bourgeois tendencies;

and it fails to concern itself with social issues. This last development suggests that the novella may no longer be capable of portraying modern life. Remak ends his essay with a summary of recent scholarship on the novella and points out that only Erné and Lockemann have accorded the frame much attention (255-62).

Hartwig Eckert seeks to delimit and to clarify the problems that arise in attempts to define the novella. Using a linguistic approach, he describes the difficulties associated with the nominalist and analytical positions. After citing the importance of Trier and Porzig's work with semantic fields for arriving at definitions, Eckert argues that the novella must be assigned to "its appropriate position within the whole field of literary genres." This position is the epic. The next step involves the identification of a "nucleus of features" that are present in all novellas. This nucleus, according to a host of critics, is the "unprecedented event." Having identified the primary characteristic, it now becomes possible to identify secondary characteristics such as medium length, a small cast of characters, a falcon, and a *Wendepunkt*. These features, Eckert emphasizes, are often derivations of the primary one — one event naturally entails a narrative of medium length that involves only a small cast of characters (1973, 167-70).

Ulrich Eisenbeiss, in a revised, published version of his dissertation directed by Friedrich Sengle, casts his spotlight on the "Idyllnovelle" of the Biedermeier period. The idyllic, in its most basic form, depicts pristine nature. This portraiture idealizes by minimizing the unpleasant and the tragic aspects of life and by emphasizing the bright, cheerful ones (1973, 11-29). The idyllic can be found in many genres, including such short prose narratives as "Erzählung," "Bild," "Studie," "Novelle," and "Idyllnovelle." Since there was no clear theory about any of these narrative types during the Biedermeier period, the genre concept of novella was at best fluid. Yet, the idea of the idyllic was quite strong and saturated many narratives of the period. Commensurate with the attitudes of the Biedermeier period, the idyllic often was expressed by a rejection of political life in favor of adopting a bucolic one (30-44).

Eisenbeiss traces the immediate origins of the "Idyllnovelle" to *Hermann und Dorothea* (1797). Goethe's idyll inspired not only a large number of verse imitations, but also led to countless prose efforts, many of which Eisenbeiss consigns to the realm of "Trivialliteratur." Serious writers of prose idylls include Tieck, Mörike, and Berthold Auerbach.

Another group of writers, Stifter, Gotthelf, Jean Paul, Arnim, Eichendorff, and Karl Immermann, while not authors of idylls as such, wrote
works that exhibit strong idyllic tendencies (45-61). Eisenbeiss describes
the "Idyllnovelle" from several viewpoints. The characters, usually from
the lower classes, are idealized as representing naive but "natural" people
who are imbued with the "true" spirit of humanity. The novellas often
exhibit a strong leaning toward realism, but this reality is also idealized.
The stories normally take place within confined areas such as houses, ga-
zebos, arbors, or immaculately kept gardens. In tone and style the
"Idyllnovelle" shows a preference for diminutives, dialects, and simple
vocabulary and syntax. The genre de-emphasizes action and, as Stifter
noted in his "Vorrede" to *Bunte Steine*, deals with commonplace events
rather than dramatic ones (61-74).

Upon analyzing the category of the wondrous ("das Wunderbare"),
Eisenbeiss notes that the penchant for realism almost precluded the totally fantastic, miraculous, or supernatural. Yet, there was a ready acceptance of highly unusual events. Tieck's comments of 1829, where he
speaks of "das Wunderbare," should be understood in this context because he emphasized that the nature of the incident is such that it could
easily have occurred. "Das Wunderbare" manifests itself in the
"Idyllnovelle" in three ways: as an event described outrightly as demonic,
magical, or supernatural (such instances are rare); as an event that may
be considered supernatural, but is actually a natural phenomenon; or as
an event that can be interpreted as either an instance of divine interces-
sion or a natural phenomenon (75-89).

In a chapter devoted to sentimentality ("Empfindsamkeit"), Eisenbeiss notes that this emotional attitude as well as the idyll trace their leg-
acy back to the eighteenth-century writer Salomon Geßner. The
"Idyllnovelle" of the Biedermeier period, however, dampened emotions,
thus making instances of sublime joy or abject sorrow rare. Jean Paul
strongly influenced this dampening, but Mörike, Gotthelf, and Stifter
also employed the same cool approach. Frequent themes associated with
sentimentality include joy, family, love, suffering, and death. The last two
themes are usually expressed in an elegiac tone (90-101). Eisenbeiss then
interprets Stifter's *Bergkristall*, emphasizing such idyllic aspects as the
hidden valley, the harmonious life of the village, the motif of lost children (symbolizing the loss of innocence), and the seemingly miraculous

yet natural circumstances that lead to the rescue of the children (102-108).

Eisenbeiss then turns to humor, noting that this theme finds its best expression in the naive, innocent, and gentle "Volkshumor" of Gotthelf. Humor has a number of functions in the novella of the period: it counterbalances the elegiac tone; it caters to the tastes of the readership (Gotthelf remarked that people want to laugh and weep); it sugarcoats didactic elements; it provides the author with a vehicle for ameliorating gruesome events; and it allows the author to distance himself from his material (109- 21). Upon turning his attention to satiric aspects of humor, Eisenbeiss implies that satire and the idyllic are mutually hostile and coexist only uneasily, if at all, in the Biedermeier novella (127-31). He concludes his study by noting that the Weltanschauung of the Biedermeier period lent itself to the idyll. With the upheavals of 1848 and the attendant change in the Zeitgeist, the "Idyllnovelle" vanished (132-33).

John Ellis, in a book completed in 1971 but not published until 1974, follows Silz's format by devoting his introduction to theory, and the text proper to novella interpretations. After reviewing recent criticism and listing standard criteria for the genre, Ellis declares that "the basic theory and its extensions are deficient in every particular." He attributes this deficiency to three factors: not all novellas show these features; several features apply to all literature; and other features are so vague that their presence or absence is indeterminable. Ellis cites several critics who have challenged elements of the standard theory and concludes that scholarship has arrived at an impasse (1-12).

After ascribing this impasse to a failure in logic, Ellis points to Ludwig Wittgenstein's work in definition theory. Confusion often reigns in literary theory because genres are identified by different criteria. For example, the sonnet is defined by formal features, the tragedy by thematic ones, the novel by length, and the fable by intent or purpose. Ellis argues that since a definition has prescriptive force, it would be a mistake to attach inappropriate descriptive elements. Thus, an attempt, for example, to describe the themes of sonnets, while perhaps interesting, would yield very little information about this genre that by definition is fourteen lines long. Another dimension of definition involves the imposition of subjective attitudes. Ellis gives as an example the word "*weed*," which is useless for taxonomy. Yet the term is useful for garden-

ers who define a weed as one of a large number of undesirable garden plants (12-15).

Ellis cautions against three errors when formulating definitions: extending definitions into inapplicable areas, confusing facts with definitions, and ignoring either dominant purpose or physical properties. "Traditional" novella theory, Ellis believes, is "logically faulty in all these respects." He finds it ironic that Wittgenstein's notion of "family resemblances" has been ignored (Ellis and Ryder wrote their works in the same year). Yet it hardly matters, because the standard features of novella theory are simply "too general and/or too vague" to distinguish one genre from another (16-17). After discussing various logical faults, Ellis comments upon Arx and Staiger's characterization of medium length (modern scholarship has ignored B. Q. Morgan's essay, which predates Arx's work by six years). Upon considering the importance of the genre for the nineteenth century, the characterization of medium length seems paltry. Yet Ellis defends it by noting that when writers in the rest of Europe were devoting their talents to novels, their German counterparts were producing narratives "of intermediate length." There subsequently arose in Germany the need to group these stories under one rubric. This need was met by the term *Novelle*. Ellis concedes that the "theoretical content" of this word "is slight," the idea itself, however, "is important" (18-20).

Ellis argues that the term *Novelle*, as used in Germany, had nothing to do with the original Italian *novella*. The word filled a vacuum and the nature of this vacuum (medium-length narratives), not the original Italian, determined the German meaning. On this basis Ellis accepts Goethe's "eine sich ereignete unerhörte Begebenheit" as a definition for works of the past, but not of contemporary ones, because Goethe himself stated that many narratives that passed for novellas were only tales ("vieles, was in Deutschland unter dem Titel Novelle geht, ist gar keine Novelle, sondern bloß Erzählung"). Ellis concludes his analysis of novella theory by dismissing the notion that the novella is a realistic, objectively narrated genre. The term *Realism* lacks precision, and every author, by the simple act of setting down his first word, embarks upon that most subjective of enterprises, the creation of a work of art. In his discussions of Realism and the objective narrative stance, Ellis finds much to criticize in Wayne Booth's influential *The Rhetoric of Fiction* (1961), because Booth devotes large parts of his book to discussions of

Realism and to various types of narration, including the objective variety (20-27). In the remainder of his book, Ellis interprets eight novellas, focusing in each on the relationship of the narrator to the story he tells.

In 1974 Judith Leibowitz, in a revised, published version of her dissertation, also analyzes narrative technique in the novella. In the introduction, which reveals a comparative rather than an exclusively German literary orientation, she cites Gerald Gillespie's comments about the paucity of criticism and the need for Anglo-American scholars to adopt the term *novella*. Leibowitz believes there are three prose genres: the short story, the novella, and the novel. She sets herself the task of defining the novella. After characterizing all past efforts to identify genre by theme as failures, and after declaring all German novella theory (both formal as well as thematic) bankrupt, Leibowitz emphasizes that a different, more productive approach is needed. This approach should concentrate upon the problem of identifying the basic purpose of the novella. The short story, she observes, limits and compresses material, whereas the novel extends and expands it. The novella undertakes both tasks and, in accomplishing this objective, often uses a "theme-complex" and a "repetitive structure." Theme-complex refers to the tendency for a novella to have either one theme or several closely related ones, thereby allowing the author to focus his attention upon one topic. The repetitive structure sharpens this focus, for it compresses the action by allowing the author to reemphasize a previously developed theme or situation. These two aspects unite to provide the genre with its distinctive purpose — to shape the narrative so that it simultaneously compresses and expands the material (9-18).

Leibowitz begins to apply her theory by analyzing eight nineteenth-century novellas, six of them German. Her goals are, first, to prove the inapplicability (hence invalidity) of standard German novella theory and, second, to identify the common relationship among the eight novellas by establishing her narrative principle of compression and expansion. At times she confounds her goals. She asserts that "traditional novella categories" such as unheard-of event, central conflict, and turning point are "irrelevant" and point to "the need for a new critical approach" (18-27). Yet, when analyzing Stifter's *Brigitta*, she is unable to refrain from identifying these characteristics (27-29). Upon interpreting Keller's *Kleider machen Leute*, Leibowitz comments: "The unusual events, turning point, and subordination of character to event make this one of the few novel-

las to fulfill traditional criteria so precisely that there is no difficulty in recognizing them" (31-32). In addition to discovering "traditional" features in the novellas she analyzes, she also finds that her principle of expansion and compression is sustained. Leibowitz tests her thesis for generic applicability by analyzing the theme-complexes of eight twentieth-century novellas, only two of which are German (51-75). In the final chapter she retests her theory by analyzing the novellas for the presence of repetitive structures (76-111). In a brief conclusion, Leibowitz states her belief that she has been able to define the genre. The distinguishing feature of the genre involves its intent "to produce the aesthetic effect of simultaneous intensity and expansion." In realization of this intent, the novella often utilizes theme-complexes and repetitive structures (112).

Leibowitz's theory is more dependent upon standard theory than is apparent at first sight. She notes that the novella incorporates the compression of the short story and the expansion of the novel. Such compression, postulated earlier by Petsch and Morgan, is repeated in textbook theory. Ryder states that the novella undertakes "the task of the novel within the scope of the short story or *Erzählung*" (1971, xxi) and can, therefore, be described by its primary characteristic of *"concentration"* (xxvii). Leibowitz's "theme-complex" is also reflected in standard theory, for Ryder observes that the novella normally depicts *"a single crucial situation or complex of situations"* (xx). Finally, Leibowitz's views about "repetitive structure" seem to restate the idea of the leitmotif, for Ryder notes that since the novella expresses so much in such short space, the "figurative devices" of leitmotifs and symbols, by "repetition and reinforcement," help to "unify and reinforce the meaning of the story" (xxiv).

The year 1975 saw the publication of three books on novella topics. Jane Brown devotes her attention almost exclusively to interpreting Goethe's novellas in *Unterhaltungen* and *Wanderjahre*. Her principal observations germane to novella theory concern the frame in *Unterhaltungen*. Upon comparing this work with *The Decameron*, she notes that the differences between these two works are greater than are the similarities. In Boccaccio's collection, the emphasis lies upon the stories; in Goethe's work the center of attention has been shifted to the frame. The whole work represents Goethe's response to the French Revolution, and the stories themselves "are subordinated as a pedagogical response to the problem posed by the frame" (5-13).

Albrecht Weber, in his introduction to *Deutsche Novellen des Realismus*, notes that the novella has almost disappeared from the contemporary German Gymnasium classroom because it is considered outdated ("antiquarisch, verstaubt, unmodern"). He regards this development as unfortunate and offers guidance to teachers who might be interested in reintroducing novellas into the secondary school curriculum. Using a practical, pedagogic approach, he first provides a brief historical survey and then enumerates twelve characteristics typical of the genre. Afterwards, he draws up a list of topics for classroom discussion and concludes his introduction by providing a sample lesson plan to be used for teaching Keller's *Kleider machen Leute* (7-18). Weber devotes the remainder of the book to providing plot summaries of novellas ranging from Tieck to Marie von Ebner-Eschenbach.

Mary Doyle Springer, in a book with an English rather than a German literary orientation, attempts to answer the question "What is a novella?" Both the short story and the novel, she remarks, have received a great deal of attention in recent decades, but "the serious study of the novella remains almost a desert area." Innocent of German novella theory, and determined to stay that way (in a footnote she refers in passing only to E. K. Bennett and John Ellis), Springer is quite optimistic that she will be able to define the genre and to classify its various forms. After commenting on E. M. Forster's discussion about the length of the novel (50,000 or more words), she provides the following definition: "*the novella is a prose fiction of a certain length (usually 15,000 to 50,000 words), a length equipped to realize several distinct formal functions better than any other length.*" This definition, she notes, is closely allied with Aristotle's notion of proper magnitude (3-9).

Upon turning to other considerations, Springer cites Sheldon Sacks's three prose forms, "*actions, apologues,* and *satires,*" as the basis of her own classification of novellas (Springer does not state clearly her reasons for choosing Sacks's classification system). The novella takes on five subforms (all derived from Sacks's original three): "1. *The serious plot of character,*" which resolves action by revealing the character, showing the character as learning, or showing the character as profiting from his learning; "2. *The degenerative or pathetic tragedy,*" which portrays the rapid degeneration of a character into misery or death; "3. *Satire,*" which chooses one object to ridicule (the novel chooses many); "4. *Apologue,*" which uses the character to illustrate the truth of a principle (apologues

are at times called allegories, fables, or parables); and "5. *The Example*," which depicts characters for didactic ends (10-13). Springer devotes the rest of her book to analyzing, under five chapter headings that correspond to the above classifications, more than one hundred Anglo-American and European novellas (18-160).

Springer's ideas about the novella, which depend on Forster for the attribute of length and on Sacks for content, do little to enrich theory. Her approach to the genre, which is international in scope yet disregards the results of two centuries of German criticism — even the material written in English — is unfortunate. Her work does show, however, that just when German scholarship seems to be deadlocking, scholars of Anglo-American letters are showing an interest in entering the fray.

In 1976 Friedrich Franz von Unruh publishes a book of interpretations, *Die unerhörte Begebenheit: Lob der Novelle*. In his foreword, which has strong existentialist overtones, Unruh describes the human condition as approaching Sartrean nausea. The contemporary individual faces a double crisis: internally, he feels homeless because he has been cast out of the cozy Ptolemaic universe and, externally, he feels a constant threat to his existence (presumably because of the cold war). Since both Christianity and Islam are rooted in a Ptolemaic universe, they are incapable of offering solace. Despite these assaults, humankind has shown its indomitable spirit through art. Dante's *Commedia*, Unruh claims, will continue to live after both heaven and hell have disappeared from the horizons of human intellect. Unruh focuses upon the novella because this genre transmits life in shorthand form (5-12).

The novella, at present declared to be dead, is ideally suited for resisting, defying, and even triumphing over fate. So noble a genre has no room in the modern literary marketplace. Today the novella is often mislabelled as a short novel, a short story, or an *Erzählung*. The nucleus of the novella, defined by Goethe as "eine sich ereignete unerhörte Begebenheit," illuminates all particulars of the genre. The novel reveals great epic breadth, but the novella is restrained, brief, dispassionate, and concerned with only essentials. Heyse noted that the contents of the novella can be summarized in a few lines, and Pongs pointed out that the genre is highly symbolistic. This symbolism elevates a unique, single incident into a realm where it gains universal validity by transforming reality into truth. Unruh states that he does not overly concern himself with theory. As a novelist, he faces a practical, two-dimensional task. On

the one hand, he feels constrained to portray the event with exactitude, knowledgeability, and felicitous detail. In doing so, he proceeds in a sober, precise manner and describes prosaic events and characters in the same fashion as would a reliable witness. On the other hand, he also knows that a writer must eradicate the aura of banality by infusing his work with spiritual or metaphysical qualities (12-16). Unruh devotes the rest of his book to interpreting thirty novellas, including non-German ones by Melville, Hemingway, Conrad, and Tanja Blixen. Although Unruh's ideas are derivative of standard novella theory, they are of interest because they represent, for the first time in decades, an author's willingness to air his views on the genre in public.

The year 1977 was most fruitful for both Anglo-American as well as German novella studies. Clements and Gibaldi, in their *Anatomy of the Novella* (which has a comparative literary leaning), disagree with Springer's assertion in *Forms of the Modern Novella* that there is no connection between the Boccaccian and the modern novella. They isolate ten structural characteristics of the genre (see the earlier discussion of the Romance novella) and then discuss a large number of themes treated in the Renaissance novellas. In their last chapter, they trace the transition from novella to short story. The key figure here is Cervantes, for in his *Novelas ejemplares* he abandons *brevitas* and expands his stories by carefully setting scenes, developing characters, and complicating plots. Clements and Gibaldi postulate that these expansions (now short stories), served as the basis for additional lengthening and led to the creation of the modern novel (216-27).

Graham Good, in yet another comparative study of the novella, uses Gerald Gillespie's call for adoption of the term "novella" as a springboard for his own study. After reviewing the work of Ellis, Leibowitz, and Springer, who fix the location of the novella between short story and novel, Good states his preference for the German classification system, which has only the novella and the novel. After studying the novellas of Boccaccio and Cervantes, Good turns to the theories of Goethe, Friedrich Schlegel, Tieck, and Heyse. He follows this analysis by discussing the work of Bruch, Grolman, and Pongs. Upon concluding his survey, Good states that there is no reason "why the theory of the novella developed in Germany should not be applicable to novellas from other countries" (1977, 197-208).

Good undertakes a brief survey of the nineteenth-century novella as it appeared in Germany (the flourishing of the genre in the post-Goethe period), Great Britain (Conrad, Kipling, Conan Doyle), France (Mérimée, Balzac, Gautier, and Maupassant), the United States (Poe), and Russia (Gogol, Turgenev, Tolstoy, and Chekhov). Good ends his essay by providing a ten-point list of characteristics that he believes are common to the novella. These characteristics, in brief, are: 1) "a common repertory of features," 2) the individual novellas of the Renaissance collections grew into connected sequences and became novels, 3) novellas contain surprising twists or novelties of plot or setting, 4) the novella has retained its "oral characteristics," 5) the novella has either an "implicit or explicit" frame, 6) the frame transmits accumulated wisdom, 7) the novella concentrates its material and is often fatalistic, 8) the novella is told from a retrospective viewpoint, 9) the novella's retention of oral qualities reflects a social dimension, and 10) the novella is "a closed form whose end is latent in its beginning" (209-11). This list, as well as the whole essay, recapitulates German novella theory. In a non-German context, Good achieves mixed results: on the one hand, he dilutes his efforts by attempting to discuss too many topics, on the other, he provides a broad overview that serves as an excellent introduction to the topic for his intended audience, Anglo-American scholars of literature.

The year 1977 also sees Josef Kunz publish the final volume of his history of the German novella, *Die deutsche Novelle im 20. Jahrhundert*. After commenting on the thematic similarities between the novella of the previous century and the current one, Kunz singles out as the distinguishing feature of the modern novella its accentuation of the individual. In his discussion of novella theory, Kunz states that theoreticians, from the very beginning, have stressed that the novella deals with remarkable yet realistic events. These events have a tragic dimension because they are connected with fate which, in its modern manifestation, has taken on a distinctive form. The individual now finds himself ensnared either by biological and psychological problems or by the undermining powers of existential Angst and alienation. Kunz, who in the first volume of his history reacted to Arx and Pabst by avoiding theory, now states that his choice of works for inclusion in this volume depended on whether they adhered to the normative principles of the genre ("das Gesetz der Gattung"). He lists these formal features as concentration upon an "unerhörte Begebenheit," the narrative stance of reportage or interior

monologue, the *Wendepunkt*, the presence of a "Pointe," and the technique of prefiguration (7-12).

In the text itself, Kunz interprets German novellas beginning with Gerhart Hauptmann's *Bahnwärter Thiel* and ending with Günter Grass's *Katz und Maus*. Kunz ends his multi-volume history of the novella by concluding, as have many critics before him, that the novella has been replaced by the short story. Chief practitioners of the new art form are Wolfgang Borchert, Heinrich Böll, Elisabeth Langgässer, and Siegfried Lenz. The novella and the short story can be differentiated by the degree of isolation depicted by the central event. In the novella the event portrays the development, resolution, and occurrence of a conflict within the pales of empirical reality and normal chronology. The central event of the short story takes place with such suddenness, and is so disconnected from everyday reality, that conflict and development lack time to materialize. Instead, the event is so radically isolated that, like a random shot in the dark, it tears a gaping hole in the continuity of normally sequenced reality and defies all understanding or explanation (228-32).

During the summer of 1977, Henry Remak, the most active of the post-war normative critics, conducted a seminar at Indiana University sponsored by The National Endowment for the Humanities. The topic, which focused on the structural elements of the German novella, led to extensive analyses and discussions of such standard elements of theory, among others, as Goethe's definition, turning point(s), irony, paradox, "Pointe," the frame, and objective narration as they related to several dozen German novellas as well as a handful each of American, French, Spanish, Italian, and Russian ones. At the end of the seminar, one of the skeptically inclined participants challenged Remak to provide a generally accepted definition of the novella (he later insisted that he was not imitating the Staiger seminar as described by Arx). Remak conceded, given the state of current scholarship, that such a task was, of course, impossible. He insisted, nevertheless, that lack of consensus hardly constituted sufficient grounds for abandoning the normative approach. To do so would be tantamount to "throwing the baby out with the bath water."

Brian Rowley, seemingly in response to John Ellis's skepticism in *Narration in the Novelle*, concedes that attempts to apply elements of standard novella theory turn out to be problematical. The turning point, for example, "is just as much at home in the drama and the novel as it is in the Novelle," whereas the falcon, as an "object-symbol," may not even

make a flyby in a novella, yet nest in a novel or a poem. Part of the problem involves the incorrect interpretation of standard features. Tieck's *Wendepunkt* is not a "turning-point," but "a complete change in direction," whereas the falcon, as a concrete symbol, is an afterthought — Heyse only demanded that a novella "should have a clear-cut profile" (1977, 4-10)

After pointing to other pitfalls, Rowley observes that critics like Ellis and Hartwig Eckert are mistaken when they assume that the fundamental task of criticism is to define the novella. The real task is that "of recognizing affinities among existing forms, and of finding a nomenclature." Using a taxonomic system adapted from biology, Rowley identifies, as have others before him, three basic genres: the lyric, dramatic, and epic. Rowley adopts Linnean binomial nomenclature and categorizes the novella as a "prose epic." In his next step he differentiates between the long and the short prose epics: the novel depicts a series of situations with a wide range of characters who are developed; the short forms depict one situation with a small cast of characters who are revealed. The novella deals with "a single central situation," with the German variety depicting it more completely than the Renaissance one. In much of Europe the prose epic split into the novel and the short story. In Germany, with *Unterhaltungen* and *Lehrjahre,* Goethe provided his countrymen with genre models — the novella and the Bildungsroman — and, in the absence of novels, novellas "expanded to fill the vacuum" (10-18).

Rowley then differentiates among short forms. The anecdote depicts bare bones, the Renaissance novella fleshes them out partially, the German novella fleshes them out fully. A corollary of this process is an increase in length. The novella, despite Ellis's arguments to the contrary, portrays the "real" and natural, whereas other short forms (ghost story, fairy tale, legend, myth) deal with the supernatural. Rowley considers those narratives that combine the real with the supernatural as hybrids and attributes their existence to two reasons. The first, from a biological viewpoint, is that two close species (lion and tiger) are easily crossbred. The other, more complex reason, involves differentiating between two realistic, short prose epics — the novella and the short story — both of which depict one event or situation. The short story, with its "low profile," depicts a situation "in which nothing very exciting happens." In the novella "something unusual or striking" occurs. The very nature of the

novellistic event puts the genre on a tightrope where, owing to its length, it walks between "the single and the multiple incident" and, owing to its subject matter, between "the feasible and the marvelous." As a consequence, the genre often depicts the paradoxical (18-23).

Rowley returns to two earlier themes by observing that the falcon, which symbolizes a remarkable incident, and the turning point, which depicts a reversal in fortune, emphasize important "aspects" (not "distinct elements") of the novella. The remarkable event, he cautions, should not be construed narrowly as "one incident," but rather as the "complete plot-nexus." The turning point, which also can be found in the novel, occurs at a much sharper angle in the novella. Rowley concludes by describing the novella as an epic that fully explores one striking yet realistic incident or situation. He concedes that these observations, while reflective of Goethe's definition, expand upon the pronouncement of 1827 by postulating a more complete development of the situation, a decisive change of direction, and, finally, they firmly ground the novella within the epic. Rowley concludes his essay by emphasizing that his remarks should be regarded as neither normative nor prescriptive (23-27).

Upon republishing an anthology of German novellas in English translation, Harry Steinhauer observes that *novella* has recently been added to the terminology of Anglo-American criticism. After tracing the novella through its Romance developments, Steinhauer notes it made its German debut with Goethe, who elevated the genre from shallow entertainment to serious literature (1977, ix-xvii). Just as Boccaccio was attacked by a host of morally outraged critics, German novellists were assailed by an army of prescriptive theoreticians. Steinhauer, who in 1970 listed twenty-nine problematic characteristics of the genre, now reduces the list to twelve. The novella, according to standard theory, displays one real but extraordinary central event that stresses fate or chaos. Since the cast of characters is small and fixed, it is accorded less priority than the event. The novella also features a compact structure, a turning point, is heavily symbolic (falcon), and displays a non-linear narrative mode. Steinhauer continues to find fault with these criteria. Yet, his earlier critical stance, that of a grudging moderate, has softened, for in addition to his original criterion of medium length, he now also accords the central event some recognition. Even more significant, he extracts from Goethe's definition of 1827 "two essential criteria:" the no-

vella "should tell an exciting story" and it should be told "as if it really had happened" (xvii-xxiii).

Martin Swales in 1977 follows in the tradition of Walter Silz by first commenting on theory and then by interpreting several novellas. He initially describes the novella as a narrative of medium length that gained prominence in the nineteenth century (3-7). After castigating both the normative and the historical approaches (the one for producing rigid results, the other for neglecting form), Swales identifies himself as a moderate: "it seems to me a falsity to reject any notion of genre as an arbitrary straitjacket, to assume that there is an infinite variety of discrete works that are created — and that exist — in a void." John Ellis, who a- nalyzed narrative technique in the novella, committed this error. Since Swales also intends to pursue the topic of narration in the novella, much of his commentary seems directed at rebutting Ellis's arguments. Swales defines narration as the "dialectical interrelationship of theory and prac- tice" and regards theory as a structural "reservoir of potentiality."

Swales describes the process of theory formulation. After a feature of the novella is initially proposed, it is subjected to debate, interpretation, modification, reinterpretation, and even misinterpretation. Such contro- versy, the very heart of theory formation, shows that there is an intense, continuing interest in the proposal. The persistence of debate and in- terest, which in some instances has lasted for two centuries, suggests that the feature lacks precision. Imprecision implies neither inapplicability nor invalidity, but suggests, instead, that the characteristic is broad enough to allow for a wide range of interpretations. This range serves the needs of different and differing constituencies (8-18).

Swales devotes a sub-chapter to each of seven criteria of the novella. These features include the central event, chance or fate, literary realism, tension between the poetic and prosaic, tension between the objective and subjective, symbolism, and the frame. The first five characteristics are thematically interrelated since they not only lead to, but foster inter- pretive diversity or pluralism. Foremost among them is the central event that Goethe described as a "Begebenheit" (event) and Tieck as a "Vorfall" (incident). While Goethe and Tieck may not have had identical ideas about the subject, they both stress that a novella deals with an am- biguous event. This event, often a manifestation of inexplicable chance or fate, disrupts a hitherto orderly world. Although highly unusual, the event is a part of everyday, empirical reality and, as a host of critics has

observed, it is also both prosaic and poetic. These mutually conflicting attributes augment ambiguity from other angles and reveal as well that the novellist faces a formidable challenge: he must somehow transform the pedestrian into the poetic. The last thematic aspect of the genre involves the tension between subjectivity and objectivity. Critics have observed that the novella resembles an objective report of an event that actually took place. Yet, owing to its brevity and compression, the novella is highly selective in presenting details. Since all narrative art is selective, the distinction between objective and subjective is not one of kind, as Ellis postulates, but one of degree. Once again, Swales emphasizes, the ambiguity of the event leads to interpretive multiplicity: the event is objective in that it actually occurred; yet, the author imposes his subjectivity by attempting in one way or another to interpret or understand it (21-38).

In explicating the two formal features of the novella, Swales notes that the symbol, sometimes called the central symbol, combines structural with thematic features. He warns that this topic must be approached with great caution because in many novellas such a symbol is either entirely missing or exceedingly ambiguous. Yet, the symbol can contribute greatly toward understanding the story, especially if it is anchored to a universal truth, as is the window beam in Gotthelf's *Die schwarze Spinne*. Swales then focuses upon the structural element of the frame. He is less concerned with the historical manifestations and influences of this device than he is with its function as an aid in interpretation. In Goethe's *Unterhaltungen*, for example, the frame is a pedagogical device because the characters within it attempt to understand and interpret the narratives. In a non-cyclical novella, the frame often functions as an intermediary between the story itself and the narrator who attempts to understand his own story (38-55).

Swales summarizes his views by emphasizing that the novella deals with a central event that is ambiguous because it reflects commonplace reality; simultaneously, it is unusual, bizarre, or unprecedented. This event acquires such great significance that Swales equates it with the novella itself. Other genres (the short story, for example) also may deal with ambiguous events, but the "crucial difference" involves the narrative stance. The novella "attempts to establish" an "interpretive relationship to the event … it describes." The short story, however, has abandoned "interpretive mediation" and simply presents an unusual event in isola-

tion (55-58). Swales devotes the main body of his book to interpreting seven German novellas. The focus of each interpretation is upon the narrative voice and how the narrator attempts to understand and interpret the ambiguity inherent in the central event.

Roland Wolff, who published his article in the same year as Swales published his book, unwittingly validates Swales's observation that individual features of the novella are subject to the process of postulation, interpretation, and reinterpretation. Wolff follows and enacts this principle when he criticizes Manfred Schunicht's essay on the theories of Tieck and Heyse. Wolff first retraces Schunicht's arguments against the *Wendepunkt*, the falcon, and all formal novella criteria. Afterwards, he summarizes Schunicht's characterizations of the novella that involve the narrator, the reader, and the structure of reality. Schunicht's description, which amounts to a "functional ... theory of the *Novelle*," reveals what Wolff believes to be a huge inconsistency — Schunicht, while attempting to reject all characterizations of the novella because they are too loose or inapplicable, himself commits the very error against which he inveighs. Wolff concludes his essay by providing a number of examples that, in his opinion, show Schunicht's descriptions to be loose, inapplicable, or erroneous (1977, 157-66).

In 1979 J. H. E. Paine publishes *Theory and Criticism of the Novella*, another comparative study. In the introduction Paine disclaims interest in formulating his own theory and instead stresses that his chief concern with genre theory involves its function as an aid in understanding literary texts (7-12). Paine devotes a lengthy section of his first chapter to summarizing German novella theory and is highly critical of what he considers the prescriptive stance of many commentators. In the survey, he cites only John Ellis with approval, because this scholar points to the inadequacy of all German novella theory (13-31). Unlike the majority of critics, Paine also devotes attention to the short prose fiction of other countries, notably to the theories of the *conte* and the *nouvelle* of France (32-47) and to the early theories of the short story of the United States (48-57). In these countries, just as in Germany, theory has produced more sound than sense.

Paine, upon turning to American criticism, begins with Henry James. This author characterized the "*nouvelle*" as "blest," because this genre, unlike the short story, allowed him to develop an idea. James also described the genre as "brief," "complicated," "multiplicitous," and "lucid."

Paine discusses the ideas of several contemporary critics and agrees with
Gerald Gillespie that the terms *nouvelle, novelette,* and *short novel* be discarded and that the term *novella* be adopted. Paine notes that Gillespie
also challenged Anglo-American critics to define this form of intermediate length prose fiction and that two critics, Mary Doyle Springer and
Judith Leibowitz, accepted this challenge (58-65).

Paine devotes his next chapter to summarizing and criticizing
Springer's classifications and arguments. Springer's principal fault lies in
forcing works into one of her five categories, thereby severely limiting
interpretive possibilities. Such an approach sacrifices understanding of
the text for the accommodation of theory (66-104). Paine follows the
chapter on Springer with one on Leibowitz. He first retraces her argument of compression and expansion as well as her ideas on theme-
complexes and repetitive structures. He follows this analysis with a summary of Leibowitz's novella interpretations. Paine observes that Leibowitz does not abandon standard German novella theory, but merely reori-
ents its thrust by rejecting prescriptive features and by accepting
descriptive ones (he does not identify which of these features is which).
Paine finds much to praise in Leibowitz's book, but he also considers her
work limited. These limitations arise because she fails to analyze any of
her novella examples in sufficient depth to test her theory fully and because her approach is too closely bound to genre constructs (strictly generic approaches tend to be too confining in scope).

Paine intends to remedy the first fault by analyzing, in depth, Joseph
Conrad's *Heart of Darkness* in light of Leibowitz's theories. He intends to
solve the second problem by incorporating into his analysis Paul Hernadi's extra-generic notions involving thematic and narrative modes and
perspectives (105-43). After devoting a lengthy chapter to Conrad's
narrative, Paine concludes that *Heart of Darkness* is a novella because it
displays many (presumably non-prescriptive) features of standard novella
theory — turning point, an unexpected event, and a frame — as well as
the "compression and expansion" required by Leibowitz (144-212). Although Paine falls into the same trap as had Leibowitz, and although he
devotes excessive space to rehearsing the ideas of Springer and Leibowitz, his work is an interesting and at times fruitful exercise in applying
German genre theory to a non-German work.

8: Contemporary Criticism (1981-1991)

THE CRITICISM OF the previous decade suggests that the riptide caused by Arx and Pabst seems to have subsided. Of the roughly twenty works reviewed, one is skeptical (Ellis), one is normative (Remak), while the majority of the remaining works are moderate. Three developments stand out: the reversal of Kunz's position, the further softening of Steinhauer's skepticism, and the five comparative or Anglo-American literary investigations, all of which seem moderate in orientation.

Such consensus proves short-lived. In 1981 Karl Konrad Polheim publishes his *Handbuch der deutschen Erzählung*. This volume, a collection of thirty-six essays by leading scholars, encapsulates the history of the medium-length German narrative. In the introduction, Polheim summarizes novella theory by listing a score of features. These criteria are not limited to the novella, but extend to all epic narrative forms and to poetry and drama as well. The only undisputed criterion that applies to the genre is that of medium length. Since the novella shares this attribute with the *Erzählung*, the main problem becomes one of differentiating between these two genres. Yet, as Polheim noted in 1964, an artistically formed *Erzählung* is a novella, whereas a novella is an artistically formed *Erzählung*. The only difference between the genres is the qualitative one imposed by scholars who insist that the novella is the superior form. Quality is not a generic attribute. Thus, when stripped of the superiority feature, the two genres are identical. Since the term *Novelle* is loaded with qualitative freight, Polheim advocates adoption of the non-prejudiced term *Erzählung* for all narratives of medium length (9-16).

The remaining essays in Polheim's handbook describe either a German literary period or the stories of one author. Since the essays focusing on authors deal only marginally, if at all, with theory, the following analyses (excepting Goethe and Tieck) will treat only essays that give an overview of the narrative within a period. Applying genre labels becomes problematic because several critics employ only the term *Erzählung*, others refer to *Novelle*, and a third group uses the two terms interchangeably. The essays by Joachim Heinzle, Willi Hirdt, Adolf Haslinger, and Jürgen Jacobs (discussed earlier) trace the history of the

medium-length narrative from the Middle Ages through the Age of Enlightenment.

These essays are followed by Werner Keller's interpretation of Goethe's *Erzählungen*. *Unterhaltungen*, Keller notes, reveals great variety in form and content: the first four narratives are ghost and love stories, the next two are novellas that emphasize moral themes, and the last is a fairy tale. The quality of the first four stories is poor, but after the baroness imposes her demands for form, the stories improve. The whole collection, nevertheless, is flawed, and is important only because it introduced the novella into Germany (72-82). Keller ends his essay by interpreting Goethe's *Novelle*, a work that he classifies as a fairy tale (83-89).

Ernst Behler lists as narratives of Romanticism such stories as folk fairy tales, artistic fairy tales, legends, novellistic stories, fables, and the fairy tale novella ("Märchennovelle"). The latter form, which dominated the era, unites the empirical realism of the novella with the fantasy of the fairy tale. This genre began in 1796 with Tieck's *Der blonde Eckbert* and ended in 1819 with Eichendorff's *Das Marmorbild* (115-20). After analyzing the ideas of individual authors, Behler describes Romantic novella theory as an attempt to bridge the gap between the prosaic, objective world and the poetic, subjective one (124-28).

Paul Gerhard Klussmann notes that Ludwig Tieck, from the beginning of his career, vacillated between polarities, mainly between the realms of reality and fantasy. Tieck found such ambivalence confirmed by his study of Shakespeare, for this author portrayed the enchanted as natural and the natural as enchanted. This dualism manifests itself in the real and in the wondrous elements of Tieck's first *Märchennovelle*, *Der blonde Eckbert*. Tieck continued to incorporate both elements into his stories until the advent of the Napoleonic wars (130-37). Upon moving to Dresden in 1819, Tieck realized that the new political and social order of Germany demanded a new artistic approach and chose the obscure novella, a narrative of 20,000 to 40,000 words. Tieck wrote more than forty novellas and his contemporaries credited him with creating the genre. In describing the novella, Tieck allowed this genre great latitude of theme, but demanded a *Wendepunkt*. This point — a manifestation of Tieck's principle of polarity — is that moment when it becomes clear that the story is both real and enchanted (137-43).

Friedrich Sengle, in his essay "Biedermeier," states that the novella has been described in several dissertations under his direction (see

Schröder, 1970 and Eisenbeiss, 1973). A crucial issue of the period involved the question whether literature was to adhere to the old religious, moral order or to the new national, political one. Biedermeier writers embraced the old (192-95). Sengle analyzes novellas by Droste, Grillparzer, Stifter, and Gotthelf and finds that these works emphasize religion and portray long periods of time that culminate in significant situations. Sengle attributes the second feature to the Biedermeierian view that an individual was not subject to constant change or redefinition as dictated by fluctuations of mood, opinion, or circumstance, but represented a central personality core that reflects a continuum. Stifter's *Brigitta* illustrates this view, since it takes a great deal of time (decades) and space (the broad Hungarian *pusta*) for the significant event (the reconciliation of Brigitta and the Major) to materialize. Sengle coins the term "Gerichtsnovelle" for a narrative that deals with divine justice. This theme, which often accentuates the demonic, can be seen in *Die Judenbuche* and in *Die schwarze Spinne*. In the former, Friedrich's mentor, his uncle Simon, is subtly associated with the devil, whereas in the latter, the devil appears in medieval times as "der Grüne," and in more modern times in less obvious guise. Both novellas show humankind's need of religious faith to battle the forces of evil. Sengle believes that the Biedermeier novella, with its emphasis on detail and metaphysical problems, differs from the standard novella in that it can hardly be classified as an epic genre. Although he considers formal genre considerations problematic, Sengle believes that the Biedermeier novella displays a certain uniformity when characterized from anthropological, religious, or stylistic viewpoints (197-205).

In an essay describing the novellas of "das junge Deutschland," a movement that paralleled the Biedermeier period, but emphasized the new political order, Helmut Koopmann quotes Heinrich Heine's question whether art and antiquity could withstand the onslaught of nature and youth. They could not. Heine's question reveals that the revolutionary spirit infusing the political arena also informed the realm of art. Goethe's famous definition of the novella was thus antiquated the moment it was uttered. The politically committed young Germans had neither the patience nor the interest to master artistic forms. Prose genres, as a result, became confused and the term *Novelle* was affixed to any work longer than an anecdote, but shorter than a novel. The most distinguished practitioners of the novella were Karl Gutzkow, Heinrich

Laube, and Theodor Mundt. As noted, Mundt, along with other writers of the period, used the novella as a medium for conveying political opinion. Since the novella of the period lacked any established features, Koopmann remarks that many pronouncements of the young Germans about the genre amount only to empty rhetoric. Yet, this disregard for standard form may have opened the door to future innovation (229-39).

Fritz Martini, who in 1960 was convinced that *Novelle* and *Erzählung* were distinct genres, in 1981 converts to skepticism by entitling his essay "Von der Erzählung im bürgerlichen Realismus." Although innumerable narratives appeared between 1850 and 1890, novella theory was based on the works of only a few famous writers. An examination of the pronouncements of the time reveals no attempt to distinguish between the novella and the *Erzählung*. These narratives, moreover, were confused with the novel. Such confusion may have been caused by the insatiable appetite of the literary market for medium-length narratives. Although Paul Heyse attempted to formulate a novella theory in 1871, Gottfried Keller in 1873 expressed contempt for authors who sought a magical elixir for the production of novellas (240-43).

Martini undertakes a survey of novella practice and theory that begins with Mundt and ends with Spielhagen (243-53). He sees, as he had earlier, the unfolding of a process whereby the individual becomes increasingly isolated. This isolation is attended by a growing determinism — the belief that an individual is a victim of social forces, psychological or physical drives, uncontrollable passions, or a flawed genetic inheritance. Simultaneously, the novella itself becomes a genre of isolation, a development that can be observed in the changes of the frame. Originally the frame brought a group of novellas together. In the Age of Realism, the frame isolates one story. Originally the frame had a social aspect — a community of narrators told each other stories. The modern frame contains only one narrator, often an outsider who tells a story about an individual who is even more isolated than is he. Such double isolation, while precluding the development of a well-rounded, unified story, faithfully mirrors the social fragmentation of the age (255-57).

Wolfgang Nehring summarizes the narrative of medium length between the years 1880 and 1920. He considers this period difficult to characterize because it either encompassed or encroached upon such diverse movements as Naturalism, Impressionism, New Romanticism, Symbolism, Expressionism, Decadence, and Jugendstil. Nehring briefly

describes the principal features of several periods. Naturalism attempted to portray the totality of life, including the lower classes, the ugly, and the immoral. Impressionism, a counter movement to Naturalism, attempted to depict life as a sequence of moments that lacked substance and that came and went with kaleidoscopic swiftness. Nehring finds New Romanticism impossible to characterize because the movement incorporated elements of a half dozen different literary styles. Symbolism has had almost no impact on prose narratives, whereas Expressionism came at the end of the period (382-84). Nehring notes that attempts to adhere to generic constructs during this era were rare and terms such as *Novelle, Kurzgeschichte, Skizze, Studie, Geschichte,* and *Erzählung* were used interchangeably. A few writers (Paul Ernst, Heinrich Hart, Robert Musil) attempted to reinvigorate and to clarify the idea of the novella, but their efforts had almost no impact on their contemporaries. Nehring devotes the remainder of his essay to listing, providing brief plot summaries, and identifying by literary "-ism" scores of narratives by dozens of authors (386-408).

Kurt Binneberg, in "Expressionismus," observes that critics consider this movement the province of poetry and drama and tend to dismiss prose works as non-expressionistic, non-existent, or of poor quality. This view is incorrect. Binneberg dates the movement as falling between 1910-1925 and notes that it embraced spiritual, artistic, ethical, and socio-critical values. The movement bridged the chasm between the age of scientific positivism and the age of irrational, subjective existentialism. The prose works of this period reveal a great variety of style and theme. Styles range from the clarity of Franz Kafka to the obscure outbursts of Kurt Corrinth. The urge for self-expression often leads authors to abandon rational motivation, cause and effect, and sequential narration. Such a narrative approach results in unmotivated, incalculable actions, simultaneous occurrence of disassociated actions, and lack of development. The themes of Expressionism include a need for community, self-revelations that approach the egomaniacal, an intense intellectualism, a hostility toward science, mood swings that range from despair to ecstasy, and portrayal of life in the huge metropolis. These spectra of style and theme make it difficult to formulate a theory of the expressionistic narrative. Yet, there seem to be two common denominators: an anti-bourgeois sentiment and an uncertainty about the nature of reality (433-35). After observing that the authors of the period used the terms *No-*

velle, Erzählung, and *Geschichte* interchangeably, Binneberg devotes the remainder of his essay to listing authors and describing their works (435-47).

Erwin Rotermund, in "Die deutsche Erzählung in den zwanziger und dreißiger Jahren," notes that this period produced many small prose texts. After commenting on the heterogeneity of these narratives, Rotermund classifies them by using Karl Mannheim's four-partite (socialist-communist, skeptical, epigonic, and radical utopian) and Alfred Döblin's tripartite (conservative, humanistic, and revolutionary) groupings (461-73). In the second part, devoted to narratives written between 1933 and 1945, Rotermund classifies authors by their political orientation (including the exiles) toward the Third Reich. Rotermund ends his essay by observing that sheer volume, a lack of critical attention, and strong, but disparate political thrusts precluded classification of the narratives of the period other than by broad theme (473-82).

Dieter Hensing, in "Die Erzählung von 1945 bis zu den späten fünziger Jahren," observes that an *Erzählung* implies a story that reflects reality. West German authors of the post-war period resisted storytelling because they lacked a firm grasp of reality. For them the crucial issue did not focus on genre, but on the problems involved in gaining a view of reality, of developing a narrative perspective, and of establishing a relationship between the narrator and the reader. In this attempt authors avoided old norms and genres and consciously attempted to create new ones. Hensing describes West German short prose efforts by analyzing selected works of Heinrich Böll, Ilse Aichinger, Hans Erich Nossack, and Siegfried Lenz (508-24). In East Germany, the literary scene was quite different since the younger writers did not experience a reality crisis as did their Western counterparts. Politically committed, these writers subordinated artistic concerns to political ones in their attempts to help transform society from bourgeois values to socialist-communist ones. Hensing concludes that West German writers destroyed traditional forms and sought to create new ones. East German artists chose traditional forms because they fostered communication and helped transmit desirable political and social views (524-27).

Polheim's handbook on the German narrative ends with "Die Erzählung der sechziger Jahre und der ersten Hälfte der siebziger Jahre." Here Hensing notes that the period 1959-1962 marks a watershed for West German literature. Many writers who were active in the previous decade

either die or become inactive and a new group of writers emerges. For this generation, the leading concern continues to be the problem of reality and its literary transmission. One group of writers focuses on contemporary political and social issues, another group involves itself with metaphysical, sociological, and historical problems about reality, and a third group views reality as surreal, absurd, or grotesque. Yet another group favors documentation and reportage and abandons story telling altogether because fiction does not portray reality. A variant of this approach combines fictional with documentary elements. In the only typological remark of his essay, Hensing notes that narratives of the period tend to be long and that the distinction between *Erzählung* and novel has become even more blurred than it had been earlier (528-33). In the remainder of his essay, Hensing analyzes representative authors and works of both East and West Germany (533-51).

Between 1981 and 1983, Margit Sinka, in three separate essays, uses elements of standard novella theory as an aid in interpreting Heinrich Böll's *Die verlorene Ehre der Katharina Blum*, Martin Walser's *Ein fliehendes Pferd*, and Adalbert Stifter's *Bergkristall*. In her analysis of *Blum*, Sinka focuses on the mainspring of the genre, "the extraordinary event" and "the problem of its explicability." The lack of a turning point, which she defines as the moment Katharina decides to murder, leads to inexplicability and, hence, to a lack of unity. Although Böll's story displays many features of the novella, the "failure to reach any conclusions" and "the escalation of tension instead of its reduction" place this work outside the confines of the traditional novella (1981, 164-71). In interpreting Walser's *Pferd*, which is subtitled *Novelle*, Sinka remarks that a novella deals with an unusual event, requires action, and attempts to explain a problematic event. Walser chose this genre in order to depict the unprecedented event of an outsider's reintegration into society (1982, 56). In her analysis of *Bergkristall*, Sinka identifies the signpost as the hitherto unidentified *Dingsymbol* that unifies the novella by giving "concrete expression to each individual aspect of the narrative" (1983, 1-13). Sinka's interpretations serve as examples of how theory, in the form of genre constructs, can be of help in understanding older as well as contemporary works.

Henry Remak, in "Die Novelle in der Klassik und Romantik" (1982), believes Goethe's definition aptly describes the core element of the novella. This genre depicts tension-filled action that unfolds in the follow-

ing sequence: dilemma, crisis, catastrophe, "Pointe," resolution, and calm reflection (Goethe's "stiller Reiz zum Nachdenken"). The concentrated narrative style employs clear language to describe inexplicable events. The novella frequently vacillates between the rational and the irrational. Since the genre portrays the event in a concrete rather than abstract fashion, it often displays a *Dingsymbol*. In musically oriented novellas, this symbol is replaced by a leitmotif. As a closed form, the novella portrays in microcosmic fashion events that have macrocosmic significance (290-93).

In 1982 James Rolleston described the short prose fiction of German exiles during the Nazi period. Suffering from the many catastrophes that attend exile, these writers often clung to form as a "locus for the self in a world without alternative roots." Since the novella is traditionally grounded in a social setting, this genre was doubly affected because the exiles were not only severed from their homelands, but also were unable to establish themselves in foreign societies. Thus, the "prerequisites for writing a *Novelle* were absent in their entirety." Exiled authors faced a choice: they could write tightly structured novellas that symbolically reconnected them with their homelands, or they could write formally less demanding, more loosely structured narratives that reflected actual experiences in their adopted countries (32-35). After noting that the short prose works of the exiles tended to be either novellas or (short) stories, Rolleston analyzes roughly twenty such narratives and concludes that the short story reflects a re-engagement with life, whereas the novella, fearing the terrors of the contemporary world, stays within the confines of the past (35-44).

Werner Strube in 1982 classifies attempts to define the genre as ontological (Johannes Klein), extensible (Walter Pabst), explicative (Joachim Müller), or utilitarian (Manfred Schunicht). Since the controversy over defining the novella arises from sharp differences over matters of substance rather than of semantics, a resolution remains unlikely. The definition of the term, Strube observes, corresponds to the user's need or intent. Klein needed a flexible definition; Pabst needed to accommodate works that already were labelled novellas; Müller wished to prevent a number of narratives from being called poor novellas and differentiated between novella and *Erzählung*; and Schunicht wished to accord short narratives maximum latitude. Strube notes that the controversy can be solved by applying Rudolf Carnap's principle of tolerance whereby all

definitions would be accepted and accorded equal footing (379-84). Strube's solution is unlikely to meet with either tolerance or acceptance.

Siegfried Weing, in "The Genesis of Goethe's Definition of the *Novelle*," attempts to determine whether Goethe's pronouncement of 1827 was a spontaneous remark intended to characterize only his *Novelle*, as Feuchtersleben originally postulated, or whether it was a careful description of a genre. After examining the definition within the wider context of Goethe's conversations, journals, correspondence, and novellas, Weing concludes that the interpretation advocating spontaneity cannot be substantiated. Goethe called his definition the real idea ("der eigentliche Begriff") in its original sense ("in jenem ursprünglichen Sinne") and referred Eckermann to the *Die Wahlverwandtschaften* of 1807 as containing an example of the genre. In this work he described the novella as an unusual event that took place (1982, 492-508).

In 1983 Henry Remak analyzes novellistic structure in the three versions of "Die Krämerin." This narrative, originally an episode from the life of the French Marshal de Bassompierre (1579-1646), was adapted by Goethe in *Unterhaltungen* and by Hugo von Hofmannsthal as "Erlebnis des Marschalls von Bassompierre." Bassompierre's two-page account of his erotic adventure contains many elements of the novella — it is, foremost, "eine sich ereignete unerhörte Begebenheit" that incorporates irony and paradox; it contains the requisite dramatic features that begin with tension and end with resolution; it contains both turning points; it emphasizes fate and action over personality; and it is told with clarity, yet remains mysterious. Remak lauds Bassompierre's story as a nigh perfect example of a novella (23-33). Since Goethe was aware of this perfection, he made only a few changes in his translation and produced a German masterpiece (33-42). Hofmannsthal spoiled this magnificent novella by subjecting it to lyrical, aesthetical, and psychological intensification and refinement (42-67). In this process he quadrupled the length, converted a novella into an impressionistic story ("Geschichte"), and, to borrow and twist a metaphor from Gottfried Keller, found and applied the elixir that converts gold into lead (67-69).

Christine Träger, in "Novellistisches Erzählen bei Goethe" (1983), credits this author with introducing the art novella ("Kunstnovelle") into Germany. Goethe's interest in this genre was prompted by his need to adopt an artistic stance to the French Revolution. Since Goethe believed the Revolution ushered in a new historical epoch, and since he witnessed

unprecedented events, he chose the novella as the medium for best mirroring this era. This choice also was prompted by the consideration that the genre first appeared during an earlier revolution, the Renaissance, and that it emphasized individuality, chance, novelty, and isolation — characteristics that also stamped the new era (182-86).

Hildburg Herbst, in "Goethe: Vater der deutschen Novelle?" (1984), lists roughly a dozen critics who answer affirmatively the question she poses in her title. She disagrees with this conclusion because authors like Meißner, LaRoche, Lenz, Merck, and Schiller wrote narratives that displayed not only a Boccaccian orientation, but in originality, significance, and perfection of form surpassed Goethe's short narratives. It was Wieland, moreover, who initially described the novella as a distinct genre in a letter to Sophie von LaRoche in 1780. Thus Goethe's chief contribution lay in neither innovative theory nor in practice, but in providing the impetus to establish the novella in Germany with his *Unterhaltungen*. This work, however, represents only Goethe's casual effort to help meet Schiller's need for material for his new journal. *Unterhaltungen* has been notoriously overrated because modern critics have fixated more upon Goethe's Olympian status in the world of German letters than they have on the quality of this work (244-53).

Gerhard Neumann believes the German novella made its debut with Schiller's "Verbrecher aus verlorener Ehre" (1786) and Goethe's *Unterhaltungen* (1795). Since both works are infused with the spirit of the French Revolution, they reflect changes that led to an accentuation of the individual and to a more subjective, autonomous self-identity. This new identity, conditioned and influenced by changing psychological, social, and economic developments (as partially described by Michel Foucault), is visible in the protagonists of both authors. Schiller portrays the highly individualistic Christian Wolff and his conflict with the new order (433-47). Goethe emphasizes the political and economic conflict between the old, feudal order and the new, democratic one. In the ghost stories, "Der Klopfgeist" and "Antonelli," economics and love play a significant role: the characters are subject to rigid economic conditions and the ghosts represent unreconciled erotic relationships. "Die Krämerin" depicts the unconditional love of a woman who is destroyed by the economic prejudice of the man. "Der Schleier" portrays a conflict between bourgeois and aristocratic values. The last two stories, "Der Prokurator" and "Ferdinand," are merchant stories that deal with the

transformation of an economic situation into a moral one — the old man buys his wife but then grants her freedom, whereas Ferdinand steals for the love of one woman and restores the money for the love of another (447-51).

The generic significance of this article lies in the reenforcement of the thesis that Goethe and Schiller adopted a new genre, the novella, to express and respond to the revolutionary spirit of the times. Yet, Neumann does not explain why both authors chose stories that predate the French Revolution — Friedrich Schwan was executed in 1760 and, in Goethe's case, one story is three centuries old and two are at least a hundred years old. Also puzzling are the assertions involving "Die Krämerin" and "Ferdinand." There is no textual evidence to suggest that the "Krämerin" is destroyed for economic reasons. Ferdinand, moreover, resolves to mend his ways and to restore the money *before* he leaves on the business trip and meets the girl who will later become his wife.

Karl Konrad Polheim in 1984 analyses Paul Ernst's novella theory. In his essay "Zur Technik der Novelle" (1901), Ernst described the genre as a strict form that portrays the fate of an individual in a single, remarkable incident that borders on the irrational. Polheim believes that Ernst's views are a collation of ideas borrowed from Goethe, Friedrich Schlegel, and Heyse. In 1923 Ernst observed that both the novella and the drama are genres of abstraction and selectivity. This pronouncement expresses an aesthetic truism, but fails to recognize that it applies to all narrative art (520-27). Polheim, in pursuit of his favorite topic, notes that the proof of any novella theory lies in its differentiation between novella and *Erzählung*. Ernst, like many other theoreticians, fails to distinguish between these genres. In the first edition of his collected works (1916), Ernst called many of his narratives novellas. In the second edition (1927), he expunged *Novelle* and substituted *Geschichte* — a development that proves to Polheim that Ernst abandoned the genre construct "novella" (529-30). At the time Ernst began to speculate about the novella, he also directed his attention to the arabesque. As with his novella theory, Ernst's notions about the arabesque are also borrowed, mainly from Friedrich Schlegel. Thus, in his career as a theoretician, Ernst initially formulated a strict definition of the novella, but transcended this narrow view by recognizing and emphasizing the *Geschichte* and the arabesque (230-37).

Henry Remak, in "Goethe and the Novella," castigates those critics who, on the one hand, deny the existence of a phenomenon that has been around for centuries, yet, on the other hand, continue to work with the genre "in practice." Much of the confusion involving the genre during the past three decades has been generated by the mistaken notion that there is a "theoretical prototype, *the* novella, and if that exclusive model is not overwhelmingly realized in every specific novella, then there is no such thing as the novella." In an attempt to resolve this confusion, Remak advocates adoption of the term *novellesque* to describe a prose story that fuses the dramatic and the epic. Characteristics of the novellesque include such features as Goethe's definition, objective narration, tension, selectivity of detail, lucidity of language, "impenetrability of events," disharmony between the rational and irrational, and a *Dingsymbol* (1984, 133-38).

Remak interprets Goethe's definition systematically. One event ("eine Begebenheit") represents "a real, compact, self-contained occurrence." If there is a series of events, it "must" exhibit "a tight sequential unity." The view that the event took place ("sich ereignet") emphasizes credibility and authenticity. The writer chooses between an actual event and a freely invented one. Remak cautions, however, that an attempt to invent a verisimilar story may lead to inauthenticity. The unprecedented ("unerhört") nature of the event "extends from the unusual ... to the totally unexpected." Again, the artist who attempts to contrive surprises will usually achieve poor results (143-52). Goethe had a strong flair for the novellesque and starts many of his stories in that vein but tends to get sidetracked by stylization and formal fatigue. Remak ends his essay with the suggestion that critics should emulate Goethe by devoting more than just lip service to the study of "the reciprocal relationships between type and text" (152-54).

Christine Träger follows her 1983 article with an identically-entitled book: *Novellistisches Erzählen bei Goethe* (1984). Here Träger repeats and develops the conclusions she drew in her essay. Träger devotes the first portion of her book to analyzing Goethe's reaction to Aristotle. Goethe had either participated in or witnessed, as he described in *Campagne in Frankreich*, many strange, unprecedented events during the French Revolution. He realized that the Revolution had suspended normality and totally changed the world. One of these changes involved aesthetics — Goethe believed the modern age had become so unpoetic that it was

impossible to write epics. Aristotle's aesthetic ideas about genre had thus become "historicized" and were only partially applicable to the current age (5-54). Goethe witnessed many sensational events and wished to portray them. He chose the novella because this genre, better than any other, lent itself to casting an unprecedented event into an artistic mold. Such casting is visible in *Unterhaltungen*, albeit only in incipient form. This work contains "unpoetic" folk stories or novellistic narratives, but not yet novellas (55-109).

By the turn of the century, Goethe was convinced that the French Revolution had killed poetry and that the new age was best expressed in prose — either the novel or novella. In 1807 he wrote several novellas, expanding one, *Die Wahlverwandtschaften*, into a novel. Goethe published these novellas individually, but later incorporated them into *Wilhelm Meisters Wanderjahre*. With these narratives Goethe strikes out in a new direction and creates the art novella ("Kunstnovelle"). None of these novellas, Träger believes, is of exceptional quality (110-75).

For much of his life Goethe emphasized analysis. In old age he turned to synthesis and attempted to express the results of this process in symbolic fashion. Part of Goethe's synthesizing involved the development of a theory in which he postulated that the three basic poetic forms — the lyric, the epic, and the dramatic — could be fused in a single work. Goethe reached the apex of his novellistic career by completing his "Jagdgeschichte" in the form of *Novelle*. In this work, Goethe put his theoretical synthesis into practice: *Novelle* contains an epic introduction, a dramatic catastrophe, and a lyrical ending — all while narrating an unheard of event in symbolic fashion. Goethe achieved formal perfection and created an ideal work of art that could not be transcended. That is why, in his conversation with Eckermann, he characterized the genre from both a theoretical and practical viewpoint and chose to entitle the work *Novelle* (176-242).

Heinrich Henel's essay, "Anfänge der deutschen Novelle," appeared posthumously in 1985. Henel believes Goethe's definition — a novella is an account of an actual, extraordinary event — has caused much confusion. While applicable to a few of Boccaccio's tales and to the stories of the "Prokurator" and the "Krämerin," the definition does not apply to Goethe's *Novelle* because this work contains not one, but five narrative components, each constituting one event. Thus, if Goethe's last novella is to be considered paradigmatic, a novella actually consists of two or more

unusual but interconnected events that took place (433-37). Henel supports his redefinition by distinguishing among anecdote, *Erzählung*, and novella. The anecdote deals with one unusual event that culminates in a "Pointe." The *Erzählung* portrays a series of events that are causally connected and unfold in chronological sequence (the early novel is a long *Erzählung*). The novella also portrays a series of events, but these events are neither causally nor chronologically connected. The hero of an *Erzählung* determines his own fate through his actions; the hero of the novella is a victim of events over which he has no control. The "Erzähler" employs an epic style to portray life as natural, rational, and normal; the novellist employs a dramatic style to depict life as mysterious, irrational, and impenetrable. In furtherance of such depiction, novellists often use symbols because their lack of precision aids the attempt to portray life as mysterious. Henel believes that it may be a mistake to use the label *Novelle* for both the Renaissance and the German narrative forms and advocates *novella* for the former and *Novelle* for the latter. Boccaccio's great achievement lay in liberating everyday, empirical reality as a fit subject for art. The German novella, while retaining Boccaccio's emphasis, also incorporated the irrational elements of the fairy tale (438-44).

Hildburg Herbst follows her essay on Goethe and the novella with a published form of her 1978 dissertation entitled *Frühe Formen der deutschen Novelle im 18. Jahrhundert* (1985). Herbst identifies her approach as historical and, after tracing the etymology and history of the novella, credits Wieland with activating the word in German. She discusses the early theoretical foundations of the genre as laid by Lessing, Wieland, the brothers Schlegel, and others. Elements of early theory include such ideas that the novella is medium long, is written in prose, exhibits a pronounced realism, narrates an unusual event, is very form conscious, reveals a strong kinship to drama, and often exhibits a turning point, a silhouette, and a frame (9-48). Herbst also explores the background of the novella from the viewpoints of several literary movements (Classicism, Pietism, Sentimentality) and the influence of genres such as the fable, the *Schwank*, and the various types of French *contes*. Other influences on the development of the novella include the appearance of many German periodicals patterned after those of Addison and Steele, the publication of anthologies that contained *Erzählungen*, *Skizzen*, *Dialoge*, and *Bagatellen*, and the growth of the publishing trade. The last development was fostered by a middle class that increasingly stressed literacy

for women, who then became consumers of such literary wares (49- 88).
In the last part of her book, Herbst interprets single novellas, written
between 1766 and 1789, by Thümmel, Wezel, Lenz, Sprickmann,
Merck, Wall, Schiller, and Meißner (89-152). Herbst repeats her earlier
conclusion that Goethe's role in the development of the novella has been
vastly overrated — the genre had existed in all but name three decades
before the appearance of *Unterhaltungen* (153-59).

Roger Paulin, in *The Brief Compass: The Nineteenth-Century German
Novelle* (1985), calls Mundt's characterization of the genre as a German
household pet incorrect because such narratives also can be found in the
United States, France, and Russia. The emphasis on prescriptive theory
and on establishing the "pure" form of the novella seem, however, to be
peculiarly German. This emphasis began in the early twentieth century
with authors and critics who were disturbed by what they perceived to be
a loss of values and a collapse of form in Naturalism and Expressionism.
Since 1945 theory has become less prescriptive and more historical in
orientation (1-10). After devoting a chapter to the historical development of the novella (11-19), Paulin notes that Goethe introduced the
genre into Germany with *Unterhaltungen*. The novella, according to
Goethe, should be pleasurable, instructive, brief, and recount a novel
event that contains a surprising twist ("geistreiche Wendung"). Paulin, a
moderate critic with latitudinarian leanings, considers Goethe's features
to be very wide "in terms of reference" and "inclusive rather than exclusive" (20-24).

Paulin also comments on the novella of the nineteenth century. In his
discussion of Romanticism, he credits Tieck with two literary innova-
tions: reintroducing the narratives from the old chapbooks and creating
the artistic fairy tale. The latter genre, as illustrated by *Eckbert*, is unique
in that it fuses the "wondrous" with the "real." In his comments on Romantic theory, he notes that the Schlegel brothers emphasize that the
novella must depict action and that, in essence, their opinions reflect the
claims of the Renaissance writers and Goethe's commentary in *Unterhaltungen*. Friedrich tends to emphasize the "tone and style" of the novella,
whereas August Wilhelm is more concerned with "subject-matter" (25-
36). In his commentary on the Biedermeier novella, Paulin notes that
Mundt, Rosenkranz, and Laube believed that the genre had become the
most popular literary form in Germany. Paulin attributes this popularity
to the development of the literary almanac ("Taschenbuch"). Publishers

mass produced such books and writers of every stripe contributed to their making. Many of these authors have sunk into well-deserved obscurity, but the stature of such artists as Tieck, Droste, Gotthelf, Stifter, Mörike, and Grillparzer has grown. The novella of the period lacked form to such an extent that "nobody seemed to know what a Novelle was and nobody seemed to care." Amidst this amorphousness two developments stand out: one involves the penchant for authenticity in the form of "true stories" and the other entails the increasing use of the frame (58-75). Gottfried Keller believed the novella of Realism focused upon the everyday world, but aimed to reproduce its more beautiful parts. Keller's view, echoed by Julian Schmidt, Gustav Freytag, Hermann Hettner, and Friedrich Theodor Vischer, finds its apex in Otto Ludwig's definition of "Poetic Realism" (76-81).

In remarks describing the relationship between the novella and the drama, Paulin states that this theme, initially introduced by A. W. Schlegel, recurs throughout the nineteenth century and culminates with Storm's remark concerning sister genres. Paulin discounts much of this notion by pointing out that dramatic features can be found in all narrative forms. Strict adherence to dramatic principles, as illustrated by Ludwig's *Zwischen Himmel und Erde*, can lead to failure. Ludwig "attempts to satisfy ... the expectations of a dramatic subject," but his novella "simply does not hold together as a story." Paulin analyzes several novellas that are based on Shakespeare's dramas and finds no strict adherence to the original: "the modern writer will simply choose ... adapt, add, combine, leave out as it suits him" (82-89).

In a chapter devoted to genre theory, Paulin stresses that comments made by Goethe, Tieck, and Heyse "were never canonical, prescriptive or definitive." Goethe's views, presented first in *Unterhaltungen* and repeated in his definition of 1827, simply reaffirm Renaissance (mainly Boccaccian) novellistic practices. Tieck believes that the genre illuminates an everyday but exceptional event and impregnates it with greater meaning than is initially apparent. The *Wendepunkt* is thus not a formal, structural device as postulated by A. W. Schlegel, it is an "*effect*" whereby the narrative intimates the existence of "a higher order or a glimpse of a truth hitherto inaccessible." Much of Heyse's theory is a restatement of ideas from Goethe and Tieck. Heyse was emphasizing neither the falcon nor the story of Federigo; he chose this tale at random to illustrate that a well-constructed novella lends itself to a brief summary. Paulin con-

cludes that Goethe, Tieck, and Heyse provide, at best, only "restatements" of older Renaissance novella practice (90-107).

John Ellis, who in 1974 accepted Goethe's remark to Eckermann as a definition for novellas of the past, in 1986 returns to the topic by asking whether this remark constituted a "well-considered attempt ... to define the Novelle." The context of the definition suggests it does not. This context involves Goethe's attempt to explain to Eckermann the totally unexpected ending of the "Jagdgeschichte." Goethe had such an unexpected ending ("unerwartet, jedoch natürlich") in mind from the moment he conceived the work thirty years previously. Several days after his discussion with Eckermann, Goethe attempted to find a title and, on the spur of the moment, delivered his definition, which "is strikingly close to his original idea for the ending." Ellis concludes that it is "a serious mistake" to accord this "off-hand" remark a central position in discussions of the genre (121-23). Ellis, in his discussion of context, does not explain Goethe's reference to the novella in *Die Wahlverwandtschaften*.

James Ritchie, in "Die strenge Novellenform im zwanzigsten Jahrhundert" (1986), observes that critics between the world wars believed the novella was on the verge of extinction. This view was fostered, on the one hand, by the formlessness attributed to Naturalism, Impressionism, and Expressionism and, on the other, by the extensive literary psychologizing inspired by Freud. Ritchie attempts to dispel this view by undertaking a selective survey of twentieth-century novellists. Paul Ernst first sounded the alarms of formlessness in *Der Weg zur Form* and offered, as a corrective, a model of neoclassicism that appealed to the National Socialist literary authorities. Several writers who followed Ernst's path incorporated racial and nationalistic ideas in their works. Yet, by no means were all novellists Nazis, for their political persuasions ranged from what Ritchie calls "decent conservatism" to "Blut-und-Boden" fanaticism. Ritchie lists as novellists of the period Emil Strauß, Rudolf Binding, Hans Grimm, Werner Bergengruen, Stefan Andres, Bruno Franck, Heinrich Mann, and Stefan Zweig. After the war, literary obituaries identified the short story as having dispatched the mortally wounded novella. Once again, the genre proved to be resilient. East Germany produced novellists such as Anna Seghers, Stephan Hermlin, and Christa Wolf, whereas West Germany witnessed novellas by Günter Grass, Peter Schneider, and Martin Walser. Ritchie believes that Grass and Walser wrote their novellas, respectively *Katz und Maus* and *Ein fliehendes Pferd*,

in response to critical accusations that their writing lacked form. Ritchie concludes that the strict novella form is showing strong signs of a comeback (252-63).

Henry Remak, the dean of contemporary novella scholars, in 1987 undertakes a structural analysis of Thomas Mann's *Der kleine Herr Friedemann, Tobias Mindernickel, Tristan,* and *Mario und der Zauberer.* His chief interest does not lie in "proving" whether these narratives are "pure" novellas, but in determing whether they exhibit novellistic features. Remak limits the scope of his structural inquiry to the individual elements of Goethe's definition of 1827. After explicating "eine Begebenheit," "sich ereignet," and "unerhört" much as he had done three years earlier, Remak systematically identifies and offers interpretive comments on these elements in the four narratives in question. He concludes his essay with the observation that Goethe's minimal definition proves quite serviceable since it provides a key to unlocking fundamental structural elements of novellistic prose narratives (103-22).

A year later Remak applies Goethe's definition, which he calls "the keystone" of novella characterizations, to two episodes from Goethe's life: "die schöne Mailänderin" described in *Italienische Reise* and the "Frankfurter Gretchen" described in *Dichtung und Wahrheit.* These episodes, while unquestionably autobiographical, exhibit strong "novellesque" features or tendencies: each deals with a unified, central event ("eine Begebenheit"), each took place ("sich ereignet,") and each is unusual ("unerhört"). Remak concludes his essay with the observation that if these two stories had been printed without the interruptions imposed by the autobiographical process, "they would be recognized as ... the most profiled and effective of Goethe's novellas" (1988, 21-54).

Brian Coghlan, in "Theodor Storms Novelle: eine Schwester des Dramas?," intersperses lengthy quotations from several Storm novellas with commentary that identifies these passages as dramatic. His first example, the scene from *Der Schimmelreiter* where Elke and Hauke declare their love for each other after the curling contest ("Eisboseln"), constitutes not only a dramatic *tableau vivant,* but also the turning point of the novella. Similar scenes can be found in Storm's other late novellas. Each instance portrays a dynamic, three dimensional tableau that, in a carefully-crafted, tension-filled moment, points to the impending conflict or catastrophe. Such scenes, which portray central events in human relationships, reveal Storm's penchant for presenting significant events in

dramatic or theatrical form and underscore his theory that the novella, as a sister of the drama, deals with the deepest human concerns (1989, 26-37).

Ulrich Karthaus finds that Günter Grass's *Katz und Maus* comes close to being a paradigm of the genre since it displays such novellistic features as objective reportage, realism, a *Dingsymbol*, a *Wendepunkt*, and even a paraphrasing of Goethe's definition. If the work did not represent more than that, it would be epigonic, since the novella, now a historic phenomenon, became extinct between the world wars. The novella proper is the account of Mahlke. His story is overlaid with another one, that of Pilenz. As the narrative unfolds the story of Mahlke (the mouse) recedes and that of Pilenz (the cat) gains ascendancy. At the end Mahlke's narrative line disappears and only that of Pilenz is left. Grass employs two different narrative techniques. He portrays Mahlke from an objective, exterior (novellistic) viewpoint that emphasizes action, whereas he describes Pilenz from a modern, interior (psychological) viewpoint that emphasizes conscious and subconscious motivation. With *Katz und Maus* Grass implies that a novella, an "unerhörte Begeben-heit," is an inadequate form for expressing the complexities of modern life (1989, 46-58).

In 1990 *Sammlung Metzler* replaced Benno von Wiese's *Novelle* (1963) with Hugo Aust's book of the same title. This handbook, while providing a fair orientation to the novella, surpasses the original in bib-liographical depth and breadth. After connecting the genre with the oral narrative (1-7), Aust provides a primer on novellistic terminology that includes such terms as *Länge, Begebenheit, unerhört, neu, Konzentration, Punkt, Symbol,* and *Rahmen* (8-19). Aust next traces the etymology of *Novelle* and summarizes the theories of the Schlegels, Tieck, Alexis, Rumohr, Reinbeck, Vischer, Hettner, Heyse, and Ernst (20-38). The chapter on theory is followed by a selective summary of novella criticism commencing with Walzel and ending with Paulin (38-51). Aust devotes the remainder of the book to tracing the historical development of the novella from its beginnings with Boccaccio to contemporary times. In his discussion of the modern novella, he disagrees with the opinion that the novella has dissolved in modern times and, in rebuttal, provides bib-liographies of novellas written between 1885-1944 (123-27) and 1945-1989 (165-67). Of interest in the second list is the fifteen-year gap that ended in 1978 with Martin Walser's *Ein fliehendes Pferd.* Walser seems to

have resurrected the genre with this work, since more than thirty-five novellas appeared in the decade following its publication. Aust lists roughly two dozen contemporary novellists and singles out Walser, Christoph Hein, Jochen Beyse, and Eva Zeller for brief commentary.

Werner Hoffmeister echoes Roger Paulin when he notes that scholars of the German novella have ignored the short to medium-length prose fiction of France, Russia, and the United States. After predicting that a comparative study would reveal that the novella was an international genre, this scholar focuses upon the early American tale between 1820-1856, because the period corresponds to the early development of the German novella (1990, 32-37). Upon comparing genres, Hoffmeister finds that the novella and the American tale share two characteristics. The first is realism, a feature described during the Renaissance as "veritas," "probabilitas," and "verisimilitudo." Identical views are expressed by Goethe ("sich ereignet"), Wieland (novellas take place "in unserer wirklichen Welt"), and A. W. Schlegel ("Wirklichkeit eines Vorfalls"). In similar fashion, Washington Irving notes that his tales provide "scenes in common life," Nathaniel Hawthorne observes that his narratives portray "pictures of actual life," and Edgar Allen Poe insists that the "unity of effect" appears only if the tale is true or verisimilar. The narratives of both countries, although at times bordering on the fantastic, remain firmly anchored in reality (37-43). The other common feature is the emphasis upon one extraordinary event which leads to terse, concentrated narration. This event is Goethe's "eine unerhörte Begebenheit," Tieck's commonplace yet wondrous incident ("alltäglich und doch wunderbar"), and Wieland's main situation ("eine Haupt-Situation"). American authors deliver the same opinion. Upon comparing the novel to the tale, Irving emphasizes concentration by remarking that in the "shorter writings every page must have its merit." Poe argues that the tale should contain no word that does not harmonize with "the one pre-established design." Hoffmeister believes that Martin Swales best described the German novella as a "marginal event" that occurs on the fringes of society. Such marginality applies not only to the German novella, but also to Irving's Ichabod Crane and Rip van Winkle, Hawthorne's Aylmer and Young Goodman Brown, and Herman Melville's Billy Budd and Bartleby (43-47). Hoffmeister's main thesis can be summarized as follows: the German novella and the early American tale

are identical genres that deal with an unprecedented event that has occurred.

Wilhelm Pötters, in a multi-faceted approach to Boccaccio's novella
theory and practice entitled *Begriff und Struktur der Novelle* (1991), undertakes a detailed study of seven Boccaccian narratives. Pötters's point
of departure involves a linguistic analysis of a sentence type that contains
a concessive clause. He provides the following example: "even though it's
raining, John is going for a walk." Such a sentence contains a generally
accepted implication or presupposition in one clause (everyone knows
rainy weather is a good reason to stay home) that is unexpectedly ne-
gated in the other (there must be some unknown reason for John not to
stay home). The in-built premise of the concessive clause and its unexpected negation in the main clause form the very nucleus of the novella
since they depict, in micro-structural form, the macro-structure of the
genre "novella" (34-36 and 49-52). The category of the unexpected,
which implies novelty, is reflected in both novella theory and practice:
Boccaccio's narratives often involve a *"fortunato avvenimento*," Marguerite de Navarre prefaces many of her stories with the term *"cas
étrange*," and Cervantes describes his novellas as *"caso extraño."* Goethe,
in modern times, defines the unexpected as "eine sich ereignete
unerhörte Begebenheit." In addition to Goethe, Pötters lists twenty-
eight other modern theoreticians and scholars who emphasize an unusual or unexpected event. Pötters believes that the explicit and implicit
meanings of all these statements can be subsumed under the rubric
"chance" (37-51).

After a sentence-by-sentence analysis of Boccaccio's falcon novella,
Pötters draws conclusions about this story that reflect and sustain standard German novella theory. He finds that this novella conforms to
Goethe's definition by depicting an "unerhörte Begebenheit." The plot
can be reduced to one sentence that simultaneously contains a concessive
clause and provides an abstract of the whole novella: "even though
Federigo wastes his fortune in a vain attempt to woo Giovanna, she
marries him anyway because the sacrifice of his last possession reveals to
her his nobility of spirit." The novella exhibits a *Wendepunkt*, located in
the middle of the story, that is inextricably interwoven with the *Dingsymbol*, the falcon. Pötters arrives at the last conclusion by counting the
number of sentences. After excluding the introduction, the novella
proper, as found in the *Codex Hamilton 90*, is composed of thirty-nine

sentences. The death of the falcon occurs in the very middle, the twentieth sentence, and divides the novella into two halves. This divide illustrates Tieck's *Wendepunkt* since the story, at this point, takes an unexpected turn ("unerwartet völlig umkehrt") and represents the hinge upon which Federigo's fortunes turn. Pötters regards the *Wendepunkt* a crucial structural element since Boccaccio employed the aesthetic principle of "*aequalitas numerosa.*" Thus, in order to achieve balance and symmetry, the two halves mirror each other — each of the nineteen sentences of the first half corresponds in reverse order to one of the nineteen sentences in the second half. To cite only two examples: the first sentence shows Federigo in the role of wastrel, the last one shows him as a good administrator husbanding his new fortune; the second sentence tells of Giovanna's being widowed, the second to last sentence tells of Giovanna's remarriage (97-108).

Pötters analyzes six other novellas and observes that Boccaccio wrote two types of novellas — those that portray an event and those that depend upon a "Pointe." In either case, the contents of the novella can be abstracted by one sentence that contains a concessive clause. All seven novellas incorporate the principle of *aequalitas numerosa* and reveal the presence of a *Wendepunkt* that in three of the cases is accompanied by a "falcon" (205-06). Pötters's analyses, although focusing upon Boccaccio, are of interest since they seem to confirm several features that play prominent roles in German novella theory.

Conclusion

THIS STUDY BEGAN with a reference to Wilhelm Meyer's early nineteenth-century description of the novella as a chameleon that continually changes colors, mocks all attempts at definition, and refuses to be clapped into the irons of theory. In language as colorful as that of Meyer, Harry Steinhauer notes five generations later that the mountain of German novella scholarship has been laboring for decades and has failed to give birth to even a mouse. Almost another generation has passed since Steinhauer's pronouncement and German scholarship, recently joined by a few Anglo-American critical efforts, is still in the throes of labor. The hairline cracks in theory, barely visible in the early nineteenth century, widened and deepened to chasms after the Second World War.

The normative assumption that the novella is a definable genre with a firm set of criteria has been severely damaged. This view, best represented by Johannes Klein, in its extreme manifestation rests upon the assumption that the novella, much like Venus emerging from the sea, descended full-grown from Mount Parnassus. Yet, this type of narrative, as is true for all artistic constructs, was first conceived by the imagination of the artist (in this instance, Boccaccio) and shaped into being by his skill and ingenuity. As with all human creations, it is subject to the ever-changing demands imposed by time, need, circumstance, and the unique talents of the individual artist.

The opposing opinion, formulated by Walter Pabst and modified by Emil Staiger and Bernhard von Arx, postulates that novellas either share no common characteristics at all or only one — that of medium length. Pabst's thesis is inconsistent in that he simultaneously seems to be advancing to and retreating from a nominalist position. Staiger and Arx, on the other hand, fail to demarcate boundaries. At what word, page, or juncture, for example, does a narrative of medium length become a short story or, moving in the other direction, a novel? Yet, even if these two critics had been able stake out clear boundaries, the next step would still have led to a rather problematic conclusion: if the prose narrative called novella can be characterized only by the criterion of length, then, by logical extension, the same criterion must hold true for the short story and the novel and the only difference among the three narrative types is

that of length. Polheim's tautological solution, that the novella and the *Erzählung* are identical, only begs the question since this narrative, whether called a novella or an *Erzählung*, has only the one clearly identifiable attribute of medium length.

The ecumenicism advocated by the moderates, that there is such a genre as the novella and that it tends to exhibit a common set of characteristics that point toward family resemblances, also leads to uncertainties. Areas of contention involve such problems as identifying, defining, and agreeing upon a list of such common features and then determining just how many of these features must be present in a work to constitute a novella. As the criticism of two centuries has shown, not even one such criterion has remained uncontested.

Hosts of critics have presented their cases, some ably, others not. No one has been able to mount an argument that is not open to challenge or doubt. Yet, after all has been said, the quite reasonable question remains: what is the novella? Since logic yields uncertainties and antinomies, and since artists seldom pay attention to the dictates of logic, the answer must be sought elsewhere. The most compelling theory seems to come from the moderates. Frank Ryder, a representative of this group, advances an argument based on empirical evidence: while the novella eludes precise definition, it nevertheless can be characterized. Thus, when an analysis of stories reveals the presence of a cluster of common thematic and formal features that combine to form a recognizable narrative configuration, we may reasonably call it a genre. These features, to name only a few, include medium length, a verisimilar but extraordinary event, a small cast of characters (usually fixed), a frame, a turning point, a central symbol, and an intrusion of chaos or the irrational into an otherwise stable, rational world. No single feature can be considered indispensable and no single narrative may exhibit all characteristics usually ascribed to a novella. Moreover, as several critics have noted, many of these criteria may also be found in other genres. Yet, despite all qualifications and exceptions, when a reader encounters a piece of prose fiction of medium length into which the artist has incorporated a relatively large number of these features, practical reason suggests that he or she has adequate cause for calling this narrative a novella.

Works Consulted

As an aid to following the text, the works consulted are listed in chronological order. For texts unavailable in the original editions, the year of initial appearance is listed in brackets after the name of the author. The year of publication for the edition cited appears in the normal bibliographical position toward the end of the entry. I have briefly annotated books that are more representative of either anthologies or primary works or of collections of essays than they are of monographs. I have found two books, Karl Konrad Polheim's *Theorie und Kritik der deutschen Novelle von Wieland bis Musil* (1970) and Josef Kunz's *Novelle* (1973), invaluable since they provide reprints of theoretical and critical materials that are either difficult to acquire or unavailable in this country. To avoid unwieldiness, I cite these reprinted materials only by author and title. Complete bibliographical information for the original editions can be found on the pages cited from Polheim and Kunz.

Aristotle. [c. 340 B.C.]. "The Art of Poetry." *Aristotle.* Translated by Philip Wheelwright, 291-325. New York: Odyssey, 1951.

Horace. [c. 14 B.C.]. "Art of Poetry." Translated by Francis Howes. *The Art of Poetry.* Ed. Albert S. Cook, 1-35. New York: G. E. Stechert, 1926.

Boccaccio, Giovanni. [c. 1352]. *Decameron.* Ed. Vittore Branca. Florence: Presso l'Accademia della Crusca, 1976. Translated by Mark Musa and Peter Bondanella under the title *The Decameron.* New York, London: W. W. Norton, 1982.

Les Cent nouvelles nouvelles. [c. 1460]. Ed. Franklin P. Sweetser. Geneva: Librairie Droz, 1966. Translated and edited by Judith Bruskin Diner under the title *The One Hundred New Tales (Les Cent nouvelles nouvelles).* New York: Garland, 1990.

Marguerite de Navarre. [1558]. *L'Heptaméron: Contes de la reine de Navarre.* Paris: Garnier, 1922. Translated by Arthur Machen under the title *The Heptameron.* New York: Knopf, 1924.

Cervantes Saavedra, Miguel de. [1613]. *Novelas ejemplares*. 2 vols. Ed. Harry Sieber. Madrid: Catedra, 1986. The "Prologue" and the novellas "Rinconete and Cortadillo," "Man of Glass," and "The Colloquy of the Dogs" have been translated by Samuel Langhorn under the title *Three Exemplary novels*. New York: The Viking Press, 1950. The novellas "The Generous Lover," "The Little Gypsy," and "The Jealous Estramaduran" have been translated by Walter K. Kelly under the title *Exemplary Novels of Cervantes*. Emmaus, Pa.: Rodale, 1952.

Wieland, Christoph Martin. [1772]. "Don Sylvio von Rosalva. Anmerkung zum I. Buch." In Polheim 1970, 1.

Schiller, Friedrich von. [1785]. "Der Verbrecher aus verlorener Ehre: Eine wahre Geschichte." Vol. 3. *Werke*. Ed. Emil Staiger, 310-31. Frankfurt a. M.: Insel, 1966.

Eschenburg, Johann Joachim. [1789]. "Entwurf einer Theorie und Literatur der schönen Wissenschaften." In Polheim 1970, 2.

Schwan, Christian Friedrich. [1791]. "Nouvelle." In Polheim 1970, 2-3.

Blanckenburg, Christian Friedrich von. [1792]. "Erzählung (Dichtkunst)." In Polheim 1970, 3.

Goethe–Schiller Briefwechsel. [1794-1795]. Ed. Walter Killy. Frankfurt a.M. and Hamburg: Fischer, 1961.

Schillers Briefe. [1794-95]. Ed. Fritz Jonas. Stuttgart: Deutsche Verlags-Anstalt, 1892-1896.

Goethe, Johann Wolfgang von. [1795]. *Unterhaltungen deutscher Ausgewanderten*. Vol. 6. *Werke*. Ed. Erich Trunz. Hamburg: Christian Wegner, 1968.

Schlegel, August Wilhelm. [1796]. "Die Horen." Vol. 4. *Sämmtliche Werke*. Ed. Eduard Böcking, 84-89. Hildesheim, New York: Georg Olms, 1971.

Schlegel, Friedrich. [1797-1798]. "Fragmente zur Literatur und Poesie." In Polheim 1970, 3-4.

___. [1798]. "Ideen zu Gedichten." In Polheim 1970, 5-6.

Schlegel, August Wilhelm. [1798]. "Vorlesungen über Philosophische Kunstlehre." In Polheim 1970, 15-16.

Schleiermacher, Friedrich. [1799-1800]. "Poesie." In Polheim 1970, 21.

Schlegel, Friedrich. [1801]. "Nachricht von den poetischen Werken des Johannes Boccaccio." In Polheim 1970, 9-14.

Schelling, Friedrich Wilhelm Joseph. [1802-1803]. "Philosophie der Kunst." In Polheim 1970, 27-28.

Schlegel, August Wilhelm. [1803-1804]. "Vorlesungen über schöne Literatur und Kunst." In Polheim 1970, 16-21.

Clodius, Christian August Heinrich. [1804]. "Entwurf einer systematischen Poetik." In Polheim 1970, 28.

Wieland, Christoph Martin. [1804]. "Die Novelle ohne Titel. Einleitung." In Polheim 1970, 1-2.

Ast, Friedrich. [1805]. "System der Kunstlehre oder Lehr- und Handbuch der Aesthetik." In Polheim 1970, 29.

Eberhard, Johann August. [1805]. "Handbuch der Aesthetik." In Polheim 1970, 30.

Bouterwerk, Friedrich. [1806]. "Aesthetik." In Polheim 1970, 30-33.

Goethe, Johann Wolfgang von. [1809]. *Die Wahlverwandtschaften*. Vol. 6. *Werke*. Ed. Benno von Wiese. Hamburg: Christian Wegner, 1968.

Schreiber, Aloys. [1809]. "Lehrbuch der Aesthetik." In Polheim 1970, 33.

Reinbeck, Georg. [1817]. "Handbuch der Sprachwissenschaft." In Polheim 1970, 33.

Nüsslein, Franz Anton. [1819]. "Lehrbuch der Kunstwissenschaft." In Polheim 1970, 39.

Schleiermacher, Friedrich. [1819]. "Ästhetik." In Polheim 1970, 22-26.

Alexis, Willibald. [1821]. "Ernst von Houwald, Der Leuchtthurm." In Polheim 1970, 39-41.

___. [1823]. "Die Schlacht bei Torgau und der Schatz der Tempelherren." In Polheim 1970, 41-42.

Rumohr, Carl Friedrich von. [1823]. "Vorbericht." In Polheim 1970, 45-47.

Alexis, Willibald. [1825]. "Über Tiecks Novellen, bei Gelegenheit seiner neuesten: 'Die Gesellschaft auf dem Lande.'" In Polheim 1970, 42-45.

Hauff, Wilhelm. [1827]. "Wilhelm Müller und Wilhelm Hauff." In Polheim 1970, 58-60.

Rosenkranz, Karl. [1827]. "Einleitung über den Roman." In Polheim 1970, 55-56.

Hauff, Wilhelm. [1828]. "Vertrauliches Schreiben an Herrn W. A. Spöttlich." In Polheim 1970, 60-64.

Mundt, Theodor. [1828]. "Zur Geschichte und Kritik der Novellen-Poesie." In Polheim 1970, 64-65.

Goethe, Johann Wolfgang von. [1829]. *Wilhelm Meisters Wanderjahre*. Vol. 8. *Werke*. Ed. Erich Trunz. Hamburg: Christian Wegner, 1967.

Tieck, Ludwig. [1829]. "Vorbericht." In Polheim 1970, 74-77.

Meyer, Wilhelm. [1829-1830]. "Drei Vorlesungen über das Wesen der epischen Poesie." In Polheim 1970, 79-82.

Immermann, Karl. [1833]. "Reisejournal." In Polheim 1970, 84-86.

Laube, Heinrich. [1833]. "Wilhelm Marsano, Die unheimlichen Gäste. Marco Doloroso. Die Abenteuer einer Nacht." In Polheim 1970, 86-89.

Mundt, Theodor. [1833]. "Über Novellenpoesie." In Polheim 1970, 64-69.

Bülow, Eduard von. [1834]. "Vorrede in: Das Novellenbuch." In Polheim 1970, 92.

Mundt, Theodor. [1834]. "Moderne Lebenswirren." In Polheim 1970, 69-71.

Gutzkow, Karl. [1835]. "David Russa, Drillinge." In Polheim 1970, 92-94.

Laube, Heinrich. [1835]. "Der Roman." In Polheim 1970, 89-91.

Rumohr, Carl Friedrich von. [1835]. "Novellen." In Polheim 1970, 47-54.

Eckermann, Johann Peter. [1836]. *Gespräche mit Goethe in den letzten Jahren seines Lebens*. Ed. H. H. Houben, 25th ed. Wiesbaden: Brockhaus, 1959.

Grillparzer, Franz. [1837]. "Tagebuchnotizen." In Polheim 1970, 96.

Mundt, Theodor. [1837]. "Die Kunst der deutschen Prosa." In Polheim 1970, 71-72.

Hebbel, Friedrich. [1838]. "Tagebuch." In Polheim 1970, 96.

___. [1838]. "Brief an E. Rousseau." In Polheim 1970, 97.

Marggraff, Hermann. [1839]. "Deutschlands jüngste Literatur- und Culturepoche." In Polheim 1970, 103-106.

Feuchtersleben, Ernst Freiherr von. [1841]. "Die Novelle. Didaskalie." In Polheim 1970, 106-12.

Hebbel, Friedrich. [1841]. "Vorwort." In Polheim 1970, 97-99.

Reinbeck, Georg. [1841]. "Einige Worte über die Theorie der Novelle." In Polheim 1970, 34-38.

Wolff, Oskar Ludwig Bernhard. [1841]. "Allgemeine Geschichte des Romans." In Polheim 1970, 112-13.

Gervinus, Georg Gottfried. [1842]. "Geschichte der deutschen Dichtung." In Polheim 1970, 113-15.

Lange, Otto. [1844]. "Deutsche Poetik." In Polheim 1970, 115.

Hettner, Hermann. [1850]. *Die romantische Schule in ihrem Zusammenhange mit Göthe und Schiller.* In Polheim 1970, 116-17.

Eichendorff, Joseph Freiherr von. [1851]. "Der deutsche Roman des achtzehnten Jahrhunderts in seinem Verhältnis zum Christentum." In Polheim 1970, 117-18.

Storm, Theodor. [1851]. "Brief an Hartmuth Brinkmann." In Polheim 1970, 118-19.

Carriere, Moriz. [1854]. "Die Poesie ...." In Polheim 1970, 121.

Tieck, Ludwig. [1854]. "Vorwort." In Polheim 1970, 77-78.

Hebbel, Friedrich. [1855]. "Brief an Arnold Schloenbach." In Polheim 1970, 101.

Köpke, R[udolf]. [1855]. "Unterhaltungen mit Tieck. 1849-1853." In Polheim 1970, 78.

Vischer, Friedrich Theodor. [1857]. "Aesthetik oder Wissenschaft des Schönen." In Polheim 1970, 122-24.

Gottschall, Rudolph. [1858]. "Poetik. Die Dichtkunst und ihre Technik." In Polheim 1970, 125-26.

Beck, Friedrich. [1862]. "Lehrbuch der Poetik." In Polheim 1970, 126.

Riehl, Wilhelm Heinrich. [1863]. "Vorwort. Geschichten aus alter Zeit." In Polheim 1970, 127.

Eckardt, Ludwig. [1865]. "Vorschule der Aesthetik." In Polheim 1970, 139-40.

Gutzkow, Karl. [1868]. "Vom Baum der Erkenntniß." In Polheim 1970, 94-95.

Oesterley, Hermann. [1870]. "Die Dichtkunst und ihre Gattungen." In Polheim 1970, 140-41.

Heyse, Paul. [1871]. "'Einleitung.' In: *Deutscher Novellenschatz.*" In Polheim 1970, 141-49.

Keller, Gottfried. [1874]. "Brief an Emil Kuh." In Polheim 1970, 157.

Riehl, Wilhelm Heinrich. [1874]. "Die Ecke. Als Vorwort." In Polheim, 1970. 127-28.

Vischer, Friedrich Theodor. [1874]. "Mein Lebensgang." In Polheim 1970, 124-25.

Heyse, Paul. [1875]. "Brief an Theodor Storm." In Polheim 1970, 157.

Keller, Gottfried. [1875]. "Brief an Friedrich Theodor Vischer." In Polheim 1970, 157-58.

Spielhagen, Friedrich. [1876]. "Novelle oder Roman?" In Polheim 1970, 160-62.

Der Briefwechsel zwischen Theodor Storm und Gottfried Keller. [1877-1887]. Ed. Peter Goldammer. Berlin and Weimar: Aufbau, 1967.

Storm, Theodor. [1881]. "Eine zurückgezogene Vorrede aus dem Jahr 1881." In Polheim 1970, 119-20.

Spielhagen, Friedrich. [1882]. "Roman oder Novelle?" In Polheim 1970, 162-66.

Fontane, Theodor. [1883]. "Rudolf Lindau. Ein Besuch." In Polheim 1970, 170-71.

Riehl, Wilhelm Heinrich. [1885]. "Novelle und Sonate." In Polheim 1970, 128-39.

Hauptmann, Gerhart. [1888]. Bahnwärter Thiel: Novellistische Studie. Stuttgart: Reclam, 1984.

Luise von François und Conrad Ferdinand Meyer: Ein Briefwechsel. [1891]. Ed. Anton Bettelheim. Berlin and Leipzig: Walter de Gruyter, 1920.

Spielhagen, Friedrich. [1895]. "Die epische Poesie und Goethe." In Polheim 1970, 167-68.

____. [1895]. "Streifblicke über den heutigen deutschen Roman." In Polheim 1970, 168.

Heyse, Paul. [1900]. "Novelle." In Polheim 1970, 150-57.

Ernst, Paul. [1901]. "Zum Handwerk der Novelle." 68-76. In Der Weg zur Form. Munich: Georg Müller, 1928.

____. [1904]. "Bemerkungen über mich selbst." 11-29. In Der Weg zur Form. Munich: Georg Müller, 1928.

Hart, Heinrich. [1905]. "Roman und Novelle." In Polheim 1970, 181-82.

Meyer, Conrad Ferdinand. 1908. Briefe Conrad Ferdinand Meyers. 2 vols. Ed. Adolf Frey. Leipzig: H. Haessel.

Biese, Alfred. 1909. Deutsche Literaturgeschichte. 3 vols. Munich: Beck.

Lukács, Georg von. [1911]. "Bürgerlichkeit und l'art pour l'art: Theodor Storm." In Polheim 1970, 183-84.

Arnold, Paul Johann. 1912. "Goethes Novellenbegriff." *Das literarische Echo* 14: 1251-54.

___. 1913. "Der Ausbau des Novellenbegriffs." *Das Literarische Echo* 15: 1676-79.

Herrigel, Hermann. 1913. "Novelle und Roman." *Das literarische Echo* 16: 81-86.

Musil, Robert. [1914]. "Die Novelle als Problem." In Polheim 1970, 184-86.

Mitchell, Robert McBurney. 1915a. "Goethe's Theory of the *Novelle*: 1785-1827." *PMLA* 30: 215-36.

___. 1915b. *Heyse and his Predecessors in the Theory of the Novelle.* Frankfurt a.M.: Joseph Baer.

Walzel, Oskar. 1915. "Die Kunstform der Novelle." *Zeitschrift für den deutschen Unterricht* 24: 161-84.

Lukács, Georg. [1916]. "Die Theorie des Romans." In Kunz 1973, 90-92.

Arnold, Paul Johann. 1921. "Tiecks Novellenbegriff." *Euphorion* 23: 258-71.

___. 1923. "Storms Novellenbegriff." *Zeitschrift für Deutschkunde* 37: 281-88.

Borcherdt, Hans Heinrich. 1926. *Geschichte des Romans und der Novelle in Deutschland.* Leipzig: J. J. Weber.

Forster, E. M. 1927. *Aspects of the Novel.* New York: Harcourt Brace.

Bruch, Bernhard. [1928]. "Novelle und Tragödie: Zwei Kunstformen und Weltanschauungen (Ein Problem aus der Geistesgeschichte des 19. und 20. Jahrhunderts)." In Kunz 1973, 118-38.

Hirsch, Arnold. 1928. *Der Gattungsbegriff "Novelle."* Berlin: Emil Ebering.

Jolles, André. [1928]. "Einleitung zu Boccaccios *Decamerone*." In Kunz 1973, 114-15.

Grolman, Adolf von. [1929]. "Die Strenge 'Novellenform' und die Problematik ihrer Zertrümmerung." In Kunz 1973, 154-66.

Pongs, Hermann. [1929]. "Über die Novelle." In *Das Bild in der Dichtung.* Vol. II, 3d ed. 97-109. Marburg: N. G. Elwert, 1967.

Jolles, André. [1930]. "Einfache Formen [Märchen und Novelle]." In Kunz 1973, 167-73.

Pongs, Hermann. [1930]. "Grundlagen der deutschen Novelle des 19. Jahrhunderts." In *Das Bild in der Dichtung*. Vol II, 3d ed. 110-83. Marburg: N. G. Elwert, 1967.

———. [1931-1932]. "Möglichkeiten des Tragischen in der Novelle." In *Das Bild in der Dichtung*. Vol II, 3d ed. 184-250. Marburg: N. G. Elwert, 1967.

Ehrismann, Gustav. 1932. *Geschichte der deutschen Literatur bis zum Ausgang des Mittelalters*. 2 vols. Munich: Beck.

Bennett, E. K. 1934. *A History of the German Novelle from Goethe to Thomas Mann*. Cambridge: Cambridge University Press. Revised and republished under the same title by H. M. Waidson. Cambridge: Cambridge University Press, 1961.

Petsch, Robert. [1934]. "Die Novelle." In Kunz 1973, 183-94.

Klein, Johannes. [1936]. "Wesen und Erscheinungsformen der deutschen Novelle." In Kunz 1973, 195-221.

Steinhauer, Harry, ed. 1936. *Die deutsche Novelle: 1880-1933*. New York: Norton. After providing an eighteen-page critical introduction to the social, political, philosophical, and literary developments in Germany during the time period indicated, Steinhauer presents an anthology of twelve novellas aimed at the student of German language and literature. Steinhauer, surprisingly, is silent on the theory of the novella.

Härlin, Erich. [1937]. "Die Form der Novelle." In: *Im Geiste von Paul Ernst. Vorträge über europäische Dichtung vornehmlich zu Novelle und Roman*. Ed. Karl August Kutzbach, 7-18. Bonn: Bouvier, 1987.

Lukács, Georg. [1939]. "Gottfried Keller und die Novelle." In Kunz 1973, 222-44.

Pongs, Hermann. [1939]. "Die Novelle und das Dämonische." In *Das Bild in der Dichtung*. Vol II, 3d ed. 251-96. Marburg: N. G. Elwert, 1967.

Auerbach, Erich. [1946]. *Mimesis: The Representation of Reality in Western Literature*. Translated by Willard R. Trask. New York: Doubleday, 1957.

Morgan, Bayard Quincy. 1946-1947. "The Novelette as a Literary Form." *Symposium* 1: 34-39.

Curtius, Ernst Robert. [1948]. *European Literature and the Latin Middle Ages*. Translated by Willard R. Trask. New York and Evanston: Harper and Row, 1963.

Boor, Helmut de. [1949]. *Die deutsche Literatur von Karl dem Grossen bis zum Beginn der höfischen Dichtung: 770-1170.* Vol. 1 of *Geschichte der deutschen Literatur von den Anfängen bis zur Gegenwart.* Munich: Beck, 1960.

Pabst, Walter. [1949]. "Die Theorie der Novelle in Deutschland (1920-1940)." In Kunz 1973, 249-93.

Burger, Heinz Otto. [1951]. "Theorie und Wissenschaft von der deutschen Novelle." In Kunz 1973, 294-318.

Newald, Richard. [1951]. *Die deutsche Literatur vom Späthumanismus zur Empfindsamkeit: 1570-1750.* Vol. 5 of *Geschichte der deutschen Literatur von den Anfängen bis zur Gegenwart.* Munich: Beck, 1965.

Arx, Bernhard von. 1953. *Novellistisches Dasein: Spielraum einer Gattung in der Goethezeit.* Zurich: Atlantis.

Boor, Helmut de. [1953]. *Die höfische Literatur — Vorbereitung, Blüte, Ausklang: 1170-1250.* Vol. 2 of *Geschichte der deutschen Literatur von den Anfängen bis zur Gegenwart.* Munich: Beck. 1960.

Pabst, Walter. [1953]. *Novellentheorie und Novellendichtung: Zur Geschichte ihrer Antinomie in den romanischen Literaturen.* 2d ed. Heidelberg: Carl Winter, 1967.

Klein, Johannes. [1954]. *Geschichte der deutschen Novelle von Goethe bis zur Gegenwart.* 4th ed. Wiesbaden: Steiner, 1960.

Kunz, Josef. [1954]. "Geschichte der deutschen Novelle vom 18. Jahrhundert bis auf die Gegenwart." In *Deutsche Philologie im Aufriß.* 2nd ed., ed. Wolfgang Stammler, 1795-1896. Berlin: Erich Schmidt, 1966.

Silz, Walter. [1954]. *Realism and Reality: Studies in the German Novelle of Poetic Realism.* Chapel Hill: The University of North Carolina Press, 1965. The "Introduction" examines the theory of the novella. The remainder of this book is devoted to interpretations of nine German novellas.

Stammler, Wolfgang. [1954]. "'Novelle:' Mittelalterliche Prosa in deutscher Sprache." In *Deutsche Philologie im Aufriß.* 2nd ed., ed. Wolfgang Stammler, 1058-62. Berlin: Erich Schmidt, 1966.

Lockemann, Fritz. [1955-1956]. "Die Bedeutung des Rahmens in der deutschen Novellendichtung." In Kunz 1973, 335-51.

Erné, Nino. 1956. *Kunst der Novelle.* Wiesbaden: Limes.

Wiese, Benno von. 1956. *Die deutsche Novelle von Goethe bis Kafka: Interpretationen.* Düsseldorf: August Bagel. The introduction analyzes the theory of the genre. The remainder of this book is devoted to interpreting seventeen German novellas.

Lockemann, Fritz. 1957. *Gestalt und Wandlungen der deutschen Novelle. Geschichte einer literarischen Gattung im neunzehnten und zwanzigsten Jahrhundert.* Munich: Max Hueber.

Newald, Richard. [1957]. *Von Klopstock bis zu Goethes Tod. Ende der Aufklärung und Vorbereitung der Klassik.* Vol. 6/1 of *Geschichte der deutschen Literatur von den Anfängen bis zur Gegenwart.* Munich: Beck, 1964.

Mackensen, Lutz. [1958]. "Die Novelle." In Kunz 1973, 391-410.

Steinhauer, Harry, ed. 1958. *Die deutsche Novelle: 1880-1950.* New York: Norton. A revision of the anthology from 1936. In his introduction Steinhauer now provides a short essay on the theory of the novella. The remainder of this anthology is devoted to presenting fifteen novellas from the time period indicated.

Ziolkowski, Theodore. 1958. "Goethe's *Unterhaltungen deutscher Ausgewanderten*: A Reappraisal." *Monatshefte* 50: 57-74.

Klein, Johannes. 1959. "Streit um die Novelle." *Welt und Wort* 14: 169-71.

Koskimies, Rafael. [1959]. "Die Theorie der Novelle." In Kunz 1973, 411-38.

Silz, Walter. 1959. "Geschichte, Theorie und Kunst der deutschen Novelle." *Der Deutschunterricht* 11: 82-100.

Martini, Fritz. [1960]. "Die deutsche Novelle im 'bürgerlichen Realismus:' Überlegungen zur geschichtlichen Bestimmung des Formtypus." In Kunz 1973, 352-90.

Mommsen, Katharina. 1960. *Goethe und 1001 Nacht.* Berlin: Akademie-Verlag.

Schunicht, Manfred. [1960]. "Der 'Falke' am 'Wendepunkt:' Zu den Novellentheorien Tiecks und Heyses." In Kunz 1973, 439-68.

Spender, Stephen, ed. [1960]. *Great German Short Stories.* New York: Dell, 1973. After an introductory orientation on the nature of the German short narrative, Spender provides an anthology of seventeen stories commencing with Büchner's "Lenz" and ending with Hildesheimer's "A World Ends." Several of these narratives, despite the title of the collection, have been traditionally considered novellas.

Booth, Wayne C. [1961]. *The Rhetoric of Fiction*. Chicago: The University of Chicago Press, 1967.

Müller, Joachim. [1961]. "Novelle und Erzählung." In Kunz 1973, 469-82.

Pongs, Hermann. 1961. *Ist die Novelle heute tot? Untersuchungen zur Novellen-Kunst Friedrich Franz von Unruhs*. Stuttgart: Silberburg, [1961].

Boor, Helmut de. 1962. *Die deutsche Literatur im späten Mittelalter. Zerfall und Neubeginn: 1250-1350*. Vol. 3/1 of *Geschichte der deutschen Literatur von den Anfängen bis zur Gegenwart*. Munich: Beck.

Mommsen, Katharina. 1962. "Nachwort." In *Johann Wolfgang von Goethe: Novellen*. Munich: Deutscher Taschenbuch Verlag. 187-99.

Remak, Henry H. H. 1962. "Theorie und Praxis der Novelle: Gottfried Keller." *Stoffe, Formen, Strukturen: Studien zur deutschen Literatur*. Ed. Albert Fuchs and Helmut Motekat, 424-39. Munich: Max Hueber.

Wiese, Benno von. [1962]. *Die deutsche Novelle von Goethe bis Kafka*. Vol. 2. Düsseldorf: August Bagel, 1964. This volume provides a different essay on the theory of the novella than does the first one. In addition, Wiese offers interpretations of fifteen German novellas not previously discussed.

Himmel, Hellmuth. 1963. *Geschichte der deutschen Novelle*. Bern: Francke.

Wiese, Benno von. 1963. *Novelle*. Stuttgart: Metzler.

Fricke, Gerhard. 1964. "Zu Sinn und Form von Goethes 'Unterhaltungen deutscher Ausgewanderten.'" In *Formenwandel: Festschrift zum 65. Geburtstag von Paul Böckmann*. Ed. Walter Seidel-Müller and Wolfgang Preisendanz, 273-93. Hamburg: Hoffmann und Campe.

Polheim, Karl Konrad. [1964]. "Novellentheorie und Novellenforschung (1945-1963)." *Deutsche Vierteljahrsschrift für Literaturwissenschaft und Geistesgeschichte* 38: 208-316. Reprinted as *Novellentheorie und Novellen-forschung: Ein Forschungsbericht (1945-1964)*. Stuttgart: Metzler, 1965.

Klein, Johannes. 1965. "Novelle." In *Reallexikon der deutschen Literaturgeschi-chte*. Vol. 2. Ed. Werner Kohlschmidt and Wolfgang Mohr, 685-701. Berlin: Walter de Gruyter.

Remak, Henry H. H. 1965. "Vinegar and Water: Allegory and Symbolism in the German *Novelle* between Keller and Bergengruen." In *Literary Symbolism: A Symposium*. Ed. Helmut Rehder, 33-62. Austin and London: University of Texas Press.

___. 1965. "Wendepunkt und Pointe in der deutschen Novelle von Keller bis Bergengruen." In *Wert und Wort: Festschrift für Else M. Fleissner*. Ed. Marion Sonnenfeld, et. al., 45-56. Aurora, New York: Wells College.

Negus, Kenneth. 1965. "Paul Heyse's *Novellentheorie*: A Revaluation." *Germanic Revue* 40: 173-91.

Kunz, Josef. 1966. *Die deutsche Novelle zwischen Klassik und Romantik*. Berlin: Erich Schmidt.

Malmede, Hans Hermann. 1966. *Wege zur Novelle: Theorie und Interpretation der Gattung Novelle in der deutschen Literaturwissenschaft*. Stuttgart, Berlin, Cologne, Mainz: W. Kohlhammer.

Staiger, Emil. 1966. "Schillers Erzählungen." Vol. 3 of *Schillers Werke*, ed. Dieter Schmidt, 510-19. Frankfurt a. M.: Insel.

Gillespie, Gerald. 1967. "Novella, Nouvelle, Novelle, Short Novel?—A Review of Terms." *Neophilologus* 51: 117-27, 225-30.

Kunz, Josef, ed. [1968]. *Novelle*. 2d ed. Darmstadt: Wissenschaftliche Buchgesellschaft, 1973. Kunz has rendered invaluable service to novella scholarship by collecting reprints of not only early statements on the novella, but also twenty-three significant critical essays. In addition, the volume provides an extensive bibliography compiled by Rainer Schönhaar.

Foulkes, A. Peter and Edgar Lohner. 1969. *Deutsche Novellen von Tieck bis Hauptmann*. Boston: Houghton Mifflin. This textbook provides an introductory essay on the genre and an anthology of nine German novellas.

Müller, Joachim. 1969. "Zur Entstehung der deutschen Novelle: Die Rahmenhandlung in Goethes *Unterhaltungen deutscher Ausgewanderten* und die Thematik der Französischen Revolution." In *Gestaltungsgeschichte und Gesellschaftsgeschichte*. Ed. Helmut Kreuzer, 152-75. Stuttgart: Metzler.

Kunz, Josef. 1970. *Die deutsche Novelle im 19. Jahrhundert*. Berlin: Schmidt.

LoCicero, Donald. 1970. *Novellentheorie: The Practicality of the Theoretical*. The Hague: Mouton.

Polheim, Karl Konrad, ed. 1970. *Theorie und Kritik der deutschen Novelle von Wieland bis Musil*. Tübingen: Niemeyer. An invaluable anthology of 125 reprints of statements germane to the theory of the novella written by 65 authors and critics between 1772 (Wieland) and 1914 (Musil).

Rowley, Brian. 1970. "The *Novelle*." In *The Romantic Period in Germany*. Ed. Siegbert Prawer, 121-46. New York: Schocken.

Rupprich, Hans. 1970. *Die deutsche Literatur vom späten Mittelalter bis zum Barock. Das ausgehende Mittelalter, Humanismus und Renaissance: 1370-1520*. Vol. 4/1 of *Geschichte der deutschen Literatur von den Anfängen bis zur Gegenwart*. Munich: Beck.

Schröder, Rolf. 1970. *Novelle und Novellentheorie in der frühen Biedermeierzeit*. Tübingen: Max Niemeyer.

Steinhauer, Harry. 1970. "Towards a Definition of the Novella." *Seminar* 6: 154-74.

Trainer, James. 1970. "The *Märchen*." In *The Romantic Period in Germany*. Ed. Siegbert Prawer, 97-120. New York: Schocken.

Ryder, Frank G. 1971. *Die Novelle*. New York: Holt. After a pithy, splendid introductory orientation to the theory of the novella, this textbook provides an annotated anthology of twelve German novellas.

Wierlacher, Alois. 1971. "Reinbecks Novellentheorie: Zur Situationsnovelle des 19. Jahrhunderts." In *Jahrbuch des Freien deutschen Hochstifts*. Ed. Detlev Lüders, 430-47. Tübingen: Max Niemeyer.

Remak, Henry H. H. 1972. "Der Rahmen in der deutschen Novelle: Dauer im Wechsel." In *Traditions and Transitions, Studies in Honor of Harold Jantz*. Ed. Liselotte E. Kurth et. al., 246-62. Munich: Delp.

Eckert, Hartwig R. 1973. "Towards a Definition of the Novelle." *New German Studies* 1: 163-72.

Eisenbeiss, Ulrich. 1973. *Das Idyllische in der Novelle der Biedermeierzeit*. Stuttgart: Kohlhammer.

Ellis, John M. 1974. *Narration in the German Novelle: Theory and Interpretation*. Cambridge: Cambridge University Press. After providing an introductory essay on the theory of the genre, Ellis interprets eight German novellas.

Leibowitz, Judith. 1974. *Narrative Purpose in the Novella*. The Hague: Mouton.

Brown, Jane K. 1975. *Goethe's Cyclical Narratives*: Die Unterhaltungen deutscher Ausgewanderten *and* Wilhelm Meisters Wanderjahre. Chapel Hill: The University of North Carolina Press.

Springer, Mary Doyle. 1975. *Forms of the Modern Novella*. Chicago: The University of Chicago Press.

Weber, Albrecht. 1975. *Deutsche Novellen des Realismus: Gattung—Geschichte—Interpretationen—Didaktik*. Munich: Ehrenwirth.

Unruh, Friedrich Franz von. 1976. *Die unerhörte Begebenheit: Lob der Novelle*. Bodman/Bodensee: Hohenstaufen. In addition to writing an introduction to the theory of the genre based principally on Goethe's definition, Unruh also provides short interpretations of 30 novellas by 23 authors, including such non-German writers as Melville, Hemingway, Conrad, and Gogol.

Clements, Robert J. and Joseph Gibaldi. 1977. *Anatomy of the Novella: The European Tale Collection from Boccaccio and Chaucer to Cervantes*. New York: New York University Press. This work is mainly devoted to an analysis of the Renaissance novellas of Italy, France, Spain, and England.

Good, Graham. 1977. "Notes on the Novella." *Novel: A Forum on Fiction* 10: 197-211.

Kunz, Josef. 1977. *Die deutsche Novelle im 20. Jahrhundert*. Berlin: Schmidt.

Rowley, Brian A. 1977. "To Define True Novellen ...: A taxonomic enquiry." *Publications of the English Goethe Society* 47: 4-27.

Steinhauer, Harry. 1977. *Twelve German Novellas*. Berkeley and Los Angeles: University of California Press. This book consists of a short essay on the theory of the genre and an anthology of German novellas in English translation.

Swales, Martin. 1977. *The German Novelle*. Princeton: Princeton University Press. In addition to three chapters of genre criticism, Swales also interprets seven German novellas.

Wolff, Roland A. 1977. "Der *Falke* am *Wendepunkt* Revisited: Some Thoughts on Schunicht's Theory and the German *Novelle* in General." *New German Studies* 5: 157-68.

Paine, J. H. E. 1979. *Theory and Criticism of the Novella*. Bonn: Bouvier.

Polheim, Karl Konrad, ed. 1981. *Handbuch der deutschen Erzählung*. Düsseldorf: Bagel. This hefty book contains a collection of thirty-five essays dealing with individual authors and literary periods. The following essays are the most germane to theory and criticism:

Polheim, Karl Konrad. "Gattungsproblematik." 9-16.

Heinzle, Joachim. "Vom Mittelalter zum Humanismus." 17-27.

Hirdt, Willi. "Boccaccio und die deutsche Kurzprosa des 16. Jahrhunderts." 28-36.

Haslinger, Adolf. "Vom Humanismus zum Barock." 37-55.

Jacobs, Jürgen. "Die deutsche Erzählung im Zeitalter der Aufklärung." 56-71.

Keller, Werner. "Johann Wolfgang von Goethe." 72-90.

Klussmann, Paul Gerhard. "Ludwig Tieck," 130-44.

Behler, Ernst. "Die Zeit der Romantik." 115-29.

Sengle, Friedrich. "Biedermeier." 192-205.

Koopmann, Helmut. "Die Novellistik des Jungen Deutschlands." 229-39.

Martini, Fritz. "Von der Erzählung im bürgerlichen Realismus." 240-57.

Nehring, Wolfgang. "Der Beginn der Moderne." 382-408.

Binneberg, Kurt. "Expressionismus." 433-47.

Rotermund, Erwin. "Die deutsche Erzählung in den zwanziger und dreißiger Jahren." 461-82.

Hensing, Dieter. "Die Erzählung von 1945 bis zu den späten fünfziger Jahren." 508-27.

___. "Die Erzählung der sechziger Jahre und der ersten Hälfte der siebziger Jahre." 528-51.

Sinka, Margit M. 1981. "Heinrich Böll's *Die verlorene Ehre der Katharina Blum* as a Novelle or How a Genre Concept Develops and Where it can Lead." *Colloquia Germanica* 14: 158-74.

Remak, Henry H. H. 1982. "Die Novelle in der Klassik und Romantik." In *Europäische Romantik I*, Vol. 14 of *Neues Handbuch der Literaturwissenschaft*. Ed. Klaus von See, 291-318. Wiesbaden: Akademische Verlagsgesellschaft Athenaion.

Rolleston, James. 1982. "Short Fiction in Exile: Exposure and Reclamation of a Tradition." In *Exile: The Writer's Experience*. Ed. John Spalek and Robert Bell, 32-47. Chapel Hill: The University of North Carolina Press.

Sinka, Margit M. 1982. "The Flight Motif in Martin Walser's *Ein fliehendes Pferd.*" *Monatshefte* 74: 47-58.

Strube, Werner. 1982. "Die komplexe Logik des Begriffs 'Novelle.' Zur Problematik der Definition literarische Gattungsbegriffe." *Germanisch-romanische Monatsschrift* 32: 379-86.

Weing, Siegfried. 1982. "The Genesis of Goethe's Definition of the *Novelle.*" *Journal of English and Germanic Philology* 81: 492-508.

Remak, Henry H. H. 1983. *Novellistische Struktur: Der Marschall von Bassompierre und die schöne Krämerin. (Bassompierre, Goethe, Hofmannsthal). Essai und kritischer Forschungsbericht*. Bern and Frankfurt a.M.: Lang.

Schulz, Gerhard. 1983. *Die deutsche Literatur zwischen Französischer Revolution und Restauration. Das Zeitalter der französischen Revolution: 1789–1806.* Vol. 7/1 of *Geschichte der deutschen Literatur von den Anfängen bis zur Gegenwart.* Munich: Beck.

Sinka, Margit M. 1983. "Unappreciated Symbol: The *Unglückssäule* in Stifter's *Bergkristall.*" *Modern Austrian Literature* 16: 1-17.

Träger, Christine. 1983. "Novellistisches Erzählen bei Goethe." *Goethe-Jahrbuch,* Weimar 100: 182-202.

Herbst, Hildburg. 1984. "Goethe: Vater der deutschen Novelle?" In *Goethe im Kontext: Kunst und Humanität, Naturwissenschaft und Politik von der Aufklärung bis zur Restauration. Ein Symposium.* Ed. Wolfgang Wittkowski, 244-59. Tübingen: Niemeyer.

Neumann, Gerhard. 1984. "Die Anfänge deutscher Novellistik: Schillers 'Verbrecher aus verlorener Ehre' — Goethes 'Unterhaltungen deutscher Ausgewanderten.'" In *Unser Commercium: Goethes und Schillers Literaturpolitik.* Ed. Wilfried Barner et al., 433-60. Stuttgart: Cotta.

Polheim, Karl Konrad. 1984. "Paul Ernst und die Novelle." *Zeitschrift für deutsche Philologie* 103: 520-38.

Remak, Henry H. H. 1984. "Goethe and the Novella." In *Johann Wolfgang von Goethe: One Hundred and Fifty Years of Continuing Vitality.* Ed. Ulrich Goebel and Wolodymyr T. Zyla, 133-55. Lubbock, Texas: Texas Tech Press.

Träger, Christine. 1984. *Novellistisches Erzählen bei Goethe.* Berlin, Weimar: Aufbau-Verlag.

Henel, Heinrich. 1985. "Anfänge der deutschen Novelle." *Monatshefte* 77: 433-48.

Herbst, Hildburg. 1985. *Frühe Formen der deutschen Novelle im 18. Jahrhundert.* Berlin: Schmidt.

Paulin, Roger. 1985. *The Brief Compass: The Nineteenth-Century German Novelle.* New York: Oxford University Press.

Ellis, John M. 1986. "How Seriously Should We Take Goethe's Definition of the Novelle?" *Goethe Yearbook III.* Ed. Thomas P. Saine, 121-23. Columbia, SC: Camden House.

Ritchie, James M. 1986. "Die strenge Novellenform im zwanzigsten Jahrhundert." In *Dichtung, Wissenschaft, Unterricht. Rüdiger Frommholz zum 60. Geburtstag.* Ed. Friedrich Kienecker and Peter Wolfersdorf, 252-64. Paderborn, Munich, Vienna, Zurich: Schöningh.

Glier, Ingeborg. 1987. *Die deutsche Literatur im späten Mittelalter. Reimpaargedichte, Drama, Prosa: 1250-1370.* Vol. 3/2 of *Geschichte der deutschen Literatur von den Anfängen bis zur Gegenwart.* Munich: Beck.

Remak, Henry H. H. 1987. "Thomas Mann als Novellist." In *Zeitgenossenschaft: Zur deutschsprachigen Literatur im 20. Jahrhundert; Festschrift für Egon Schwarz zum 65. Geburtstag.* Ed. Paul Michael Lützeler, et. al., 103-22. Frankfurt, a.M.: Athenäum.

___. 1988. "Autobiography or Fiction? Johann Wolfgang and Johann Caspar Goethe's 'Schöne Mailänderin' and the 'Frankfurter Gretchen' as Novellas." In *Goethe in Italy, 1786-1986.* Ed. Gerhart Hoffmeister, 21-54. Amsterdam: Rodopi.

Coghlan, Brian. 1989. "Theodor Storms Novelle: eine Schwester des Dramas?" *Schriften der Theodor-Storm Gesellschaft* 38: 26-38.

Karthaus, Ulrich. 1989. "Günter Grass: *Katz und Maus* — das Ende einer Gattung?" In *Über Grenzen: Polnisch-deutsche Beiträge zur deutschen Literatur nach 1945.* Ed. Wolfgang Braungart, 46-58. Frankfurt a.M., Bern, New York, Paris: Lang.

Schulz, Gerhard. 1989. *Die deutsche Literatur zwischen Französischer Revolution und Restauration. Das Zeitalter der napoleonischen Kriege und der Restauration: 1806-1830.* Vol. 7/2 of *Geschichte der deutschen Literatur von den Anfängen bis zur Gegenwart.* Munich: Beck.

Aust, Hugo. 1990. *Novelle.* Stuttgart: Metzler.

Hoffmeister, Werner. 1990. "Die deutsche Novelle und die amerikanische 'Tale': Ansätze zu einem gattungstypologischen Vergleich." *German Quarterly* 63: 32-49.

Jørgensen, Sven Aage, Klaus Bohnen, and Per Ohrgaard. 1990. *Aufklärung, Sturm und Drang, frühe Klassik: 1740-1789.* Vol. 6 of *Geschichte der deutschen Literatur von den Anfängen bis zur Gegenwart.* Munich: Beck.

Pötters, Wilhelm. 1991. *Begriff und Struktur der Novelle: Linguistische Betrachtungen zu Boccaccios "Falken."* Tübingen: Niemeyer.

Index

Abraham a Sancta Clara 14

Action 28, 30, 33, 45, 49, 54, 55, 59, 61, 64, 72, 89, 126, 142, 143, 145, 151

Addison, Joseph and Richard Steele 15, 150

— *The Spectator* 15

— *The Tatler* 15

Adoption of novella 1, 3, 18, 24, 32, 46, 45, 63, 67, 77

Adventure story (Abenteuererzählung) 46, 56

Aeneas Silvius 11, 64

— *Eurialis und Lucretia* 11, 64

Aequalitas numerosa 158

Aesop 11

Aichinger, Ilse 102

Alexis, Willibald 33, 34, 35, 155, 163

Alf laila wa laila (see *Arabian Nights*)

Alfonsi, Petrus 2, 11

— *Disciplina clericalis* 2, 11

Allegory 38, 104, 127

Andres, Stefan 153

Anecdote 2, 24, 27, 31, 32, 35, 37, 40, 44, 45, 48, 55, 56, 64, 65, 72, 86, 87, 102, 105, 114

Anglo-American scholarship 127, 128, 129, 132, 137

Anti-novella (Gegennovelle) 90

Anton Ulrich von Braunschweig 13, 14

Anzengruber, Ludwig 51

Apologue 126

Apuleius 2

— *Metamorphoseon libri XI* 2

Arabesque 147

Arabian Nights 3, 8, 21, 22, 24, 92, 98

Aristotle 2, 22, 25, 28, 29, 30, 32, 33, 35, 36, 37, 40, 42, 63, 126, 148–49, 161

Arnim, Achim von 64, 80, 83

— *Isabella von Aegypten* 64

— *Der tolle Invalide auf dem Forte Ratonneau* 64, 80

Arnold, Paul 55, 61, 167

Art novella (Kunstnovelle) 67, 145, 149

Arx, Bernhard von 16, 78–81, 103, 106, 111, 123, 137, 159, 169

Ast, Friedrich 31, 163

Auerbach, Berthold 70, 120

Auerbach, Erich 5, 168

Aue, Hartmann von 10, 11

— *Der arme Heinrich* 10, 11, 71

Aust, Hugo 3, 11, 14, 16, 155–56, 177

Bagatelle 150

Balzac, Honoré de 129

Bandello, Matteo 14

Baroque 13–14, 15

Basile, Giambattista 68

Bassompierre, François de 21, 25, 145

Baudri of Bourgueil 2

Bebel, Heinrich 12

— *Facetiae* 12

Beck, Friedrich 45, 165

Begebenheit (*see* event)

Behler, Ernst 138, 175

Bel parlare 91, 93

Bennett, E. K. 1, 16, 69–71, 126, 168

Bertuch, Friedrich Justin 16

— *Blaue Bibliothek aller Nationen* 16

Beyse, Jochen 156

Biedermeier 37–43, 113–115, 120–22, 138–39, 151

Biese, Alfred 35, 166

Bilateral structure 97, 100

Binding, Rudolf 153

Binneberg, Kurt 141–42, 175

Binomial nomenclature 131

Blanckenburg, Christian Friedrich von 18, 162

Blixen, Tanja 128

Boccaccio, Giovanni xi, 1, 3, 4–5, 8, 9, 10, 11, 12, 13, 14, 19, 22, 24, 27, 28, 38, 44, 47, 49, 53, 55, 64, 65, 67, 68, 71, 77, 78, 85, 86, 88, 91, 92, 108, 115, 125, 128, 132, 150, 155, 157–58, 159, 161
— *The Decameron* xi, 1, 3, 4–5, 11, 12, 13, 18, 24, 28, 53, 56, 62, 64, 67, 69, 75, 85, 91, 92, 110, 119, 125, 157–58, 161

Böll, Heinrich 102, 130, 143
— Die verlorene Ehre der Katharina Blum 143

Booth, Wayne C. 123, 171

Borcherdt, Hans Heinrich 61, 167

Borchert, Wolfgang 130

Bouterwek, Friedrich 31, 163

Bovet, Felix 51

Brentano, Clemens 80, 119
— *Geschichte vom braven Kasperl und dem schönen Annerl* 80, 119

Brown, Jane K. 125, 173

Bruch, Bernhard 62, 68, 69, 70, 77, 167

Büchner, Georg 74, 99
— *Lenz* 74, 99

Bülow, Eduard von 39, 164

Burger, Heinz Otto xii, 77, 169

Capriccio 47

Carnap, Rudolf 144

Carriere, Moriz 44, 165

Catastrophe 6, 29, 41, 50, 65, 82, 94, 100, 144, 149, 154

Les Cent nouvelles nouvelles 4–5, 9, 11, 19, 23, 25, 161

Cervantes Saavedra, Miguel de 1, 4, 6, 7, 13, 14, 18, 25, 28, 33, 42, 43, 53, 67, 68, 71, 72, 128, 157, 162
— *Don Quixote* 14

— *Novelas ejemplares* 1, 4, 6, 8, 13, 14, 18, 24, 53, 67, 128, 162

Chance/fate 20, 36, 43, 44, 46, 47, 54, 55, 58, 61, 62, 65, 66, 68, 69, 70, 71, 73, 75, 82, 83, 88, 97, 98, 100, 103, 109, 110, 111, 127, 129, 132, 133, 145, 146, 147, 157

Chaos in novella 75, 82, 85, 88, 90, 100, 117, 132, 160

Characters in novella 34, 40, 48, 50, 59, 82, 98, 108, 111, 120, 121, 126
— Developing 40, 47, 59, 82
— Fixed 30, 34, 40, 48, 52, 59, 84, 117, 132, 160
— Number 22, 49, 50, 51, 52, 76, 120, 131, 132, 160
— Type 22, 37, 44, 115

Character novella 67, 68, 72, 89, 107

Chekhov, Anton Pablovich 88, 129

Cicero 1

Clairon, Hippolyte 21, 25

Classicism 83, 150

Clements, Robert J. and Joseph Gibaldi 1, 3, 4, 7–9, 25, 37, 128, 174

Clodius, Christian August Heinrich 31, 163

Cochem, Martin Linius von 14

Codex Hamilton 90 157–58

Coghlan, Brian 154–55, 177

Comedy 30

Comparative studies 124, 127, 128, 135, 137, 156

Conan Doyle, Arthur 129

Conceit 6, 21

Concessive clause 157

Conflict 46, 48, 49, 50, 53, 55, 61, 62, 82, 94, 95, 109, 110, 111, 124, 154

Conrad, Joseph 86, 109, 128, 129, 136
— *Heart of Darkness* 136

Conte (*also see* philosophical tale) 15, 93, 94, 109, 135, 150

Cornice (*see* frame)

Corrinth, Kurt 141

Crime story (Kriminalgeschichte) 16, 26

Crystallization point (Kristallations-punkt) 86, 90
Cuento 108
Cultural-historical novella (Kulturges-chichtlichenovelle) 114
Curtius, Ernst Robert 3, 168

Daimonic 73–75, 82, 83, 99, 100
Dante Alighieri 2, 4, 9, 127
— *The Divine Comedy* 2, 9, 127
Death/decline of novella 54, 55–56, 66, 70–71, 88, 89, 95, 100, 101, 102, 127, 130, 153, 155
Delectatio 2, 7, 25
Demonic 73, 74–75, 139
Determinism 98, 111, 140
Diderot, Denis 118
Discussion novella 114
Döblin, Alfred 142
Doppelgänger 111
der Doppelte Boden (*see* narration)
Dorfnovelle (*see* village novella)
Droste-Hülshoff, Annette von 70, 84, 139, 151
— *Die Judenbuche* 84, 139

East German writers 142, 153
Eberhard, Johann August 31, 163
Ebers, Georg 49, 60
Ebner-Eschenbach, Marie von 126
Eckardt, Ludwig 45, 165
Eckartshausen, Karl von 9, 15
Eckermann, Johann Peter 25, 26, 34, 40, 60, 145, 153, 164
Eckert, Hartwig 120, 131, 173
Ehrismann, Gustav 3, 10, 168
Eichendorff, Joseph Freiherr von 42, 83, 138, 165
— *Das Marmorbild* 138
Eisenbeiss, Ulrich 120–22, 139, 173
Elixir 48, 140
Ellis, John M. 122–24, 126, 130, 131, 133, 134, 135, 137, 153, 173, 176
Empfindsamkeit (*see* sentimentality)
Enlightenment 137

Epic 22, 30, 32, 36, 40, 41, 42, 44, 61, 64, 82, 99, 118, 120, 131, 132, 137, 139, 149
Epigone 52, 111, 155
Erotic/bawdy 4, 8, 12, 20, 25, 28, 42, 54
Erné, Nino 85–89, 120, 169
Ernst, Paul 53–54, 55, 56, 60, 72, 77, 140, 147, 153, 155, 166
Erzählung xii, 24, 28, 34, 39, 42, 44, 45, 46, 52, 85, 108, 114, 140, 141, 142, 143, 144, 147, 150, 160
Eschenburg, Johann Joachim 18, 162
Etymology of novella 1, 32, 33, 35, 37, 43, 56, 63, 77, 93, 123, 155
Event (Begebenheit) 10, 18, 23, 35, 36, 42, 46, 49, 52, 57, 61, 62, 63, 64, 68, 69, 72, 73, 80, 85, 89, 90, 92, 93, 98, 99, 103, 107, 108, 109, 110, 111, 112, 118, 120, 121, 124, 128, 132, 133, 134, 136, 143, 146, 147, 148, 149–50, 154–55, 157, 160
— Authenticity 152
— Central 63, 84, 94, 95, 100, 109, 132, 133, 139
— Priority 63, 68, 117, 124
— "Real"/occurred 5, 6, 7, 8, 20, 21, 22, 24, 25, 27, 28, 29, 31, 32, 33, 35, 37, 38, 51, 55, 63, 68, 69, 71, 93, 114, 129, 134, 145, 157
— Verisimilar 25, 33, 76, 84, 91, 117, 119, 148, 160
Exemplum 2, 6, 13, 14, 127
Exiled writers 142, 144
Existentialism 88, 127, 129, 141
Expressionism 83, 95, 140–41, 141–42, 151, 153
Eyb, Albrecht von 11
— *Das Ehebüchlein* 11

Fable xi, 1, 2, 10, 11, 56, 118, 122, 127, 138, 150
Fabliaux 3, 77
Façade novella 65, 66

Fairy tale (Märchen) 8, 10, 15–16, 20, 23, 24, 26, 41, 42, 45, 61, 68, 79, 80, 85, 99, 111, 113, 131, 138, 150
— Kunstmärchen 113, 138, 151
— Volksmärchen 113, 138
Fairy tale novella
— Märchennovelle 87, 94, 113, 114, 138
— Novellenmärchen 113
Falcon (see symbol)
Falcon theory 35, 47, 105, 112
Family portrait (Familiengemälde) 23, 26
Family resemblance 117, 123, 160
Fate (see chance)
Fate novella (Schicksalsnovelle) 65, 67, 72
Faulkner, William 88, 109
— A Rose for Emily 88
Feuchtersleben, Ernst Freiherr von 40–41, 60, 145, 164
Feyerabend, Sigmund 12
— Kurtzweilige und Laecherliche Geschicht.... 12
Folk novella 149
Fontane, Theodor 51, 166
Form 27, 28, 33, 34, 35, 37, 44, 49, 52, 54, 56, 57, 58, 62, 64, 65, 66, 68, 69, 71, 72, 77, 78, 81, 82, 84, 88, 90, 91, 93, 95, 97, 99, 100, 102, 104, 107–108, 109, 111, 119, 129, 131, 138, 139, 144, 147, 152, 153–54
Forschungsbericht xii, 76, 77, 102–103
Forster, E. M. 126, 127, 167
Foucault, Michel 146
Foulkes, Peter A. and Edgar Lohner 3, 110, 172
Frame/cornice (Rahmen) xi, 3, 7, 8–9, 19, 25, 52, 60, 62, 64, 78, 82, 84–85, 86, 90, 91, 92, 93, 98, 109, 110–11, 118–20, 129, 130, 133, 134, 136, 140, 149, 150, 152, 155, 160

Franck, Bruno 153
Franck, Hans 65, 66
— Südseeinsel 65
François, Luise von 47, 166
French Revolution 16, 19, 71, 75, 82, 85, 110, 125, 145, 146–47, 148–49
Freud, Sigmund 153
Frey, Jakob 12
Gartengesellschaft 12
Freytag, Gustav 50, 151
Fricke, Gerhart 102, 171
Function of novella 2, 3, 4, 5, 7, 12, 13, 23, 66, 111
— edify 2, 3, 4, 5, 6, 13, 23
— entertain 2, 3, 4, 5, 6, 7, 14, 18, 19, 20, 22, 23, 24, 25, 29, 53, 66, 69, 79, 91, 92, 99, 109, 110, 115, 116, 132

Gautier, Théophile 129
Geistergeschichte (see ghost story)
Geistesgeschichte 58, 62
Gerichtsnovelle (see justice novella)
Gervinus, Georg Gottfried 42, 43, 165
Die Geschichte von den sieben Weisen 3, 10
Gesellschaftsnovelle (see social novella)
Geßner, Salomon 121
Gesta Romanorum 3
Ghost story (Geistergeschichte) 102, 131, 138, 146
Gide, André 109
Gillespie, Gerald 108–109, 124, 128, 136, 172
Goethe, Johann Wolfgang von xi, 3, 4, 9, 10, 11, 13, 19–26, 27, 28, 31, 32, 33, 34, 37, 42, 46, 52, 53, 58, 60, 70, 72, 73, 77, 78, 79, 82, 85, 90, 91, 92, 107–108, 112, 129, 145–46, 148–49, 150–51, 156, 157, 162, 163, 164
— Annalen 24
— "Antonelli" 21, 146

— *Campagne in Frankreich* 148
— "Ferdinand" 23, 26, 27, 35–36, 61, 146–47
— "Frankfurter Gretchen" 154
— *Hermann und Dorothea* 120
— "Das Klopfen" 21, 146
— "Die Krämerin" 21, 145, 146, 149
— *Die Leiden des jungen Werthers* 63
— "Das Märchen" 23, 26
— *Novelle* 40, 43, 52, 58, 64, 78, 107–108, 112, 138, 149
— "Die pilgernde Törin" 25
— "Der Prokurator" 11, 21, 23, 25, 26, 146–47, 149
— "Der Schleier" 21, 146
— "Die schöne Mailänderin" 154
— *Tag- und Jahresheften* 24
— *Unterhaltungen deutscher Ausgewanderten* 9, 11, 19–24, 26, 28, 30, 31, 32, 35, 40, 55, 57, 58, 60, 67, 69, 75, 78, 85, 90, 91, 92, 97, 98, 101, 102, 109, 110–11, 112, 113, 119, 125, 131, 134, 138, 145, 146, 148, 149, 151, 152, 162
— *Die Wahlverwandtschaften* 24, 25, 31, 67, 145, 149, 153, 163
— *Wilhelm Meisters Wanderjahre* 24, 25, 26, 40, 79, 125, 149, 164
— "Die wunderlichen Nachbarskinder" 24, 25, 26, 31, 40, 112
Goethe's definition xi, 24–25, 26, 34, 35, 40, 50, 52, 58, 60, 61, 62, 64, 68, 71, 78, 87, 89, 92, 93–94, 100, 101, 106, 108, 109, 110, 119, 123, 127, 130, 132–33, 139, 143, 145, 148, 149–50, 151, 152, 153, 154, 155, 156, 157
Gogol, Nikolai 129
Good, Graham 129, 174
Gotthelf, Jeremias 70, 74–75, 119, 121, 122, 139, 152
— *Die schwarze Spinne* 74–75, 119, 134, 139
Gottschall, Rudolf 45, 165
Grass, Günter 102, 130, 153, 155

— *Katz und Maus* 102, 130, 153, 155
Grillparzer, Franz 39, 70, 84, 139, 152, 164
— *Der arme Spielmann* 39, 84
— *Das Kloster bei Sendomir* 39
Grimm, Hans 69, 153
— *Der Richter in der Karu* 69
Grimmelshausen, Hans Jakob Christoffel von 13, 14, 25
— *Abenteuerlicher Simplicius Simplizissimus* 14
— *Landstörtzerin Courasche* 13
— *Der seltsame Springinsfeld* 13
— *Das wunderbarliche Vogelnest* 13
Grolman, Adolf von 66, 69, 77, 167
Gross, Erhart 11
Grundmotiv (*see* plot)
Gutzkow, Karl 39, 45–46, 139, 164, 165

Härlin, Erich 72, 168
Harsdörffer, Georg Phillip von 13, 14
— *Frauenzimmer-Gesprächsspiele* 14
— *Der Große Schauplatz Lust- und Lehrreicher Geschichte* 14
— *Der Schauplatz jämmerlicher Mordgeschichte* 14
Hart, Heinrich 54–55, 56, 141, 166
Haslinger, Adolf 11, 13, 14, 138, 174
Hauff, Wilhelm 34, 163
Hauptmann, Gerhart 52, 130, 166
— *Bahnwärter Thiel* 52, 130, 166
Hawthorne, Nathaniel 156
Hebbel, Friedrich 40, 164, 165
Hegel, Friedrich 96
Hein, Christoph 156
Heine, Heinrich 139
Heinzle, Joachim 10, 11, 138, 174
Hemingway, Ernest 88, 109, 128
— "A Clean, Well-Lighted Place" 88
— *49 Stories* 88
— *The Old Man and the Sea* 88, 109
Henel, Heinrich 149–50, 176
Henry, O. 88, 93
Hensing, Dieter 142–43, 175

Herbst, Hildburg 146, 150–51, 176
Hermlin, Stefan 153
Hernadi, Paul 136
Herodotus 2
Herrigel, Hermann 56, 167
Hettner, Hermann 43, 152, 155, 165
Heyse, Paul xi, 46–47, 48, 49, 50, 52–53, 55, 56, 59, 60, 65, 66, 70, 71, 93–94, 96, 98, 101, 105–106, 112, 127, 131, 135, 140, 152, 155, 165, 166
— *Deutscher Novellenschatz* (with Hermann Kurz) 46, 47, 105, 112
— *Zei Gefangene* 65
Himmel, Hellmuth 3, 10, 13, 15, 16, 17, 101, 171
Hirdt, Willi 9, 12–13, 138, 174
Hirsch, Arnold 1, 3, 11, 16, 32, 63–64, 69, 77, 114, 167
Historical critics xi, 102, 103, 113, 117, 133, 151
History (as substitute term for novella) xi, 1, 6, 12, 14, 108
Hoffmann, Ernst Theodor Amadeus 67, 80–81, 83, 87
Hoffmeister, Werner 18, 156–57, 177
Hofmannsthal, Hugo von 145
— "Erlebnis des Marschalls von Bassompierre" 145
Homer 32
— *The Iliad* 32
— *The Odyssey* 32
Horace 7, 161
Humanism 10, 11, 25
Humboldt, Wilhelm von 34
Humor 4, 29, 30, 44, 51, 54, 82, 98, 122

Idyll/idyllic/Idyllnovella 41, 72, 114, 120–22
Immermann, Karl Leberecht 38, 164
Impressionism 56, 83, 95, 140–41, 153
Individual, emphasis on 67, 73, 76, 85, 98, 106, 110, 119, 129, 146

Irony 27, 53, 60, 65, 69, 100, 105, 130, 145
Irrational 82, 83, 98, 117, 144, 147, 150, 160
Irving, Washington 156
Isolated characters 6, 68, 72, 82, 83, 85, 94, 130, 135, 140, 146

Jacobs, Jürgen 15, 16, 138, 174
James, Henry 109, 135
Jean Paul 121
John of Salisbury 2
Jolles, André 63, 68, 167
Jørgensen, Sven Aage, Klaus Bohnen, and Per Ohrgaard 15, 177
Jugendstil 140
das junge Deutschland (*see* young Germany)
Justice novella (Gerichtsnovelle) 139
Justinian Code 1, 77

Kafka, Franz 99, 141
— *In der Strafkolonie* 99
Kaiserchronik 11
— "Annolied" 10
Karthaus, Ulrich 155, 177
Kayser, Wolfgang 118
Keller, Gottfried 48, 50, 51, 53, 57, 70, 73, 100, 104, 106, 124, 140, 152, 165, 166
— *Kleider machen Leute* 124, 126
— *Romeo und Julia auf dem Dorfe* 73, 104, 106
Keller, Werner 138, 175
Kipling, Rudyard 129
Klein, Johannes 9, 10, 17, 77, 81–82, 93, 103–104, 107, 144, 159, 168, 169, 170, 171
Kleist, Heinrich von 39, 41, 46, 64, 65, 66, 68, 69, 70, 75, 79, 83, 89, 91, 105
— *Das Erdbeben in Chili* 64, 65, 75
— *Die Marquise von O* … 64, 66
— *Michael Kohlhaas* 75, 89, 105–106
— *Die Verlobung in St. Domingo* 69

Klussmann, Paul Gerhard 138, 175
Koopmann, Helmut 139–40, 175
Köpke, Rudolf 44, 165
Körner, Christian Gottfried 19
Koskimies, Rafael 93–94, 170
Kotzebue, August von 38
Kriminalgeschichte (*see* crime story)
Kristallationspunkt (*see* crystallization point)
Kulturgeschichtlichenovelle (*see* cultural-historical novella)
Kunstmärchen (*see* fairy tale)
Kunstnovelle (*see* art novella)
Kunz, Josef 16, 82–83, 106, 109–110, 111, 129–30, 137, 162, 169, 172
Kurzgeschichte (*see* short story)

La Fontaine, Jean de 68
Lais 3, 77
Langbein, August 9
Lange, Otto 42, 165
Langgässer, Elisabeth 130
Language (polite) in novellas 5, 8, 25, 118
LaRoche, Sophie von 15, 18, 146
— *Moralische Erzählungen im Geschmack Marmontels* 15
Latitudinarian critics xii, 115, 116, 117, 159
Laube, Heinrich 38, 140, 164
Lazarillo de Tormes 14
Legend 2, 10, 41, 81, 131, 138
Legend novella 94
Leibowitz, Judith 124–25, 136, 173
Leitmotif 71, 72, 84, 89, 98, 103, 125, 144
Length of novella 5, 8, 18, 24, 33, 41, 42, 43, 47, 53, 54, 55, 56, 71, 76, 78, 79, 81, 84, 88, 89, 91, 92, 101, 106, 107, 108, 109, 114, 115, 116, 120, 123, 126, 128, 131, 132, 133, 137, 139, 140, 150, 155, 159–60
Lenz, Jakob Michael Reinhold 16, 146, 151
— *Zerbin* 16

Lenz, Siegfried 130
Lessing, Gotthold Ephraim 1, 18, 150
— *Nathan der Weise* 18
Liechtensee, Johann Talitz von 13
Lindau, Rudolf 51
Lindner, Michael 12
— *Katzipori* 12
— *Rastbüchlein* 12
Linnaeus, Carolus 131
Literaturwissenschaft 58, 59
LoCicero, Donald 111–12, 172
Lockemann, Fritz 84–85, 90, 120, 169, 170
Lohenstein, Daniel Caspar von 14
Ludwig, Otto 70, 84, 152
— *Zwischen Himmel und Erde* 152
Lukács, Georg 55, 56, 60, 69, 73, 77, 167, 168
Lundorf, Michael Kaspar 13
Lyric 64, 149

Mackensen, Lutz 91–92, 170
Malmede, Hans Hermann 106–108, 172
Mann, Heinrich 153
Mann, Thomas 64, 109, 154
— *Der kleine Herr Friedemann* 154
— *Mario und der Zauberer* 154
— *Tobias Mindernickel* 154
— *Der Tod in Venedig* 64
— *Tristan* 154
Mannheim, Karl 141
Märchen (*see* fairy tale)
Marggraff, Hermann 40, 164
Marguerite de Navarre 4, 6–7, 8, 9, 21, 24, 25, 110, 157, 162
— *The Heptameron* 4, 6–7, 9, 24, 162
Marmontel, Jean-François 15, 21
— *Contes moraux* 15
Martini, Fritz 96, 97–98, 101, 103, 140, 170, 175
Maupassant, Guy de 53, 55, 88, 102, 109, 129
Meißner, August Gottlieb 9, 15, 16, 146, 151

— *Skizzen* 16
Melville, Herman 128, 156
Memel, Petrus de 13
Merck, Johann Heinrich 15, 146, 151
Mérimée, Prosper 53, 63, 86, 88, 129
— *Carmen* 63, 86
— *Lokis* 86
— *Vénus d'Ille* 86–87
Metaphor 64, 66, 104, 105
Metaphysical aspects 69, 105, 143
Metaphysical novella 69
Meyer, Conrad Ferdinand 51–52, 54, 60, 70, 84, 86, 104, 166
— *Der Heilige* 84
— *Die Hochzeit des Mönchs* 60
— *Die Versuchung des Pescara* 52, 54, 104
Meyer, Wilhelm xi, 36, 159, 164
Middle Ages 10, 71, 103, 138
Midpoint (Mittelpunkt) 35, 37, 43, 44, 46, 48, 65, 71, 72, 107, 108
Milieu 53
Mitchell, McBurney 1, 58–59, 167
Moderate critics xii, 57, 77, 96, 102, 117, 132, 133, 137, 151, 160
Mood (Stimmung) 44, 55, 61, 111, 115
Mood novella (Stimmungsnovelle) 55, 61, 67
Mommsen, Katharina 98, 170, 171
Montanus, Martin 12
— *Wegkürzer* 12
Moral tale (Moralische Erzählung) 15, 16, 17, 23, 26, 33
Moralizing in novella 6, 12, 13, 25, 36, 46, 69, 71, 138, 147
Morgan, Bayard Quincy 76, 123, 125, 168
Mörike, Eduard 70, 74, 120, 121, 152
— *Mozart auf der Reise nach Prag* 74
Moriz von Craon 10
Müller, Joachim 99, 110–11, 144, 171, 172
Mundt, Theodor 34, 35, 37–38, 42, 48, 59, 101, 114, 140, 151, 164

Musäus, Johann Karl August 16
— *Volksmärchen der Deutschen* 16
Musil, Robert 56, 57, 141, 167
Musset, Alfred de 53
Myth 2, 10, 74, 85, 131

Napoleon/Napoleonic wars 138
Narration
— objective 51, 64, 73, 83, 84, 105, 124, 155
— objective/subjective 27, 29, 45, 51, 55, 61, 62, 64, 65, 66, 97, 98, 109, 118, 119, 123, 130, 133, 134, 138, 148, 155
Narrative
— compression/concentration 32, 33, 42, 47, 58, 88, 92, 95, 105, 107, 109, 119, 124–25, 129, 134, 136, 144, 155, 156
— double plane (der doppelte Boden) 86–87
— technique/perspective 7, 21, 22, 29, 82, 84, 89, 97, 101, 118, 124, 128, 130, 132, 134–35, 141
Narrator 7, 8, 21, 61, 86, 90, 93, 97, 98, 111, 124, 134–35. 150
National Endowment for the Humanities 130
Naturalism 52, 53, 83, 84, 95, 110, 140–41, 151, 153
Negus, Kenneth 105–106, 111, 172
Nehring, Wolfgang 52, 140, 175
Neumann, Gerhard 146–47, 176
New Romanticism 140–41
Newald, Richard 12, 13, 14, 15, 16, 169, 170
Normative/rigorist critics xii, 57, 102, 103, 115, 117, 130, 133, 137, 159
Norms 5, 41, 115, 129, 142
Nouvelle 136
Novalis 58
Novelette 76
Novella compared with:
— Anecdote 71, 81, 90, 92, 94, 131, 150

— Ballad 72, 95
— Drama 18, 27, 30, 32, 36, 42, 45, 49, 50, 52, 53, 54, 57, 62, 63, 68, 72, 73, 76, 94, 109, 118, 152, 154
— Erzählung 64, 72, 85, 91, 98, 99, 103, 108, 117, 137, 150
— Fairy tale 68, 80, 81, 113
— Geschichte 91
— Novel 18, 26, 29, 31, 32, 34–35, 37, 38–39, 40, 41, 42, 43, 44, 45, 46, 47–48, 48–49, 50–51, 54, 55, 56, 57, 59, 61, 63, 64, 71, 73, 76, 92, 111, 118, 125, 127
— Short story 76, 81–82, 90, 92, 94–95, 117, 125, 130, 131–32, 134
Novella-novel (Novellenroman) 38, 94
Novellenmärchen (see fairy tale novella)
Novellesque 148
Il Novellino 91
Novellistic narration (novellistisches Erzählen) 89, 93, 100, 101, 107, 149
Novelty 20, 23, 27, 44, 109, 157
Numerus perfectissimus 9
Nüsslein, Franz Anton 32, 163

Oesterley, Hermann 46, 165
Oral tradition of novella 2, 7, 8, 42, 60, 86, 91, 118, 129, 155
Origin of novella xi, 1-17, 33, 68, 71, 85, 86, 91, 101, 103, 106
Ovid 1

Pabst, Walter xi, xii, 3, 4–7, 10, 76, 92, 103, 106, 110, 116, 117, 137, 144, 159, 169
Paine, J. H. E. 135–36, 174
Panchatantra 3
Pannwitz, Herr von 21, 25
Parable xi, 2, 56, 108, 127
Paradox 58, 105, 130, 132, 145
Pauli, Johannes 12
— Schimpf und Ernst 12

Paulin, Roger 9, 15, 16, 151–53, 155, 156, 176
Pedagogy xii, 2, 6, 66, 73, 77, 102, 111, 116, 125, 126, 134
Perrault, Charles 16, 58
Petrarch 11
— Griseldis 11
Petriconi, Hellmuth 77
Petronius 2
— Satyricon 2
Petsch, Robert 71, 77, 107, 125, 168
Pfeil, Johann Gottlob Benjamin 15
Philosophical tale (conte philosophique) 15
Pietism 150
Pirandello, Luigi 88, 102
Pliny 1
Plot (Grundmotiv) 47, 71, 105–106
Poe, Edgar Allen 129, 156
Poetic Realism 43–52, 70, 83–84, 95, 110, 152
Poggio Bracciolini 5, 11, 12
— Liber Facetiarum 5
Pointe 37, 44, 45, 54, 56, 62–63, 67, 72, 87, 88, 90, 99, 105, 109, 130, 144, 149, 158
Polheim, Karl Konrad xii, 102–103, 113, 117, 137, 147, 160, 162, 171, 172, 174, 176
Pongs, Hermann 64–66, 67–68, 68–69, 70, 72, 73–75, 77, 100, 105, 107, 127, 167, 168, 171
Positivism 141
Pötters, Wilhelm 157–58, 177
Precursors of novella 2-3
Predigtmärlein 14
Prefiguration 130
Probabilitas 8
Problem novella 69
Prodesse 2, 7, 25
Proem 1, 7, 12, 23
Profile 71, 99, 131
Protestant Reformation 12
Psychological novella 67, 68, 70
Punktualität 96

Quality of novella
— Poor (examples) 33, 34, 36, 39, 40, 44, 46, 51, 102, 114, 141, 144
— Superior (as genre) 38, 39, 45, 46, 85, 95, 99, 127, 137

Raabe, Wilhelm 70, 119
— *Elsi von der Tanne* 119
— *Des Reiches Krone* 70
Racconto 108
Radical critics 77, 96
Rahmen (*see* frame/cornice)
Ramdohr, Friedrich Wilhelm 15
— *Moralische Erzählungen* 15
Rationalism 38
Realism 21, 46, 58, 61, 70, 73, 79, 81, 83, 94, 99, 109, 111, 113, 114, 121, 123–24, 126, 130, 131, 133, 138, 140, 155, 156
Reinbeck, Georg von 32, 41–42, 43, 118, 155, 163, 164
Remak, Henry H. H. 100, 104–105, 118–20, 130, 137, 143–44, 145, 148, 154, 171, 173
Renaissance/Romance novella 3–9, 11, 14, 25, 26, 37, 54, 59, 66, 68, 69, 77, 78, 94, 109, 111, 128, 131, 146, 152–53
Repetitive structure 124–25, 136
Reversal (*see also* turning point) 30, 54, 62
Riehl, Wilhelm Heinrich von 45, 48, 51, 165, 166
— *Geschichten aus alter Zeit* 45
Rigorist critics (*see* normative)
Rist, Johann 13
Ritchie, James 153, 176
Rolleston, James 144, 175
Romannovelle (*see* novella-novel)
Romanticism/Romantics 38, 42, 43, 46, 56, 67, 68, 70, 72, 74, 79, 80, 82, 83, 84, 87, 94, 111, 138, 151
Romanzo 100
Rosenkranz, Karl 34, 163
Rotermund, Erwin 142, 175

Rowley, Brian 113, 130–32, 172, 174
Rubble story (Trümmergeschichte) 89
Rumohr, Carl Friedrich von 33, 39, 155, 163, 164
Rupprich, Hans 11, 173
Ryder, Frank 117, 123, 125, 160, 173

Sacks, Sheldon 126, 127
Saga 41, 45
Sandrubs, Lazarus 13
das Sanfte Gesetz (*see* Stifter)
Sartre, Jean-Paul 88, 127
— *The Wall* 88
Satire 6, 34, 39, 48, 51, 57, 122, 126
Schelling, Friedrich Wilhelm Joseph 31, 163
Schicksalsnovelle (*see* fate novella)
Schiller, Friedrich von 16–17, 19, 21, 102, 146, 151, 162
— *Die Horen* 19, 23, 28
— *Der Verbrecher aus verlorener Ehre* 16–17, 146, 162
Schlegel, August Wilhelm 26–30, 32, 33, 35, 36, 37, 58, 60, 69, 101, 112, 150, 151, 152, 155, 156, 162, 163
Schlegel, Friedrich 26–30, 32, 33, 37, 51, 58, 60, 64, 101, 147, 150, 151, 155, 162
Schleiermacher, Friedrich 32, 162, 163
Schlüsselfelder, Heinrich 1, 11
Schneider, Peter 153
Schnitzler, Arthur 71
Schnurre, Wolfdietrich 102
Schopenhauer, Arthur 70
Schreiber, Aloys 31, 163
Schröder, Rolf 113–15, 139, 173
Schumann, Valentin 12
— *Nachtbüchlein* 12
Schunicht, Manfred 96–97, 112, 135, 144, 170
Schwan, Christian Friedrich 18, 162
Schwan, Friedrich 16, 147
Schwank/Schwankliteratur 12, 13, 14, 44, 64, 65, 81, 150

Seghers, Anna 153
Sengle, Friedrich 113, 138–39, 175
Sentimentality (Empfindsamkeit) 121, 150
Sercambi, Giovanni 53, 54
Shakespeare, William 27, 30, 77, 138, 152
Short story (Kurzgeschichte) 52, 71, 88, 89, 102, 136, 140, 144
Von den sieben weisen Meistern 3, 9
Silhouette 47, 53, 59, 65, 84, 89, 92, 105, 150
Silz, Walter 9, 10, 83–84, 94–95, 117, 133, 169, 170
Sinka, Margit 143, 175, 176
Situation 18, 32, 43, 44, 57, 125, 131, 156
Skeptical critics xi, 63, 92, 93, 96, 100, 115, 117, 137
Sketch, prose 52, 53, 54, 114, 141, 150
Social aspects of novella 19, 25, 27, 31, 46, 53, 60, 66, 71, 73, 85, 89, 91, 92, 102, 109, 110, 115, 119, 120, 129, 140, 144
Social novella (Gesellschaftsnovelle) 64, 67, 68
Solger, Karl Wilhelm Ferdinand 96, 97, 113
Sonata 51
Sonnet 122
Sorel, Charles 14
Spender, Stephen 99, 170
Spielhagen, Friedrich 48–49, 50–51, 52, 59, 140, 166
Spielmann 10
Spiess, Christian Heinrich 9, 15, 16
— *Selbstmörderbiographien* 16
Sprickmann, Anton Mathias 151
Springer, Mary Doyle 126–27, 128, 136, 173
Staiger, Emil 17, 78, 92, 111, 116, 123, 159, 172
Stammler, Wolfgang 10, 11, 82, 169

Steinhauer, Harry 13, 92, 115–16, 117, 132–33, 168, 170, 173, 174
Steinhöwel, Heinrich 11
— *Buch und Leben des Fabeldichters Esopi* 11
Stifter, Adalbert 70, 99, 112, 121, 139, 143, 152
— *Abdias* 70
— *Bergkristall* 121, 143
— *Brigitta* 99, 125, 139
— *Bunte Steine* 112, 121
— das sanfte Gesetz 112, 121
Stimmung (*see* mood)
Stimmungsnovelle (*see* mood novella)
Storm, Theodor 43, 48, 49–50, 51, 55, 60, 61, 70, 72, 84, 104, 118, 119, 154–55, 165, 166
— *Zur Chronik von Grieshuus* 50
— *Draußen im Heidedorf* 61
— *Der Schimmelreiter* 61, 70, 84, 104, 119, 154
Straparola, Gian Francesco 68
Strauß, Emil 153
Der Stricker 10
— *Die Schwäncke des Pfaffen Amis* 10
Strube, Werner 144–45, 175
Supernatural 67, 69, 73, 75, 80, 81, 87, 113, 121, 131
Surreal 95, 99, 143
Swales, Martin 133–35, 158, 174
Symbol/Symbolism 70, 71, 75, 78, 89, 91, 95, 98, 104, 105, 107, 108, 109, 117, 127, 131, 133, 134, 140, 141, 149, 155, 160
— Falcon (Falken) 47, 48, 50, 53, 59, 65, 66, 67, 68, 71, 78, 84, 89, 92, 93–94, 96, 100, 101, 103, 105, 107, 120, 130, 132, 152, 157–58
— Object (Dingsymbol) xi, 47, 65, 66, 69, 71, 74, 90, 96, 98, 100, 101, 103, 105, 106, 107, 130, 143, 144, 148, 155
Symbolon 66

Tale xii, 2, 156–57

Taschenbücher 26, 113–14, 151
Taxonomy 122, 131
Templin, Prokop von 14
Theme-complex 124–25, 136
Theory formation xi, 133, 135
Thümmel, Moritz August von 151
Tieck, Ludwig xi, 10, 33, 34, 35, 36, 37–38, 40, 42, 43, 44, 46, 53, 55, 59, 60, 61, 62, 67, 69, 73, 79, 83, 96, 97, 101, 104, 112, 113–14, 120, 121, 126, 135, 138, 151, 152, 155, 156, 164, 165
— *Der Aufruhr in den Cevennen* 37, 79
— *Der blonde Eckbert* 138, 151
— *Der fünfzehnte November* 112
— *Der Gelehrte* 112
— *Die Gemälde* 33
— *Die Verlobung* 112
— *Die wilde Engländerin* 61
Tolstoy, Leo 129
Tragedy/tragic 29, 30, 32, 62, 63, 68, 69, 70, 74, 75, 82, 98, 122, 126
Träger, Christine 145–46, 148–49, 175
Trainer, James 113, 173
Troubadour 3
Trümmergeschichte (*see* rubble story)
Turgenev, Ivan 51, 53, 86, 129
Turning point (Wendepunkt) xi, 30, 35, 36, 43, 44, 45, 49, 57, 58, 59, 62, 67, 69, 73, 78, 79, 84, 85, 88, 89, 90, 94, 97, 100, 101, 103, 104, 107, 109, 110, 112, 114, 117, 120, 124, 130, 131, 132, 135, 136, 138, 143, 145, 150, 152, 155, 157–58, 160
— auflösend 104–105, 117, 145
— auslösend 104, 117, 145
Tuti-Nameh 3

Ulenhart, Niclas 14
— *Historie von Isaak Winckelfelder und Jobst von der Schneid* 14

Unity 8, 9, 22, 25, 27, 32, 38, 55, 56, 58, 61, 62, 66, 78, 92, 97, 99, 102, 140
Unruh, Friedrich Franz von 100, 127–28, 174
Urform/Urnovelle 5, 7, 17, 43, 64, 77, 93, 102, 103, 115–16, 148
Utilitas 2, 7, 12, 13, 15, 25

Verisimilitude 8, 113, 156
Veritas 8
Verse novella 10, 71
Village novella (Dorfnovelle) 70
Virgil 1
Vischer, Friedrich Theodor 44–45, 47–48, 59, 118, 152, 165, 166
— *Auch Einer* 47
Volksmärchen (*see* fairy tale)
Voltaire 15
— *Candide* 15
— *Zadig* 15

Wall, Anton 15, 151
— *Bagatellen* 15
Walser, Martin 143, 153, 155–56
— *Ein fliehendes Pferd* 143, 153, 155–56
Walzel, Oskar 59–60, 77, 107, 167
Weber, Albrecht 126, 173
Weing, Siegfried 145, 175
Wendepunkt (*see* turning point)
Wernher der Gärtner 10
— *Meier Helmbrecht* 10, 11
West German writers 142, 153
Wezel, Johann Carl 9, 15, 151
Wickram, Jörg 12
— *Rollwagen-Büchlein* 12
Wieland, Christoph Martin xi, 10, 15, 16, 18, 29, 31, 42, 53, 68, 101, 118, 146, 150, 156, 162, 163
— *Die Abenteuer des Don Sylvio von Rosalva* 18, 162
— *Dschinnistan* 16
— *Koxkox und Kikequetzel* 15
— *Die Novelle ohne Titel* 31, 163

Wierlacher, Alois 118–19, 173
Wiese, Benno von 13, 17, 89–90, 93, 100–101, 101–102, 107–108, 177, 155, 170, 171
Wildonie, Herrand von 10
— *diu getriu kone* 10
Wittgenstein, Ludwig 122, 123
Wolf, Christa 153
Wolff, Oskar Ludwig Bernhard 42, 164
Wolff, Roland A. 135, 174
Wondrous (das Wunderbare) 18, 29, 35, 53, 61, 67, 68, 75, 80, 83, 88, 112, 121, 138, 151, 156
Würzburg, Konrad von 10, 11
— *Engelhard* 10
— *Herzmäre* 11
Wyle, Niklas von 11
— *Translatzion oder Tütschungen* 11

Young Germany (das junge Deutschland) 37–43, 69, 139–40

Zeitroman 51, 56
Zeller, Eva 156
Ziolkowski, Theodore 92, 170
Zweig, Stefan 153